State Violence in East Asia

STATE VIOLENCE
IN EAST ASIA

Edited by

N. GANESAN

and

SUNG CHULL KIM

UNIVERSITY PRESS OF KENTUCKY

Scholarly publisher for the Commonwealth,
serving Bellarmine University, Berea College, Centre College of Kentucky,
Eastern Kentucky University, The Filson Historical Society, Georgetown
College, Kentucky Historical Society, Kentucky State University,
Morehead State University, Murray State University, Northern Kentucky
University, Transylvania University, University of Kentucky, University of
Louisville, and Western Kentucky University.

Editorial and Sales Offices: The University Press of Kentucky
663 South Limestone Street, Lexington, Kentucky 40508-4008
www.kentuckypress.com

17 16 15 14 13   5 4 3 2 1

Library of Congress Cataloging-in-Publication Data

State violence in East Asia / edited by N. Ganesan and Sung Chull Kim.
    p. cm. -- (Asia in the new millennium)
  Includes bibliographical references and index.
  ISBN 978-0-8131-3679-0 (alk. paper) — ISBN 978-0-8131-3680-6 (pdf) —
  ISBN 978-0-8131-4061-2 (epub)
  1. Political violence—East Asia. 2. Political violence—Southeast Asia.
3. State-sponsored terrorism—East Asia. 4. State-sponsored terrorism—
Southeast Asia. I. Ganesan, N. (Narayanan), 1958- II. Kim, Sung Chull, 1956-
III. Series: Asia in the new millennium.
  HN720.5.Z9S73 2013
  322.4'2095—dc23   2012043601

This book is printed on acid-free paper meeting the requirements of the American
National Standard for Permanence in Paper for Printed Library Materials.

∞

Manufactured in the United States of America.

Member of the Association of
American University Presses

Contents

Note on Romanization

In romanization of Korean sources and Korean names, the McCune-Reischauer system is used; exceptions are some already commonly used spellings. In the Japanese case, the Hepburn system is adopted. In the Chinese case, the Pinyin system is adopted. Following the traditions of these countries, the family name appears first with the given name following; however, the spellings of personal names that appear in works in English are cited as in the originals.

For the Indonesian case, the spelling of personal names, organizations, and publications prevalent at the time under discussion is retained. Sukarno's name was spelled with a *u,* but Soeharto's name was officially spelled with the older *oe.* In the Thai case, the guidelines of the Royal Institute, outlined in "Principles of Romanization for Thai Script by Transcription Method," have been followed. The only exceptions to this are the names of individuals; if there is already a romanized name in use, that one is used in lieu of imposing the Royal Institute guidelines. In the Burmese case, all political groups have official names in both English and Burmese, so their official names are adopted. For personal names, the method used by the government media is followed.

Abbreviations

AFP	Armed Forces of the Philippines (Philippines)
ASEAN	Association of Southeast Asian Nations
Baperki	Badan Permusyawaratan Kewarganegaraan (Consultative Body for Indonesian Citizenship)
BCP	Burma Communist Party
BLDP	Buddhist Liberal Democratic Party (Cambodia)
BSPP	Burma Socialist Program Party
BTI	Barisan Tani Indonesia (Indonesian Peasants' Front)
CAC	Cabinet Action Committee (Philippines)
CCP	Chinese Communist Party
CGDK	Coalition Government of Democratic Kampuchea
CMC	Citizens' Mendiola Commission (Philippines)
CPK	Communist Party of Kampuchea
CPP	Cambodian People's Party
CPT	Communist Party of Thailand
CRPP	Committee Representing People's Parliament (Myanmar)
CSOC	Communist Suppression Operations Command (Thailand)
DLP	Democratic Liberal Party (Korea)
ECCC	Extraordinary Chambers in the Court of Cambodia
EDSA	Epifanio de los Santos Avenue (Philippines)
FUNCINPEC	Front Uni National pour un Cambodge Indépendant, Neutrale, Pacifique, et Coopératif (National United Front for an Independent, Neutral, Peaceful, and Cooperative Cambodia)
IATFAR	Inter-Agency Task Force on Agrarian Reform (Philippines)
IPKI	Ikatan Pendukung Kemerdekaan Indonesia (League of Upholders of Indonesian Independence)
ISOC	Internal Security Operations Command (Thailand)

KCIA	Korean Central Intelligence Agency
KMP	Kilusang Magbubukid ng Pilipinas (Farmers Movement of the Philippines)
KNU	Karen National Union (Myanmar)
Komnas HAM	Komisi Nasional Hak Asasi Manusia (Indonesian National Commission on Human Rights)
KOTI	Supreme Operations Command (Indonesia)
KPNLF	Khmer People's National Liberation Front
MPRS	Majelis Permusyawaratan Rakyat Sementara (People's Consultative Assembly) (Indonesia)
NBI	National Bureau of Investigation (Philippines)
NDF	National Democratic Front (Myanmar)
NHK	Nippon Hoso Kyokai (Japan Broadcasting Corporation)
NLD	National League for Democracy (Myanmar)
NPA	New People's Army (Philippines)
NSCT	National Student Center of Thailand
NSL	National Security Law (Korea)
NU	Nahdlatul Ulama (Indonesia)
NUP	National Union Party (Myanmar)
PKI	Partai Komunis Indonesia (Indonesian Communist Party)
PNI	Partai Nasional Indonesia (Indonesian National Party)
PRRI	Pemerintahan Revolusioner Republik Indonesia
RIT	Rangoon Institute of Technology
RPKAD	Resimen Para Komando Angkatan Darat (Kostrad and Army Para Commando Regiment) (Indonesia)
SLORC	State Law and Order Restoration Council (Myanmar)
SNLD	Shan National League for Democracy (Myanmar)
SOC	State of Cambodia
SPDC	State Peace and Development Council (Myanmar)
SPT	Socialist Party of Thailand
SWC	Special Warfare Command (Korea)
TRC	Truth and Reconciliation Committee (South Africa)
UF	United Front against Dictatorship (Thailand)
UNTAC	United Nations Transitional Authority in Cambodia
USCAR	United States Civil Administration of the Ryukyu Islands (Japan)

USDA	Union Solidarity and Development Association (Myanmar)
USDP	Union Solidarity and Development Party (Myanmar)
VOA	Voice of America

Introduction

Conceiving State Violence, Justice, and Transition in East Asia

Sung Chull Kim and N. Ganesan

The collaborative research presented in this volume is about the dark side of political history in East Asian countries. It deals with the worst cases of state violence in East Asia, most of which were underresearched for different reasons. The eight cases examined in this comparative study include the Japanese military's killing of Okinawans (1945), the Indonesian counterrevolutionary massacre (1965–1968), the Phatthalung Red Drum incident in Thailand (1972–1975), the Khmer Rouge's mass killings in Cambodia (1975–1978), the Kwangju incident in Korea (1980), the Mendiola Bridge incident in the Philippines (1987), the suppression of the democratic movement in Myanmar (1988), and the Tiananmen incident in China (1989). The cases chosen here are representative in illustrating victimization of the people by military or authoritarian regimes during the Cold War. (The Okinawan case occurred during the wartime period, but narratives about it were long suppressed because of the Cold War divide.) The cases show that state violence derived from a sense of threat among the ruling elite, who believed that there was a strong conflation between state and regime security. In all cases, the modality of violence was basically exemplary and demonstrative as lessons to challengers, even if combined with an instrumental element in varying degrees. This volume does not include cases of violence targeting specific ethnic minorities. Although such ethnic violence might be another important research topic, particularly in the multiethnic Southeast Asian context, the state violence examined in this volume targeted regime challengers in general rather than specific ethnic groups.

Since the Cold War period, most countries dealt with in this volume have not been considered globally significant in the political, economic, and cultural realms. For this reason, most cases of state violence in these countries, unlike in Eastern European and Latin American countries, have not received proper public and international attention.[1] Calling attention to a situation that has been ignored for decades, this volume intends to investigate these cases with a measure of empirical rigor. It aims to not only identify the nature of state violence but to analyze the relationship between state violence and the legitimacy of the existent regime and those coming afterward. It is also interested in detailing how individual countries have dealt with past state violence in different ways in order to arrive at a typology of sorts.

It is necessary, above all, to clarify where this study is situated in relation to the study of violence in general. First, this research focuses on *state violence* rather than on political violence in general, which has been a frequently studied subject in the social sciences. *Political violence* is a more inclusive term than *state violence*. The former encompasses all kinds of politically related violence: the political opposition's violent actions, ethnic electoral violence, violent secessionist movements, as well as state-led mass killings. State violence, as a form of political violence, refers to the more narrowly defined aggression that is led by the state in an abstract sense and actually performed by its apparatuses, such as the military, the police, and other security agencies.

The state violence discussed here involved mass killing, the magnitude of which ranged from tens of people (the Mendiola killings in the post-Marcos Philippines) to millions (the mass killings in Cambodia under the Khmer Rouge). The individual cases detail how each state possessed a monopoly on the use of force and exercised it brutally. There was no real competing political entity in relation to the use of force, even if there were different perceptions of threat or crisis, case by case, between challengers and detractors. A state, in an ideal situation, has a legitimate monopoly of the use of violence, to use Max Weber's term.[2] But the states and their apparatuses under discussion here, whether they had an authoritarian or military regime or some combination thereof, never legitimately used violence from the perspective of human rights or international law or even the official legal standards of the perpetrators themselves. The state violence here differs from the violence that originates from civil war and revolution, in which Charles Tilly's notion of multiple sovereigns contending with each other may be relevant.[3] In other words, the state violence examined in this volume refers to the state's utilization of its apparatus—the military, the police, and security agencies—in order to maintain the unilaterally defined order of the society in question.

Second, inasmuch as this volume is concerned with the violence perpetrated on the people the state was formed to protect, there have to be sustained efforts to observe the ramifications of past violence and ways of settling related issues. These analyses are indispensably related to the examination of political transition: that is, how the legitimacy of regimes changes over time; how resolution of violence takes place today; and, if there has been no ostensible change of regime or of the viewpoint of the past, why such a situation has persisted.

Here transitional justice seems a useful tool to examine postviolence resolution. The notion of transitional justice is widely accepted in examining approaches to applying justice to past evils. There are two different approaches to the issue of transitional justice: one focuses on *punitive* legal means of dealing with offenders, and the other stresses *reconciliatory* means of including past wrongdoers in the new society in order to obtain broader peace and stability. Transitional justice is useful in examining cases in which new rules prevail over old regimes and in which an existing regime at least intends to make a compromise in relation to its own past violence. An important question that arises here is what motivates justice, either punitive or reconciliatory, to prevail. There are also related questions. What prevents the process of settlement from beginning? What are the necessary structural requirements for the process to commence?

One may reasonably generalize that the resolution of past violence is closely intertwined with democratization and that resolution and democratization mutually reinforce each other rather than one being a precondition for the other. The Kwangju case in Korea is a model case of the mutually reinforcing relationship between democratization and the resolution of state violence. And little progress in the resolution of state violence, particularly in Myanmar and China, is related to the continued authoritarian nature of the political process in these countries. Conversely, however, Thailand is an example of a state where democratization has not addressed past examples of state violence. Similarly, Cambodia presents anther counterintuitive example: the Hun Sen government, whose leaders are accused of having been involved in past state violence, has agreed to prosecute those responsible for past crimes.

Given their different backgrounds, the individual cases may follow different paths of settlement, whereby the state makes amends to the victims of violence. Resolution can begin with something as simple as an apology or ritualistic practices, even without truth-telling exercises and legal verdicts. It can develop into a much more targeted approach, such as reparation to the victims of violence and, where possible, either including them in mainstream society or building a monument in their honor. Or resolution can take place after truth commissions have been held or the legal accountability of those responsible for state violence has been assessed, as in the UN-sponsored tribunal in Cambodia now taking place. What should be noted is that regimes in democratic transition are more likely to admit to state-led violence and to make amends afterward. In instances where efforts toward resolution of violence have not been addressed, it is necessary to identify the major reasons why even a minimal level of state effort to obtain some recognition of past misdeeds and compromise has not been forthcoming.

In connection with the points mentioned above, this volume addresses four overarching questions.

- First, why did the state use violence against a particular group of people?
- Second, how has the violence been treated afterward by the society?
- Third, what has been the path of resolution? Or alternatively, why has the violence not yet become an item on the public agenda?
- Fourth, what is the relationship between political transition and the resolution of violence?

Bringing the Study of State Violence Back In

Despite the brutality of the violence and the illegitimacy of the relevant nondemocratic regimes, most cases in this volume have not been seriously investigated from a comparative perspective. There are a couple of reasons for this seeming neglect. First, the Cold War situation, which significantly reified state and national security, impeded the mood of the study of state-led violence. A few scholars, such as Barry Buzan, tried to inspire a new conceptualization of security, differentiating security along a range of various referent objects, from individual to national and international ones.[4] These scholars have also made efforts to redress this imbalance over the past two decades. But the state has long been considered the most important referent object for security in the academic community.

The Khmer Rouge massacre and the Tiananmen incident did draw exceptional international attention. The dreadful mass executions conducted by the Khmer Rouge came to special attention in the wake of the Vietnamese invasion of Cambodia in 1978 and the Sino-Vietnamese War in 1979, in which the Soviet Union and China competed for respective spheres of influence over Indochina. The Tiananmen incident captured international attention owing in part to the mass media's widespread coverage and to the euphoria associated with the erosion of communism in Eastern Europe. Even such international attention to developments in Cambodia and China, however, was unable to induce systematic research on the ways and means of state involvement in violence and on its aftermath. That is, the dominance of state security, or national security, in the Cold War situation impeded international attention to atrocious violence led by the state.

Second, the lasting underinvestigation of state violence has been associated with the Cold War divide itself. Most cases show that the Cold War situation *justified* state violence for decades. Ideological persuasion, particularly anticommunist sentiment, rendered state violence legitimate in the name of order, at least in the eyes of perpetrators. The Indonesian army's counterrevolutionary operations, which occurred alongside the escalating Vietnam War in the mid-1960s, ruthlessly targeted so-called communists regardless of the reality of their affiliation and sympathies. The Red Drum massacre in Phatthalung in the 1970s was closely related to anticommunist operations in Thailand, while the 1980 Kwangju uprising in Korea, at its initial stage, was depicted in the state-controlled media as a riot instigated by impure elements, meaning procommunists or subversives. In these cases, the regimes were basically authoritarian, but they had external political legitimacy that derived from the Cold War divide. For ideological reasons, the prevailing us-them dichotomy tarred the victims as deserving of their miserable fate after the violence.

The Okinawan case also is true in this respect, no exception to the impact of the Cold War divide on the delay of thorough and objective research. The Japanese army's mass killing of Okinawans occurred at the final stage of the Pacific War, and the postwar democratic regime in Japan might have had a chance to conduct truth-finding work about the incident. The Okinawa incident, however, could not become a public agenda item for a long time during the Cold War. The US military administration in Japan between 1945 and 1972 and the continued US presence afterward delayed the emergence of an Okinawan identity, as Hirofumi Hayashi notes in his contribution to this volume. The security of Japan and the importance of the US-Japan alliance were also main issues for both policymakers and academics. To make matters worse, the government's revisionist interpretation of the incident came in 1983, when the Ministry of Education requested that the Okinawa incident be termed a mass suicide.[5]

However, the end of the Cold War divide two decades ago reversed this situation. The notion of security received new attention from the academic community and became omnipresent in the social sciences. Human security in particular, where the referent objects are individuals and groups of people, became an indispensable part of the research agenda. In the 1990s, civilian vulnerability—mass casualties in the Rwandan civil war and the Kosovo conflict—called special attention to human security needs. The frame of reference effectively shifted from the state to its inhabitants, who were now treated as intrinsically deserving of protection by the state and its agencies. Consequently, the state and its agencies could also be held to account if such security was not provided.

Now it is time to shed light on such state violence from a comparative perspective. The examination of the cases focused on in this volume may benefit from the changed international environment and the gradual political transitions in the countries under investigation. Stabilized security in Cambodia and democratization in Indonesia, the Philippines, and Thailand are encouraging signs in the movement to uncover the dark history of these countries. The resolution to the Kwangju incident, which coincided with democratic consolidation in Korea, provides a model for comparison. The significance of the Tiananmen incident in China lies elsewhere: that is, we need to analyze why Tiananmen has not become a public agenda item notwithstanding the rapidly changing nature of Chinese society.

IDENTIFYING VICTIMS AND PERPETRATORS

The initial question arising from an examination of state violence is: who were the victims, and who were the perpetrators? This question is not simple enough to be answered straightforwardly. It is no overstatement that all inquiries about past violence start with this question and end with it as well. The most debatable question that should be addressed in this regard is *why the state targeted the specific groups* under investigation. There might be variations among cases: some accounts, for example, stress the power-competition explanation, emphasizing the military's perception of the threat posed by students' challenge amid a power vacuum, as in the Kwangju case in Korea; some stress the cultural explanation, emphasizing the elite's anger over a shaming challenge to patrimonial governance, as in the Chinese tradition.[6] But these accounts still do not address a key question regarding victims and perpetrators: who stood behind the weapons, and, more important, why did they use a specific form of violence against their particular victims? The latter question considers the issue of threat perception, as well as the recourses and resources available to those in power.

Violence, to use Hannah Arendt's term, is a means to multiply natural strength and to keep the power structure intact.[7] Accordingly, there should be a certain relationship between how rulers perceive challengers and how they use violence in a given situation. If the rulers view a certain peripheral group's actions, whether demonstrations or clandestine organization-building activities, as an existential threat to state sovereignty per se, it is highly probable that they will exercise instrumental violence, as Vincent Boudreau notes in this volume. On the other hand, if the rulers regard the crisis situation as a challenge to the rules of the regime, they may either use exemplary violence or loosen the tightened control. A delicate point here is that rulers as offenders often view the challengers' situation differently from what the challengers originally intended. For instance, the Cold War divide rendered the military leaders in Korea suspicious that the demonstration in Kwangju was instigated by procommunist elements; the anticommunist ideology prevalent in the 1960s drove Indonesian military officers to undertake cruel counterinsurgency measures and to unfairly persecute several hundreds of thousands of men and women, most of whom were innocent of any crime except being members of the Indonesian Communist Party (Partai Komunis Indonesia,

PKI) or its sympathizers. It is fair to say that most cases of state violence involve a serious *perceptual gap* between the perpetrators of violence and those subjected to it, in relation to threat, order, loyalty, and governance.

The question of who were the victims of violence and who were the perpetrators becomes a very hard-pressing one, as any attempt toward resolution invariably enters into a stage of either assessing victims' and perpetrators' versions of the truth or prosecuting perpetrators. In naming victims and perpetrators, there are a number of stumbling blocks. Since the violence in these cases is state led, to name both victims and perpetrators is a "fundamentally political task."[8] Without the approval and assistance of rulers, whether initiated by the new regime or with the cooperation of the old regime, naming victims and offenders is almost impossible. In particular, naming specific people—who ordered or endorsed violence—is a prohibitively difficult task. Even with their identification, assigning all responsibility for the calamity to a single individual is not enough.[9] This is because institutional arrangements must have facilitated such a situation. To make the question more complicated, if the resolution adopts a moderate approach toward the perpetrators, then how a given society deals with those who may say "we were all victims"—that is, that the victims of violence include those who were forced to become evildoers at a particular juncture—is an unavoidable issue.[10] The Khmer Rouge massacre in Cambodia is a good example: layers of orders and hierarchy were involved in executing the mass killing, as well as in causing deaths through starvation and disease, blurring the blade-cut line of responsibility; this was particularly true for the rank-and-file officials who were involved in the massacre but did not know about or predict the chains of atrocity and their consequences.

Counting the number of victims is also related to the settlement of past violence. This issue is problematic both in the process of calling for any form of perpetrator responsibility and in the process of applying criminal justice to perpetrators. It is probable that contentious numbers may haunt perpetrators and that discourses within a society may fall into a numbers game.[11] When the state considers reparation to victims, the numbers issue again becomes contentious, because of the significance of who will be entitled to reparations and who will be excluded. Unlike the issue of identifying victims and perpetrators, however, the numbers question is not a politically divisive, polarizing issue in a society in transition.

THE AFTERMATH OF VIOLENCE: THE JUSTIFIED, FEARED, AND FORGOTTEN PAST

Continued repression is a typical means of quelling any possible distur-bance after the outbreak of state violence, but it is not the only means of doing so. First, the perpetrators in some cases examined here refuse to admit culpability, justifying the violence in the name of protecting integral state sovereignty. Consequently, the victims become double vic-tims: once because of the physical and psychological wounds inflicted by the violence and again because of society's—not to mention the perpe-trators'—treatment of the victims as an "enemy outside" and "enemy of the order."[12] Those who risk association with the victims of violence are labeled subversives, raising suspicion that their behavior is also detrimen-tal to the integrity of the state. The Thai military's repression has been described as a counterinsurgency measure, the Myanmar oppression has been justified for maintaining order within the state, and the demonstra-tion at Tiananmen Square in China is still described as a disturbance of state order.

Because of the state's monopoly on the means of violence and its abil-ity to determine the tone and temper of state-society relations afterward, the victims of violence do not have recourse to shelter within broader society. This dynamic alerts us to another important aspect of states that use violence against their own citizens. Such states invariably con-flate state and regime security: threats perceived by the regime in power are automatically assumed to constitute threats to the state as well. This conflation is naturally interactive with strengthening regime legitimacy. More important, and within a broader context, such definitions also heavily influence the structuration of state-society relations. The regime's discourse and location of the context for the perpetration of violence sim-ply collapse different layers and levels of society into regime-defined con-ceptions of proper and subversive behavior.

Second, fear, for both perpetrators and victims, leaves the postvio-lence situation unchanged in most instances. One explanation for this may be that just as fear of being ostracized makes victims remain silent, so fear of losing privileges and being subjected to punitive justice renders perpetrators equally resistant to settlement of past violence. Victims who did not lose their lives have often been heavily monitored, their move-ments restricted accordingly. Many of them have also been subjected to lengthy periods of detention and even internal political exile, as in the case of Buru Island in Indonesia, the whole of which was designated as a prison colony. For the perpetrators, the fear is political rather than psychological or cultural.[13] A rereading of the past may well render them liable to criminal prosecution. Consequently, it is not uncommon for perpetrators of state violence to destroy evidence that may implicate them, as shown in the cases of Thailand and Indonesia. In Indonesia, the Suharto-led regime actually imposed a ban on research and study of the period leading up to the violence against the PKI.

Finally, the emergence of regulated space maintained by the regime is another reason why past violence has not become a public agenda item. Within this regulated space, the rulers as offenders provide both victims and related groups with various incentives that may be more rewarding than remembering the violence and advocating some form of settlement. Some cases vividly illustrate the types of incentives involved. The reparation to the Okinawan victims in postwar Japan was intended, even if not successful, to create an official memory of them as loyal citizens who fought for the country, rather than as civilians who were killed by the imperial army. The donation to Buddhist monks and temples in postviolence Myanmar, which exceeded normal practices, was apparently aimed at inducing broader support from one of the country's most influential social and legitimizing groups. The rapid economic growth in reformist China not only benefited all Chinese people but also gradually marginalized critics of the regime. In other words, oppression is not the only means by which an unresolved situation is perpetuated; such regulated space also allows rulers to design many means to legitimate the violence afterward. It is difficult to predict how long such regulated space will survive, but it seems clearly to function to alienate victims from many segments of society, watering down the memories of the incident and invariably delaying its resolution.

Divergent Paths of Resolution

Most cases examined in this volume, except Korea and Cambodia, have not reached the point of resolution for the various reasons discussed above. Here it is necessary to start with an examination of the theoretical implications of the two different types of transitional justice if we are to understand the possible paths of resolution that individual postviolence cases are likely to follow.[14] The ongoing UN-sponsored tribunal in Cambodia stands for the initial stages of retributive justice, whereas the step-by-step resolution of the Kwangju incident, running parallel with democratization in the 1980s and the 1990s, represents an admixture of retributive justice and more restorative, reconciliatory justice.

Retributive justice, advocated mostly by legal scholars, maintains that prosecution is a precondition for other elements of resolution, such as repentance, reparation, and reconciliation. The central goals are to punish the perpetrators on the one hand and to reinstate the lost honor and human rights of the victims on the other. Standards of justice are situated within an international framework, that is, the international legal context of human rights.[15] The advocates of retributive justice by and large place less emphasis on the institution as a context for the occurrence of state violence; they are also less concerned about social rehabilitation within a broader context. In the same vein, for these advocates, there is little room for forgiveness and reintegration within a more conciliatory framework.

On the other hand, advocates of restorative justice are mainly concerned with justice's transformative effect in relation to both perpetrators and the society at large. For them, resolution of the violence should be an impetus for the attitudinal and behavioral change of past offenders and for reintegrating them into a new society. Therefore, restorative justice is more closely related to forbearance and social unity than to any other forms of settlement, and for this reason, it is frequently called *reconciliation*. Reconciliation here presupposes "a condition of mutual respect among former enemies" and requires "reciprocal recognition of moral worth and dignity of others," to cite Ernesto Verdeja's normative definition.[16] But reconciliation also has limitations. If the transformative effect of reconciliation is overly emphasized, then resolution of past violence may become a soft option without extensive truth-finding. No doubt, excessive concern about harmony and social consensus invites criticism from advocates of human rights, as well as victims of state violence.

There is quite an interesting parallel between the retributive-restorative dichotomy and the liberal-nonliberal distinction in such matters. The advocacy of retributive justice is akin to the liberal tradition, emphasizing protection of individual human rights and punitive measures over the violation of these rights, whereas advocacy of restorative justice prioritizes restoration of social unity rather than penalizing measures. The retributive-restorative distinction also parallels, if not in exactly the same way, the private-public distinction. Whereas retributive justice values rights at the individual level, restorative justice essentially concerns the public nature of justice. The logic of the latter is that the wounds were inflicted in the name of public order, so that justice over the past public—meaning the old regime—is a crucial part of justice.[17] In this logic, individual rights are relatively, if not absolutely, given less priority than the question of the legitimacy of the old regime.[18]

It is notable that just as the retributive-restorative dichotomy raises an intense theoretical debate, it brings about an equally difficult choice in the real world. In more than half of the cases around the world in the midst of the justice question, particularly in Latin America and Eastern Europe, the path of reconciliation has been taken. Ideally, retributive justice and reconciliatory measures should go hand-in-hand; they should be complementary. Probably the most idealistic approach is to begin with truth-telling and accountability for reinstating victims' political rights and saving them from the stigma of "enemy of the order," then moving to reparation, repentance, conditional amnesty, and forgiveness. In reality, however, the political elite are tempted to take the "second-best choice": social unity and reconciliation. This is so because they want to avoid social polarization in dealing with past violence.[19] Even after regime transition, vestiges of the past are never totally displaced, and members of the previous regime often remain in positions of power and influence. This is especially the case if a military authoritarian regime was previously in power. The military's notion of discipline and solidarity often makes it difficult for perpetrators to be criminally prosecuted. Rank-and-file loyalties and the military's corporate image may also affect the form of resolution that is available. In fact, it is not uncommon for such regimes, or senior individuals within them, to arrange for immunity or impunity prior to regime transition.

Is there any practical need for truth-telling and its instrument, the truth commission, in the process of the resolution of past violence? The truth commission eventually aims at reconciliation even if it pursues strict punitive justice over perpetrators at the initial stage; the establishment of a truth commission presupposes—probably with the exception of the imprisonment of top commanders—such ensuing processes as offenders' repentance, victims' forgiveness, and amnesty from the succeeding regime. The success or failure of a truth commission depends on appraisals of its role. For instance, there are diverging views on the Truth and Reconciliation Committee (TRC) in South Africa. Advocates of human rights groups particularly have charged that the TRC watered down the legal standards of criminal justice and failed to play its expected role in restoring the victims' rights.[20] Furthermore, when the truth commission is considered a state-manipulated ritual and as presenting a spectacular scene of the victims' pain and suffering, it will be subject to severe public criticism. Such ritualistic public testimony may overly individualize political calamity and thus ignore the deeper structure of violence.[21] Even if such appraisals or criticisms are not within the mainstream, the role of truth commissions, whether for postviolence resolution in a broader sense or for the healing of victims' wounds in a narrower sense, remains controversial.

The truth commission is not the only solution to past violence, but its value in regard to democratic practices should not be ignored. On the one hand, truth-telling, as Leigh Payne aptly notes, might justify violence if the offenders speak only about the crimes they wish to confess. In this case, the victims of past evils are victimized again rather than healed by such perpetrators' self-justification. On the other hand, truth-telling and truth commissions, as Payne argues, may contribute to democratization. Telling the story of the horrible experience of the victims; confessing to crimes, even if the narrative is incomplete; feeling repentance and remorse—all these actions open up some new space where a possible "contentious coexistence" may be created.[22] The victims, who have been treated as the enemy outside, and the evildoers, who are now the enemy of justice, may be situated together with a new value: mutual accommodation. In this respect, Kirk Simpson notes the need for "communicative justice," through which public democratic deliberation and communication take place among all people, offenders as well as victims. Borrowing Jürgen Habermas's notion of communicative action in the public sphere, Simpson maintains that communicative justice is the core aspect of transition to peace and reconciliation.[23]

In sum, dealing with past violence in East Asia (especially the unsettled cases of the Philippines, Myanmar, Thailand, Okinawa, China, and Indonesia), societies must pass through both contentious debates and hard-pressing political choices regarding the questions of retributive-versus-restorative justice and punitive-versus-reconciliatory resolution. The backdrop of this bifurcation may be relevant to the nature of state–

civil society relations at the particular juncture of the resolution of the past violence—for instance, whether or not state–civil society relations have changed since the occurrence of violence. In other words, understanding why a certain country takes a specific path—in relation to the resolution of past violence—must go hand in hand with understanding changes in state-society relations and democratization. If a country has no other way forward but to accept the international arrangement of resolution, then postviolence settlement is highly likely to begin with retributive justice. The ongoing trials in Cambodia illustrate just such an outcome.

The Relationship between Political Transition and Resolution

Does the resolution of state violence bring about political transition, or does political transition provide an appropriate environment for resolution? What, if any, is the cause-and-effect relationship between the two? If the relationship is not one of cause and effect, how is one relevant to or interactive with the other?

To postulate: the resolution of past violence, either punitive or reconciliatory, is an inevitable step in creating new social relations, one that may truly take place in the process of transition. The analysis of state violence and its resolution is logically associated with an understanding of political change. On the one hand, reconciliatory resolution, as well as punitive justice in some sense, will likely promote new democratic practices and end the state's illegitimate use of violence and its old practices of transgressing human rights. On the other hand, room for the resolution of past violence is more likely created when the old regime breaks down or when the existing regime concedes to allow truth-telling. In the particular case of the existing regime's concession, such regimes tend to take preemptive moves to prevent harsher retributive justice by later rulers.[24] For example, an authoritarian regime may pass laws that admit, even if incompletely, its misdeeds and pardon those associated with state violence prior to a transfer of power, and the succeeding regime may acquiesce to such a request.

An empirical question arises from this ongoing discussion. Why is a new regime—or a newly emerging order—more likely to make the practical choice of restorative, reconciliatory resolution rather than rigid, victim-centered retributive justice in dealing with the past? In the majority of state-violence cases, as exemplified in Spain, Chile, El Salvador, Brazil, and Poland, restorative reconciliation has been chosen.[25] One answer might lie in the presumption that reconciliation will be more viable in the long run.[26] It may be more practical and feasible to draw a consensus for social unity holding that perpetrators are fallible human beings who should be given a chance to contribute to reconstruction.[27]

The more convincing answer, however, lies in the fact that transition in general involves many forms of institutionalization, such as introduction of an electoral system, consolidation of the rule of law, and establishment of power-transition rules; in turn, institutionalization entails various forms of negotiation, and bargaining and compromise are at the heart of the transition.[28] In this context, the resolution of the past violence tends to become one of several subjects of negotiation, a situation that both victims of violence and advocates of human rights sometimes do not expect to materialize. Also, resolution tends to become a topic of the *pact* between the opposition and the state in place—whether a rising new regime or the decaying old regime. According to Guillermo O'Donnell and Philippe C. Schmitter, such a pact is desirable for democratic transition, more effective than continuous contention with a divisive agenda.[29] The important point is something more than what is desirable; it is an empirical question of under what conditions transition is more likely to be successful, as exemplified by the TRC in South Africa and by the May 18 special laws in Korea. As opposed to the successful cases, the Argentine case is instructive in another sense. The Raul Alfonsin administration's rigid retributive justice for the crimes of the "dirty war," which was led by the military regime of 1976 to 1980 and brought about more than nine thousand deaths, ended in failure in 1989. In this case, overly restrictive, punitive justice arrived at an impasse, ironically polarizing the society because of the vestiges of military power and failing to properly respond to mounting public expectations in a time-constrained situation.[30]

Particularly in the cases of Indonesia, Thailand, the Philippines, Myanmar, and China, the military has remained a significant feature of the state apparatus, either dominating or sustaining order within society, while showing varying degrees of change in its role since its involvement in state violence; therefore, the form of the military's engagement in the institutionalization of political transition deserves special attention in relation to the resolution of past violence. There should be increasing legitimacy concerns within the military regarding the process of institutionalization, and such concerns must be closely associated with changes in the apparatus's perception of the threat and of the opposition, as Alfred Stephan notes.[31] Further, the military's readiness to shift its major focus from the domestic order to its own professionalism is a key indicator of institutionalization, allowing means toward the resolution of past violence to be deliberated.[32] In addition, the resolution of state violence depends on the relative empowerment of civil society at the time of transition, either positioning past state violence for punitive justice or arriving at compromise and reconciliation through negotiation and bargaining with the main perpetrator—the military, in most unresolved cases. It seems that the success or failure of resolution depends on the proximity of justice in application to each country's unique mode of transition rather than on the form of justice per se. Consequently, it is difficult to be prescriptive with regard to what models should be adopted in the East Asian cases. The natural fear deriving from any judgment of this sort, especially when longer-term reconciliation between the state and society is desired, is that the perpetrators of violence will be pardoned during the process of resolution on the utilitarian premise of achieving the greatest good for the greatest number.

NOTES

1. For an extensive discussion of the relationship among global significance, public awareness of state violence, and the ensuing alteration of state behavior, see James Ron, "Varying Methods of State Violence," *International Organization* 51, no. 2 (1997): 275–300.

2. H. H. Gerth and C. Wright Mills, eds., *From Max Weber: Essays in Sociology* (Oxford: Oxford University Press, 1958), 78, 124.

3. Charles Tilly, *From Mobilization to Revolution* (Reading, MA: Addison-Wesley, 1978).

4. See Barry Buzan, *People, States, and Fear: The National Security Problems in International Relations* (London: Harvester Wheatsheaf, 1983).

5. For details on the Cold War situation and the Japanese government's ideological disposition, which impeded extensive research on Okinawa and other Japanese war-crime issues, see Yoshiko Nozaki, *War Memory, Nationalism and Education in Postwar Japan, 1945–2007: The Japanese History Textbook Controversy and Ienaga Saburo's Court Challenges* (London and New York: Routledge, 2008).

6. Particularly for the Chinese case, see Jeffrey Wasserstrom, *Student Protests in Twentieth-Century China* (Stanford: Stanford University Press, 1991); L. H. M.

Ling, "Rationalizations for State Violence in Chinese Politics: The Hegemony of Parental Governance," *Journal of Peace Research* 31, no. 4 (1994): 393–405.

7. Hannah Arendt, "From *On Violence*," in *Violence in War and Peace: An Anthology*, ed. Nancy Scheper-Hughes and Philippe Bourgois (Oxford: Blackwell, 2004), 239.

8. Jemma Purdey, "Problematizing the Place of Victims in *Reformasi* Indonesia: A Contested Truth about the May 1998 Violence," *Asian Survey* 42, no. 4 (2002): 621.

9. Ibid., 617.

10. Katherine E. McGregor, "Confronting the Past in Contemporary Indonesia: The Anti-Communist Killings of 1965–66 and the Role of the Nahdlatul Ulama," *Critical Asian Studies* 41, no. 2 (2009): 195–224.

11. One exemplary case of the numbers game concerns the number of casualties of the Nanjing massacre. The notion of the numbers game was inspired by Iris Chang, *Rape of Nanking: The Forgotten Holocaust of World War II* (New York: Basic Books, 1997); for details of the ongoing game, see Peter H. Gries, *China's New Nationalism: Pride, Politics, and Diplomacy* (Berkeley and London: University of California Press, 2004).

12. Daniel Philpott, "Beyond Politics as Usual: Is Reconciliation Compatible with Liberalism?" in *The Politics of Past Evil: Religion, Reconciliation, and the Dilemmas of Transitional Justice*, ed. Daniel Philpott (Notre Dame: University of Notre Dame Press, 2006), 17.

13. Brandon Hamber, "Flying Flags of Fear: The Role of Fear in the Process of Political Transition," *Journal of Human Rights* 5 (2006): 127–42.

14. For a comprehensive discussion of the retributive-restorative distinction, see Mark R. Amstutz, "Restorative Justice, Political Forgiveness, and the Possibility of Political Reconciliation," in Philpott, *Politics of Past Evil*, 165–67.

15. Vikki Bell and Kirsten Campbell, "Out of Conflict: Peace, Change and Justice," *Social and Legal Studies* 13, no. 3 (2004): 299–301.

16. Ernesto Verdeja, *Unchopping a Tree: Reconciliation in the Aftermath of Political Violence* (Philadelphia: Temple University Press, 2009), 3.

17. Philpott, "Beyond Politics as Usual," 29.

18. For discussion of the conditions for successful retributive justice in particular, see Ellen L. Lutz and Caitlin Reiger, "Conclusion," in *Prosecuting Heads of State*, ed. Ellen L. Lutz and Caitlin Reiger (Cambridge and New York: Cambridge University Press, 2009), 275–93.

19. Philpott, "Beyond Politics as Usual," 17–19, 37.

20. Amstutz, "Restorative Justice," 175.

21. Michael Humphrey, "From Victim to Victimhood: Truth Commissions and Trials as Rituals of Political Transition and Individual Healing," *Australian Journal of Anthropology* 13, no. 2 (2003): 171–87.

22. Leigh A. Payne, *Unsettling Accounts: Neither Truth nor Reconciliation in Confessions of State Violence* (Durham: Duke University Press, 2008).

23. Kirk Simpson, "Victims of Political Violence: A Habermasian Model of Truth Recovery," *Journal of Human Rights* 6 (2007): 325–43.

24. For self-punitive, preemptive moves, see Jon Elster, *Closing Books: Transitional Justice in Historical Perspective* (Cambridge: Cambridge University Press, 2004), 258.

25. Paloma Aguilar, "Justice, Politics and Memory in the Spanish Transition," in *The Politics of Memory: Transitional Justice in Democratizing Societies,* ed. A. Barahona de Brito, C. Gonzalez Enriquez, and Paloma Aguilar (Oxford: Oxford University Press, 2001), 92–118; Lavinia Stan, "Truth Commissions in Post-Communism: The Overlooked Solution?" *Open Political Science Journal* 2 (2009): 1–13.

26. See A. James McAdams, "The Double Demands of Reconciliation: The Case of Unified Germany," in Philpott, *Politics of Past Evil,* 129.

27. Ibid., 149.

28. Helga A. Welsh, "Political Transition Process in Central and Eastern Europe," *Comparative Politics* 26, no. 4 (1994): 391.

29. Guillermo O'Donnell and Philippe C. Schmitter, *Transitions from Authoritarian Rule: Tentative Conclusion about Uncertain Democracies* (Baltimore: Johns Hopkins University Press, 1984).

30. Amstutz, "Restorative Justice," 169–72.

31. Alfred Stephan, *Rethinking Military Politics: Brazil and the Southern Cone* (Princeton: Princeton University Press, 1988), 64–66.

32. For the significance of the military's professionalism in transition, see Juan J. Linz and Alfred Stephan, *Problems of Democratic Transition and Consolidation: Southern Europe, South American and Post-Communist Europe* (Baltimore and London: Johns Hopkins University Press, 1996), 219–20; Deborah L. Norden, "Democratic Consolidation and Military Professionalism: Argentina in the 1980s," *Journal of Interamerican Studies and World Affairs* 32, no. 3 (1990): 151–76; J. Samuel Fitch, "Military Professionalism, National Security and Democracy: Lessons from the Latin American Experience," *Pacific Focus* 4, no. 2 (1989): 99–147.

1

Interpreting State Violence in Asian Settings

Vince Boudreau

In this chapter I set out to analyze state violence in terms of the social and political role it plays—seeking to uncover its logic and objectives, rather than regarding it as fundamentally aberrant. Indeed, a long and strong tradition exists in the theoretical literature that examines state violence as instrumental to a host of political processes, in ways that implicitly argue for this kind of interpretive effort. An analysis of violence is central: to Barrington Moore's passages from tradition to modernity; to any number of state-building accounts; to the struggle for democracy, enfranchisement, and representation; and to the defense of authoritarian orders under attack.[1] Here I explore the logic of state violence in Asia, paying particular attention to its relationship to larger political processes and primarily to questions of the relationship between state power and political challengers. In this account, I investigate both the conditions that produce different forms of violence and the trajectory of violent legacies in political power and contention moving forward. Where efforts to reconcile past acts of violence take place, what prompts those efforts? Where states are able to move forward without explicitly dealing with a violent history, how is that possible? And, where the unresolved memory of violence rises as part of an effort to displace unjust authority, what conditions seem to make that possible?

The chapter proceeds in three substantive parts. In the first section, I set the stage for the examination of state violence, beginning by theorizing the situations that influence the character and intensity of that violence and the particular elements of the Asian state-building process that drive violence in different directions from that associated with oft-analyzed European state building. In the next section, I examine in a more sustained way how violence can be expected to vary in the Asian context, situating patterns of attack against larger political processes in Asia and using that contextualization to differentiate among Asian cases. In the third section, I examine the legacies of state violence, exploring the often complicated relationship among punishment, reconciliation, and forgetfulness, all of which play a part in the varied trajectories of violence in the life of a nation.

While this article represents but a preliminary discussion, I hope these ideas will help future examinations of state violence in several ways. First, we may be in a better position to make sense of state violence if we inquire after its logic rather than its magnitude. My assumptions here are twofold. On the one hand, the immediate logic of state violence reflects authorities' efforts to deal with a challenge to existing or emergent power—to build the state, enforce its rules, or gain and defend power within that system. But because such political actors must ultimately look to construct a viable future for their regime, the question of reconciling the victims and witnesses of violence to the resulting political settlement is never too distant. Crisis and political exigency may, under conditions we will examine, suppress those considerations. But state actors cannot ignore questions of reconciliation, and such questions often shape both how violence unfolds and how it is subsequently dealt with.

Three short-term factors influence patterns of violence. *First,* what larger political processes set the tone for violence? State agents act violently for a variety of reasons, including that individual actors are untrained or poorly disciplined. But big political processes like state building, regime construction, or crisis management also motivate and shape violence, and such processes call forth distinct patterns of violence. *Second* and within those processes, what specific tasks does violence seek to accomplish? Violence may eliminate challengers and subversives, may establish hegemony by displacing loyalties, or may change political behavior. It has, that is, both instrumental and exemplary purposes: it torches and teaches. While these objectives mingle in many cases, tracing them through specific episodes of state attack helps one situate the violence politically.

Finally, how does the relationship between the targets of violence and the larger political community influence state attacks? Targets may represent large blocs of cosmopolitan society—as when a regime has a narrow social base—or can be smaller and more isolated groups within that society. They may also be geographically or categorically distinct from majority populations (or from populations that control the state). They may, *third,* be factions of the state or have a distinct organizational or institutional locus. Because violence can undercut an opponent or spur massive countermobilization, the relationship between those targeted by violence and other significant political communities will influence violent strategies.

In addition to these three factors, however, a *fourth,* long-run consideration influences violence. State actors also take into account longer-term needs to reconcile the political community to acts of state violence. Such objectives influence both how authorities restrain and explain violence and how violence is treated in historical memory and national courts. Questions of how to reconcile violence (in the broadest possible terms, to include cases in which it is ignored or forgotten) require attention to another set of actors, for *political* violence always plays out in relation to larger publics. For these publics, violence varies along two dimensions: it is a more or less visible spectacle, enacted in communities that are more or less different or distinct from their own. Such considerations help direct violence in specific directions. In some cases, the narrative of violence coalesces around the theme of eliminating unreconcilable subversives; in others it will be explained as a step toward a well-ordered political community. Sometimes, it will be ignored entirely.

STATES, REGIMES, AND VIOLENCE: THEORETICAL CONSIDERATIONS

If the threat of violence underlies the authority of even the most established and settled states, naked violence is never, in the long term, a stable or efficient foundation for governance.[2] The direction and intensity of state violence will depend on the kinds of challenges that authorities face and the sorts of resources (both coercive and noncoercive) that they have at their disposal. Accordingly, violence associated with state emergence, struggles for state control, over unstable or contested regimes, and in settled regimes will vary. Distinctions between state building, regime construction and politics under settled regimes influence state violence and so constitute key elements of my argument here.

States and Regimes

State building, and particularly the expanding geographic scope of state authority, involves more or less direct efforts to bring people living *outside* state authority *under* state control and includes the construction of institutions and capacities that enable those efforts.[3] Coercion moves center stage in these processes as authorities dismount or subsume rival centers of power, direct authority away from local social actors, and extract resources to enhance their power.[4] Regime construction, in contrast, involves the regularization of rules for the exercise of power, including the principles according to which leaders are selected; how governments are structured; who has access to political, social, and civil rights; and how protected those rights will be.[5] Regimes benefit from their ability to clarify rules and meet popular expectations, provide services, and produce stronger normative resonance and active social support.[6] The movement from state building, to regime construction, to politics under more settled political arrangements both narrows the range of what is contested between states and society and provides authorities with an increasingly broad range of noncoercive tools to use against dissidents and rebels.

Differences between dynamics of state building and regime construction or maintenance inform authorities' use of coercion. The initial resources that aspiring authorities bring to state building tilt heavily toward the coercive and extractive. Men are pressed into military service, taxes are forcibly extracted from agricultural classes, and local rulers are dismounted or subsumed over a superordinate authority structure. Little initial effort may be made to explain or justify these moves—superior force, in the Hobbesian world of early state building, provides its own justificatory framework. As state hegemony becomes a more settled matter, new questions arise about the rules that will govern the political community. At such moments, incumbents can often reinforce their position through nationalist appeals, the invocation of patriotic norms, the provision of real or illusory participatory opportunities, and the distribution of resources.[7] As rules and institutions regularize expectations and generate legitimacy, noncoercive means of control proliferate, and the character of conflict between authorities and opponents should shift.[8] Early state building occasions more generally zero-sum conflicts over who will rule, while the potential for compromise, cooptation, and side payments grows more robust in negotiations over the regime and in later expansions of state power. This is not to say that violence necessarily diminishes in the process—but the logic of how authorities respond to recalcitrants unfolds against new conditions. Governments engage dissidents in the context of other citizens, some who strongly support the regime, some who may sympathize with dissidents, and many who will be on the fence. State coercion will strive both to punish or discipline those who resist government authority and to demonstrate the advantages of compliance to those who could go either way. Indeed, in such cases, indiscriminate or excessive regime violence may undercut rather than enhance government power and stability. States with shallower reservoirs of legitimacy or slimmer resources to distribute may locate violence more centrally in their control repertoire—but the strategy will have costs and reflects already diminished resources available to those in more stable governments.

Naturally, state violence is not confined to the relationships between government authorities and societies: sharp conflict sometimes also emerges for control within states and regimes. When state actors seek to shoulder one another aside, they may fall back upon more instrumental coercion, reminiscent of early state building and far less concerned with demonstrating or enforcing modes of behavior—for such struggles take place among specific contestants, and those who wield violence have no need to specify categories of activity as their targets. As in early state building, the architects of this violence use it initially to resolve an immediate challenge or displace a proximate rival—but of course the scope of that violence depends on the size and solidity of social support for one or another challenge to state power. In many such cases—one thinks of most Thai military coups, as well as similar episodes in Korea and the Philippines—instrumental violence takes place within a narrow circle of direct aspirants to state power.[9] But follow-up activity, often designed to solidify a new regime around the new set of state leaders, can expand across society. In Indonesia, small circles of conspirators were linked to larger, less involved social groups.[10] In either case, direct and instrumental violence resolves the contest for who will control the state; victors and victims may then subsequently think about the longer-term legacy of the violence, its victims, and the political community.

While we can attempt to separate state building, regime construction, and internal state power struggles analytically, activities often over-lap these seemingly discrete categories. Efforts to establish new rules or arrangements of power may require authorities to construct a new appa-ratus to exercise that power and, in the process, displace rivals (classic state-building activity). Those constructing state institutions may in the process also lay down and communicate the rules that govern them (and so set forth elements of the regime). Shortly, I will make the case that the extent and nature of the overlap are part of what distinguishes state-building activity in Asia—but the precise differentiation of coercion into categories of either state building or regime construction will not always be possible. Hence, rather than thinking about state building and regime construction as utterly distinct, it makes more sense to regard them as different but related elements of the extension and defense of political hegemony—an extension that relies on some combination of norma-tive appeals, the provision of services and certainty, and coercion. Still, rewards await those who try to sort out differences between state building and regime construction or to disentangle different elements of the pro-cess: figuring out what authorities are trying to do will help us understand how violence is likely to take place. For our purposes, state building and regime formation/defense will operate as a kind of habitat that organizes more discrete elements of the relationship among different parties to state violence.

Instrumental and Exemplary Violence

Moving down the ladder of abstraction from the larger political processes in which violence is embedded, we next consider state violence in rela-tionship to the specific tasks it accomplishes on the ground and the kinds of opponents it engages. Working for the moment in a typology mode that will briefly ignore intermediate or mixed cases, we can describe some violence as *instrumental* and other violence as *exemplary*.[11] Instrumental violence sets out directly to neutralize or displace a threat or challenge. Instrumental violence in state building targets rival centers of power. It puts down rebels and replaces rival authorities with state institutions and agents. Instrumental violence directly disrupts, disaggregates, or elimi-nates political targets. Authorities troubled by communists may round them up for detention or murder. Ethnic cleansing is direct violence, as are campaigns to disarm militia. Instrumental violence—to the extent that it is purely instrumental—does not primarily attempt to "teach" people but to pacify them. Violence that seeks to delineate proper modes of political conduct, and to advertise those sanctions that will be visited on those who ignore such modes, is exemplary. Exemplary violence has both primary targets (in relation to whom it has instrumental effects) and secondary audiences: people who are not directly involved in the attack as victims or perpetrators, but who take lessons from it. Exemplary violence in defense of a (new or old) political regime seeks to influence both primary and secondary audiences—punishing the former but teaching the latter.

As with state building and regime construction, distinctions between exemplary and instrumental violence are almost never absolute. At least *some* exemplary and instrumental objectives animate most violence. What I have called exemplary violence is almost always, in some measure, also instrumental: broadly explained and publicized sanctions on labor organizing or peasant land occupation may both discourage the diffusion of that activity *and* temporarily or permanently eliminate specific rule breakers.[12] Similarly, instrumental violence can always be regarded by bystanders in exemplary terms—as they try to figure out why one or another group came under attack.[13] Rather than encouraging an effort to identify two clearly separate species of violence, therefore, the concepts help us interpret political influences that operate within violence, including the interaction of instrumental and demonstrative objectives.

The clearest observable implication of the difference between instrumental and exemplary violence lies in targeting strategies. Instrumental violence will typically involve proscription of a certain kind of person, actor, or organization. Some will be categorically proscribed—as communists or enemy nationals. Some will be proscribed for membership in organizations that have been identified, tout court, as subversive or terrorist—rather than for specific transgressions. Exemplary violence takes greater care to specify proscribed activity in its identification of targets, and in this specification, it also lays out the terms of reconciliation or rehabilitation. In this sense, exemplary violence attempts to create a political alignment that isolates state targets and drives more citizens into compliance with regime rules. Instrumental violence more often accepts the existing battle lines in society—either because a proscribed group is so isolated that its attack will not mobilize support or because even a large and centrally situated group is deemed to be a fundamental threat.

Reconciliation

A final key element in the interpretation of violence lies in the relation-ship between that violence and the prospects of political reconciliation. Reconciliation is, of course, a tricky thing, requiring that people facing each other across a divide of injury and recrimination decide to close that gap. Several things make it easier to contemplate this kind of closure, including the passage of time and the demonstrated ability of a violence-inscribed order to represent the interests and safeguard the well-being of even those targeted by that initial violence. Several things make it harder to close the gap, including the persistence of categorical differences, par-ticularly when those also indicate categorical inequality, across the locus of violence. Different modes of violence also influence the magnitude of a reconciliation project—and we expect people specifically targeted for sanction or elimination to be less reconcilable to violence than those pre-sented as having violated a given set of rules.

Two important considerations follow. The first emerges from the dif-ferences between exemplary and instrumental violence. Exemplary vio-lence may be reconciled over time, as people adapt to the new regime and new principles of behavior become routine and accepted. As new political orders emerge and strengthen, they can retrospectively cast regime-changing violence as law enforcement. The extent to which the regime succeeds in contextualizing violence in this way will likely reflect, in part, the extent to which the regime acquires broad legitimacy. More instrumental violence needs to make the case that a certain class of peo-ple needed to be attacked—and that can be a tougher argument to make, for the specific targeting of individuals requires some clear discussion of why such people require sanction. Particularly where liberal or inclusive norms play some part in the legitimation strategy, it may pull against the unresolved legacies of violence in the past—particularly when the victims of that violence survive or have committed advocates.

This brings us to the second consideration: how the spatial and cat-egorical relationships between victims and perpetrators influence the prospect of reconciliation. Three considerations concern us here. First, individuals who are targeted because of ascriptive attributes—ethnicity, religion, and the like—will be least easily reconciled to that violence. Second, victims who cluster in identifiable regions will be harder to rec-oncile, at least to the extent that those regional distinctions persist over time. Finally, organizations and political parties that are targeted by violence will demand an accounting when they continue to exist and retain some power. It may be, of course, that such groups will disappear, remain politically marginalized, or go into hiding. But if they remain they will be difficult constituencies to reconcile without substantial effort. In all of these instances, the victims of violence, or their representatives, play primary roles in demanding restitution and justice. But whole categories of citizens, as we have seen, also interact with the politics of violence in other ways. Cosmopolitan citizens are also often the targets of government explanations about why a particular region, a given ethnicity, or a far-flung political movement posed a danger and needed to be targeted. In such cases, a discourse of security may replace a discourse of justice. Instrumental attacks on subversives may be packaged in exemplary terms for other citizens or may be presented as government protection against internal subversion.

This point underscores a basic difference between violence that takes place against mainstream cosmopolitan populations and violence that targets more marginal or region-specific groups. Urban centers and mainstream populations are often more politically significant in national power calculations, and violence against such groups must be justified to those populations—or presented in terms of overwhelming state need and power. Similarly intensive but more removed violence can be presented in different ways to different populations—as the act of an intractable, invincible state to targets in the periphery and as a defending power, rooting out subversion, to urban populations. For analysts of state violence, this means paying close attention to how state strategies to explain and reconcile violence take place across variegated settings.

These considerations interact in processes of reconciliation in ways that we can preview and anticipate here—but that play out in complicated ways in each case. While a fully formed theory of state violence in different settings is beyond my grasp here, it is possible to lay out some assumptions about the pressures driving violence in one direction or another and the pressures that guide reconciliation strategies. First, violence against cosmopolitan populations, given their political centrality, will require more immediate reconciliation than violence against populations that are further removed or isolated; that means a more careful effort to calibrate and explain that violence. Accordingly, instrumental violence must carefully discriminate subversives from citizens, and exemplary violence will come under pressure to be consistently and clearly applied. As a general rule, the broader the range of potential targets, the more we would expect violence against cosmopolitan targets to present itself in exemplary terms. In contrast, violence deployed against more categorically or geographically distinct groups will need less immediate reconciliation; other things being equal, this drives it in directions that are less restrained. Norms of proper conduct may be less important in peripheral communities than sheer domination, and that should make violence more instrumental and of a less exemplary direction.[14] We expect to more frequently encounter stories of individuals being branded as subversive people, rather than being held to account because they have violated specific laws or rules of conduct.

Strategies to explain, discuss, and justify violence—all part of larger reconciliation strategies—should also vary depending on the population in question. Among central populations, exemplary violence will be packaged as measures to ensure law and order and will seek support among the same populations that states attack; rhetorical strategies to present violence will very much resemble a campaign for the political loyalties of people and represent a warning for those whose loyalties may be suspect. Instrumental violence in such settings will most likely be framed as identifying subversives and running them to ground—in the process, offering an interpretation of bystanders as endangered by the targets of violence and protected by its perpetrators. In rare cases, such as the Khmer Rouge massacres that Sorpong Peou describes in this collection, changing regimes is conceived in terms of eliminating those who engage in regime practices; in such settings, widespread violence often regards people engaged in some practice (capitalism in the Cambodian case) as if that practice were an ascriptive, irredeemable element of their identity.[15] In either case, the reconciliation of violence that occurs in cosmopolitan settings will need to be more contemporary with the violence itself and framed as efforts to protect society against threats. It will also offer some set of rules that witnesses can adopt to avoid running afoul of the state.

Violence that targets more distinct or marginal groups is potentially separate from these same cosmopolitan audiences and witnesses, and this allows state agents to develop dual reconciliation strategies: one for cosmopolitan audiences and one for those more categorically similar to victims. Under some circumstances, this violence will be secreted away from cosmopolitan audiences but well known and advertised among those it targets—a pattern clearly in evidence in the Red Drum killings.[16] In other cases, it will be presented to national audiences as restoring law and order in the periphery but understood by those in the peripheries as campaigns against people of specific types—something we see both in contemporary Thai violence in Patani and in histories of counterinsurgency in Mindanao, East Timor, and elsewhere.

Naturally, these reflections merely suggest things an interpretation of violence should account for—whether the violence is hidden or advertised, whether the victims are presented as criminals or subversives, and whether attacks or descriptions of attacks stress prohibited activity or contaminating people. Interpreting reconciliation strategies and violence in any case requires analysis of political and social circumstances—but the effort begins by asking about how forms of violence and social relationships interact.

State Building in Asia and Beyond

It is possible to regard state-building and regime-construction processes as a kind of habitat, within which authorities attempt a range of specific tasks and encounter a range of challenges. In general, I have suggested that violence attached to state building is more likely to be *instrumental* and that violence associated with changes in the political regime should tend toward the *exemplary*. That is, when state control is seriously at issue, authorities will seek directly to disrupt, undercut, or eliminate alternative centers of power. One probably should also expect fairly direct, instrumental violence in cases where rival authorities compete for control over the state. The construction or defense of a regime, in contrast, will utilize violence tending toward exemplary modalities. Regime-changing violence often targets people living in the same political space as those who are expected ultimately to accept that violence as just: often, of course, they are one and the same. Working to establish this new political ordering, authorities attempt to justify violence in terms of proper conduct and the greater good. New regime rules may undercut rivals—but they also must form the foundation for new political support and an emergent hegemony. Hence, even where regime-changing violence first appears as ad hoc or random attacks, it will need to evolve in more categorical and consistently applied sanctions.[17]

It follows that different patterns of state building—and its different relationship with regime construction—will set up different patterns of violence. Where states expand geographically to add peripheries to thoroughly penetrated central realms (a pattern of expansion that accompanied colonial conquest and postcolonial state building in many Southeast Asian countries), central authorities need to explain violence against national peripheries to centrally situated populations, but not (at least initially) to the victims of that violence. This situation probably generates relatively little pressure to moderate the violence itself and may open rather crude justificatory strategies in relations to central populations. Where state building concentrates on central populations—deepening, for instance, the penetration of state agencies among those populations— it may need more thoroughly to explain and justify violence as it goes along, which may work to moderate violence. In such cases, state building and regime construction move forward more or less apace with one another, and that synchronicity should drive violence in exemplary directions. In this sense, the relationship between the victims of violence and other populations depends on patterns of state building—something I discuss shortly.

STATE BUILDING AND VIOLENCE IN ASIA AND IN GENERAL

Classic accounts of state building often present a kind of segregated relationship between the high periods of state violence and eras when the legitimation of that order receives greater attention. In Europe, for example, the active application of state violence recedes into reservoirs of legitimate coercive *capacity* as efforts to fortify government move from martial to civic postures. Tilly's organized criminals and racketeers eventually extend democratic rights to their populations; as they do so, state violence shifts to a less proximate tool of governance.[18] The boundary between exclusion and inclusion may routinely be enforced by state violence: against new immigrants to a nation-state, against disenfranchised populations clamoring for representation, against labor and farm workers seeking greater protection. But by the time these struggles for enfranchisement were taking place, the broader social pact—that state power will be legitimized through some form of consultation, participation, and performance—had displaced naked state violence as the core mediating relationship between states and societies.[19] The varieties of rules through which this pact took shape represented the range of political regimes. In such accounts, state and regime building are largely separate and sequenced processes: new states first establish hegemony and then figure out how to arrange and signal regime rules and, eventually, how to make those rules palatable.[20] Moreover, state building and regime construction in Europe often took place in a context of largely unmobilized societies and before working people were incorporated into their political systems.[21] In early state building, an originally limited coercive network developed a new scale and a programmatic scope, displacing contenders but not penetrating too deeply into society. Subsequent periods of enfranchisement and mobilization were separated from initial state building in space and time.

In respect to both factors, the Asian cases that most concern us here present very different dynamics. First, historical pressures in many Asian cases conspired to more closely embroil state building and regime construction. Models of what states were had become more elaborated and available by the twentieth century.[22] While benefiting from the advantages of later development, this meant that Asian states never stood so far apart from the regulation of social life as they had in Europe. Second, colonial resources and activity frequently created a diverse entourage of potential state leaders bidding to take charge of things when Europeans departed.[23] A host of what had been later entrants to the Western political scene existed at independence: mobilized social groups, participating citizens, civil organization, schools and universities, clear ideas about human and participatory rights, some transnational networks, and the pale shadow of global civil society.[24] The former element of the Asian political scene made for a more diverse competition for state power. The latter made the separation of state- and regime-building processes untenable for very long.

World time and the location of many such struggles in the aftermath of colonialism explain important elements of the difference. The rather late decolonization across much of Asia (no less than the top-down Meiji modernization in Japan) took place in a world with clear and fully elaborated models of what states were and what they were supposed to do. Many of these functions included institutions and practices designed to harness the energies and participation of mass populations. In cases like Siam, Burma, and Japan, local efforts imitated earlier European or American developments, introducing mass conscription or education for bureaucratic service.[25] Elsewhere, the occupation and attempted reani-

mation of abandoned colonial structure transmitted a colonial framework for state rule to local actors. But the process also called forth a range
of different aspirants to state leadership and to full citizenship: nationalist movements and their leaders, men with significant martial accom-
plishment, members of the old (or newly burnished) nobility, those with
experience and standing in the colonial administration, graduates of new
and modern schools.[26] The sequence reverses a classic precedent—where
the imagination *of* rule and the capacity *to* rule traveled together. Initial
European competition around state building hence took place between
those who could direct the new apparatus and those who held to other,
more localized modes of rule. In Asia, the possibility of a national state,
from the outset, had a range of diverse contenders for the position of state
leader.

   This more fully elaborated idea of national states also deeply influenced politics among elite aspirants to state power; two elements of this
influence are most immediately important. First, while all settings did
not produce the full cast of potential characters, virtually nowhere did
the drama emerge among only a single *kind* of aspirant. The contest
was therefore both over the identity of rulers and over the modalities of
power and rule: about both the state and the character of the regime.
The dynamic, I should emphasize, was profoundly connected to colonialism, as an examination of Southeast Asia's one *un*colonized country, Thailand, demonstrates. Anderson's description of political murders
in modern Siam, moving as it does from the homogenous ranks of the
royal family to a more diverse set of aspiring parliamentarians, feels in
some ways distinctly Shakespearian: Rosencrantz and Guildenstern were
collateral damage in ways that Aung San or Sukarno clearly were *not*.[27]
Across much of the region, contests for state power were not restricted
to a single kind of elite but took place, and *specifically targeted,* different
kinds of actors, including mobilized social actors.

   These differences also meant that contests for control among different
kinds of aspiring elites were always simultaneously contests to determine
the nature of politics under emerging political arrangements, because different contestants would build on different modalities of power: bureau-
crats controlled administration and organizations; soldiers controlled
martial resources and often also national organizations of command and
control. Nationalist leaders may have particular appeal in urban centers,
while traditional authorities often had a particular appeal among rural

populations. In this sense, efforts to build a state apparatus were simultaneously contests between different visions of the regime.

Important and distinct considerations also emerge on the social side of the contest with new states. Asian states in struggles to maintain their position often did so from within relationships with mobilized and, in some ways, empowered societies. Where anticolonial movements played large roles in independence processes, they produced social legacies connected to at least some new elites. Activists and social movements nurtured ideas about class or national rights and had organizational and political capacities within easy reach. Particularly in later episodes of state violence, moreover, social groups began to draw on other resources in the contest with state authorities. By the middle 1970s at least, the ideological foundations of universal human or citizenship rights informed social engagement with state authorities. The mobilization of society also accelerated the need for regime-building efforts to rationalize and justify patterns of rule, efforts that were more often postponed in earlier European cases.

International dynamics also shaped state violence in Asia. International influences often intervened to strengthen states in Cold War proxy struggles but also made some efforts to constrain state violence in the century's last decades. Just as the Nuremberg trials had done for war crimes, so the South African transition adopted a formal process of resolution. Now the idea of formal processes dealing with violence became a standard element of the political repertoire. These elements of the social situation made the application of state violence more potentially costly to state builders, more dissonant to existing social orientations, and more in need of calibration and then formal reconciliation than violence during the high age of European state building.

For all these reasons, Asian state violence stood in a closer and more insistent relationship to regime construction than had been the case in Europe. Still, while Asian authorities often could not separate state building and regime construction temporally, they generally lacked the resources to accomplish the entire project at once. The solution has often been to separate state building and regime construction spatially and in categorical terms. As central states built outward, crude and more coercive-dependent elements of state building often targeted different populations from regime-constructing activity. When sorely pressed, authorities naturally responded to proximate and dangerous threats in ways that pushed the justificatory effort onto the back burner. But state actors who commit violence against societies will need to anticipate the larger political consequences of that violence, and in the effort to interpret these politics, we also find clues that distinctive patterns of violence itself depend on some path from raw coercion to a more durable regime. In investigating this violence, analysts should ask about the larger contest in which attackers and targets find themselves and then about the relationship between different patterns of attack and the relationship to efforts to reconcile social groups to those attacks.

Differentiating among Asian Cases

The time has come to trace out some of the important variations in the relationship between state building and regime construction across Asian cases and to seek the relationship between these differences and patterns of violence. While an involved discussion of these different trajectories would take us too far afield, we can outline four important modalities of state building in Asia, fostered by different relationships between state building and colonialism, the presence or absence of precolonial great societies, modernization processes, and political mobilization.[28] Each variation is set up by different concentrations of power and different strategies to expand and build state power and regime compliance. It hardly bears mentioning that the following categories are schematic: different state-building projects combine elements of the four following variants, either simultaneously or in sequence. Still, as heuristics, they help sort out some of the major battles associated with the construction of the state.

In some Asian states (often but not always where strong premodern states established a territorial template and organizational tradition) state building does not look entirely distinct from what appears in Europe. In places like Korea, Japan, and China, modern state institutions emerged atop earlier forms of absolutism and were followed by regimes developed to regulate mass participation in modern politics—in ways that separate the processes temporally, as we noted in the European pattern. In such cases, later state-building efforts are often associated with international competition and the drive to establish a modern military/industrial infrastructure. We would expect violence in such settings to initially serve exemplary aims—to teach the rules of the new system to populations whose membership in the political community or acceptance of the state is less in question—or to supplant one regime with another. Even colonialism within Asia, such as the Japanese imperial effort in Korea, worked mainly to change a regime and to deepen control, rather than to incorporate new territory.[29] Under such conditions, early episodes of violence should be public and associated (in state descriptions). Where sharp challenges emerge to regime norms or rules, the violence may occur on a broader scale—as was directed against students and other protesters who had gathered in central Beijing—but the logic of the violence still seeks to regulate behavior, and even widespread or coordinated resistance may be described as essentially criminal.[30] And though violence may be central in putting down immediate challenges, the state's ability to construct a counternarrative (i.e., collective good or rising prosperity) is an important element of the regime of control. This will have important implications for the probability that state violence will be the subject of legal or social processes at reconciliation or transitional justice.

In other cases, the modern state is a colonial imposition, without deep roots in the national territory, although it may be set down upon the remnants of an older aristocracy or bureaucracy. Even where state building is not a colonial enterprise, as in Thailand, these processes represent the rapid replacement of an old model of political authority with the new, well-elaborated model of rational institutions exercising political hegemony to the limits of their political territory. It is these latter-day state impositions that cast Asia in the starkest contrast with European processes, because they emerge more nearly alongside efforts to contain and direct more mobilized societies and only shortly before more modern norms of political and human rights.[31]

Differences, however, exist among this set of cases. In some, the state apparatus sets down in a central enclave and then builds toward peripheral territories. This lateral state expansion over unincorporated peripheries represents fairly easy challenges for those seeking to reconcile its violence with the larger narrative of the political community. Physically marginal populations need not so urgently be reconciled to the violence they suffer: their very marginalization allows that element of regime construction to follow state building at some later time. Violence will likely be direct and instrumental, targeting subversive people or categories. In the immediate term, reconciliation efforts may, rather, target central populations. But especially where categorical differences between victims and this audience overlie their spatial segregation, such efforts may succeed simply by representing peripheries as populated by politically dangerous others—may, that is, present far-flung violence as protecting closer, more incorporated populations. For as long as central actors are unwilling to make the defense of peripheral populations an important political priority, and central authorities are not strongly moved to communicate a regular regime in the periphery, this violence will fall under few pressures toward moderation. If Thai violence against southern Muslims or Filipino violence against Moros can be seen as targeting a national "other," then not only will exemplary lessons in that region not have broader application, but the violence may be justified as protecting the national center from subversive peripheries.

In other places, the colonial state is established more laterally across the territorial expanse and then needs to work to build stronger dominion over the populations it may but nominally rule. In some ways, this pattern of state building and regime construction presents the greatest challenge to authorities, because of the physical proximity of those who suffer violence and audiences that authorities would like to understand violence. While some share of people in Manila, Bangkok, and Jakarta will tolerate violence in Mindanao, Patani, and Aceh merely because of its physical remove from their lives, violence that picks off one's neighbors is harder to ignore. The options for violence that must be reconciled to attentive bystander populations are several-fold. Where state authority predates the development of a new regime, violence may attempt to get populations to do something new—such as join a new export-oriented economy in a docile fashion—or refrain from making claims for expanded economic or political rights. Authorities can rely on established or emergent political norms to make their case and treat the targets of violence as criminals that endanger the welfare of everyone else. This kind of justification emerges in the bureaucratic authoritarian phases of South Korean and Japanese development and may well be part of most authoritarian and state-led industrialization efforts.[32]

Where state building is more contested and ongoing, however, authorities may be driven to adopt broader and more categorical violence—requiring a more robust, more threatened narrative. In such cases, targeting strategies may be justified as efforts to eliminate subversives and subversion presented as a broader concern. Authoritarian repression and violence against new social forces, making new claims on or resisting the expansion of the state, often draw this kind of fire: the declaration of martial law in either the Philippines or South Korea, Thai repression in 1976, and the Indonesian politicide in 1965–1966 all follow this pattern. Where society is deeply divided by categorical cleavages, authorities may recruit social allies for this violence; where such divisions do not exist, the job may fall more squarely on security-force shoulders. Postconflict cases may contain such differences as well—because that conflict may help create and ossify newly categorical identities (collaborator, class traitor, counterrevolutionary). Instrumental Cambodian and Vietnamese state violence against kinds of people operated not so much along categories of ethnic or linguistic identity, but in categories of action that acquired something like permanence in their political climate.

The real tension emerges, of course, when authorities perceive cat-egorical adversaries (accurately or not) but are constrained from openly inflicting categorical violence—where, that is, the rhetoric of liberal gover-nance exists in tension with authorities' sense of the real balance of power. Mobilized populations and regime authorities alike profess their accep-tance of norms supporting civil liberties, participation, and human rights —but these norms could not constrain the authorities' state-building process. Under such constraints, state actors may develop other strate-gies. They may, first, broaden action-based sanctions, codified in more authoritarian legal structures, to provide cover for attacks on subversives. This approach, however, has drawbacks: by narrowing the scope of what is permissible, the regime may make new enemies among populations inclined to desire greater, rather than more constrained freedoms. Pro-hibitions on assembly, on speech, on publication, and on movement are famous irritants to the middle class and predictable accelerants to regime-threatening democracy movements. Legal regulations applied inconsis-tently or with clear bias (even those regulations designed to enhance state power) can provide ideological resources to opponents.

Alternately, they may embrace the strategies of a dirty war—rhetorically honoring legal norms but violating them in practice and in secret. Such acts of violence operate at both exemplary and instrumental levels—sending a message and eliminating subversives. The message-sending, exemplary aspect of violence in such cases often follows a dis-tinct protocol: authorities need to preserve the façade of legal probity and so approach the killings as mysterious or as the act of undisciplined men driven to the (understandable) limits of their patience. Authorities may say relatively little about the violence—such silence conveys a deeply ominous threat: that the legal system cannot bind state actors and cannot protect regime opponents. Violence that is not claimed or justified demonstrates a separation between the needs of conformity to a political regime and the interests of state officials. Because state actors never claim the acts as policy, they need not justify it. Because the attacks occur under mysterious circumstances—in which perpetrators are either unknown or driven past the limits of discipline by passion or confusion—one never knows exactly what triggers the violence. Hence, unlike purely exemplary violence, which clearly communicates the message to refrain from a set of proscribed activities, the ambiguity of this message sets out to cultivate a paralyzing fear. One never knows, with finality, whether specific kinds of people were targeted or specific acts were being proscribed.

By examining the pressures that setting exerts on authorities and social forces, I aspire less to predict political outcomes than to unearth influence on the trajectory of violence and to draw out questions one might most fruitfully ask of these situations and to introduce the relationship between the application and the justification of violence as a key analytical consideration. This relationship will likely be influenced by different situations of state and regime construction—but these broad organizing statements cannot replace specific empirical investigation. In each setting, analysts will want to know what is being taught and what audiences are relevant in that instruction. Are regimes constructed simultaneously across a country's geographical expanse—or is the process staged? Where, for instance, a central state authority has penetrated into the periphery, what kind of regime will it eventually seek to propagate? Exemplary, regime-teaching violence in the countryside may exist in the service of a significantly more brutal regime than that in the cities. Are the same regimes in play in the hinterland as those that hold sway at the center? These questions need consideration in the full light of specific circumstances that obtain in any situation and should direct empirical investigation toward clear questions of what violence means to its various perpetrators, targets, and audiences.

JUSTIFICATION, RECONCILIATION, AND RETRIBUTION: LEGACIES OF VIOLENCE

For centuries, state violence against populations, even that violence associated with state building, was dealt with in one of three ways. At least some violence gets assimilated in a country's historical narrative, emerging as part of the challenges the nation faced (at worst, imperfect responses to difficult choices) rather than as injustice. Some violence remains unreconciled and unsettled and can provide the ideological basis for future mobilization against authorities, given a certain conjunction of opportunity and framing. Other violence is simply forgotten. Where pressure emerges to redress legacies of violence, it typically reflects the efforts of some persistently aggrieved population with some access to political resources and an ability to link its grievances to that violence. Much is forgotten, however: think how ridiculous a movement demanding redress for the victims of the French Revolution's terror or the English enclosures would seem.

In the contemporary world, international norms protecting civil and human rights have created more pressure for justice to victims of state violence, and this development changed the very nature of reconciliation. Earlier processes reconciled—or failed to reconcile—the victims of violence to the political community and its norms, and the hardships that some individuals shouldered are ransomed by the virtues of that community. More contemporary processes reconcile different members of the political community to one another: the victims and the perpetrators of violence. To be sure, state violence may still be shamefully ignored, its memory left to recede and its urgency diminishing over time. But in such cases, it now makes sense to ask why citizens take the path of neglect and forgetfulness, rather than something else. But less is forgotten these days, and authorities who simply hope their crimes will go undiscovered run higher risks today than ever before. Peripheries are more able to report on circumstances in their communities, and domestic and transnational advocacy networks are more available to transmit and amplify that information. So what explains the different careers that state violence has experienced in the popular, political, and judicial memory? The answer, I believe, is entangled in two things—power relationships in which state actors are involved and the nature of the violence itself.

The legacy of violence will partly depend on the political processes under which accusations of violence emerge. Perpetrators who remain in power when the violence comes to light have the resources of incumbency to frame or obscure elements of that violence, to figure out how to win the support of those touched by repression, or to intimidate people away from raising the subject. In other settings, accounts of violence may emerge in the context of regimes genuinely struggling against an opposition. Finally, the violence may emerge in the context of regime transitions or in post-transitional settlements; each situation influences how and whether violence will be reconciled.

While the perpetrators of state violence remain in power, they will struggle with their critics over the legacy of that violence. The outcome of that struggle can yield an acceptance of that violence as anything from legitimately rule enforcing or state building to criminal. Where it eventually lands along this continuum reflects both the balance of power between the regime and its critics (who controls the narrative?) and elements of the violence itself. The more violence transgresses political norms, the harder it will be to dispel: analysts should therefore think about the relationship between violence and emergent regimes. On the other hand, even strongly transgressive violence can be suppressed or ignored when significant spatial or categorical distance between the victims of that violence and cosmopolitan communities exists. State violence against marginal populations may not trigger strong outrage. Years of Indonesian state violence in East Timor and Aceh attracted relatively little outrage among Javanese activists, partially because its victims were successfully portrayed as endangering the unity of the Indonesian republic—a set of norms to which Indonesians were deeply committed.

Where the violence targets populations that are less marginal, and where it seems to undercut the regime's own rules, it can provide oppositions their greatest and most powerful resources. Norms and rules, even those inscribed by regime violence, take on a life independent from regime intentions. Once some framework for permissible political behavior gains currency, the regime ceases exclusively to own it—it becomes, rather, available for expropriation by others, including democracy or reform movements. Gaps between state violence and accepted political norms can increase calls that violence be accounted for and may also underwrite sharp antiregime mobilization. Hence, we expect to find particularly explosive and insistent calls for justice and reconciliation where specific *individuals* are targeted by regimes that formally proscribe modes of *activity* or when those proscriptions become, in their application, blurred and ambiguous. In the first instance, this violence represents the unequal application of the law and, in the second, ambiguity in the law itself. Both represent fodder for those wishing to challenge the regime.

In fact, reactions to unjust regime violence often represent seminal elements of regime transitions, particularly those that involve strong mass mobilization. But is there any way of anticipating what kind of treatment violence will receive in a post-transition environment? Many who theorize about the politics of political transitions worry that overly strict transitional justice risks triggering a hard-line backlash against democracy itself. Some concern themselves most with the prospect that armed forces fearing prosecution for human rights violations will roll back democracy to protect themselves. Others worry that transitional justice that purges the ranks of the old regime will deprive the new government of necessary expertise and experience.[33] Both calculations approach the question in terms of how disruptive the prosecution of those responsible for violence will be. To these established considerations, the foregoing discussion adds the issue of how central past violence was to the formative experience of those building the new regime. How fundamentally did violence transgress the old regime, and how integrated (categorically and spatially) were the sites of violence to the opposition movement? In the immediate aftermath of a transition, the more state violence has undercut established norms, and the more directly it attacked enfranchised, politically powerful populations, the more we would expect that it would demand some accounting. Where the perpetrators of violence hold powerful positions in the post-transition government, we would expect the accounting to move toward nonpunitive reconciliations modes and, where they are less central, toward retribution.

What are the chances that even horrific violence may go unpunished and unreconciled, after a transition? Between exemplary and instrumental violence, the former will be less likely to lead to transitional justice processes for two main reasons. First, exemplary violence aimed at restricting, altering, or criminalizing modes of behavior produces social change: people learn to live with (and according to) prevailing laws. In time, a regime of permitted and proscribed activity produces people who have succeeded by navigating that minefield of proscriptions. Even when violence encounters great resistance, expectations can in time reconverge around new norms, particularly if they are consistently applied. People can learn to navigate new sets of rules, and some may even prosper. Children of the Indonesian new order, of Philippine martial law, or of China's People's Republic may do quite well under the rules—and all authorities need is for some members of society to support the new rule of law to make a justificatory effort viable. Over time, that is, an order inscribed by initial violence can accommodate and assimilate a broad range of social forces and actors.

Second, violence applied consistently to proscribe a specific kind of activity or behavior eventually shapes politics toward modes that authorities will expect to dominate.[34] Such proscriptions underpin a more or less permanent tension in dissident tactics: forms of struggle must thread a line between disruption and recruitment. To do this, dissidents create enough trouble to pressure authorities while alienating (with that trouble) as few potential recruits as possible. Some potential supporters on the *issues* will always break ranks with a movement or dissident group on how justified a disruptive tactic might be. This tension provides an opportunity for state repression and violence to divide dissidents from potential supporters, because it emphasizes the long-term power of the rule of law that *most* citizens will support under *most* conditions. Importantly, this dynamic helps explain the opportunities that authorities have to use violence on procedural grounds against individuals who are not in any obvious way isolated politically. For both reasons, as time elapses between the commission of violence and the regime transition, we grow less and less likely to inspire any effort at reconciliation or transitional justice.

Reconciliation processes are far more likely when a regime has attacked categories of people rather than categories of action. Where the violence has some ascriptive or affiliative foundation, it will not modify target behavior or seek to do so. Moreover, proscriptions on kinds of people strike at some of the fundamental beliefs of liberal or democratizing settings (settings most likely to produce a reconciliation process). For both reasons, this particular kind of violence appears most likely to produce some sort of accounting—a reconciliation process or a prosecution.

And yet, truth and reconciliation committees, or other modes of transitional justice, have been comparatively rare in Asia. What accounts for this rarity? One answer is that in many transitional governments, veterans of the old regime occupy strong veto points in the new regime and can roll back democracy to avert a prosecutorial threat. This suggests that one potentially fruitful avenue for research would be the exploration of the relationship between modes of transition and the subsequent position of security forces in the new government. Do Asian political transitions tend to leave more of those who wielded violence in power than elsewhere—something that Valerie Bunce identified as important in differentiating Latin American and Eastern European transitions?[35] Even in the most prominent mass-driven transitions in contemporary Southeast Asia—in the Philippines and Indonesia—huge sections of the pre-transition regime make their way into the new arrangement. In such cases, the requirements of a peaceful future often lead new governments to tread lightly on the ghosts of the past—for better or for worse.

One additional class of answers can be drawn from the foregoing discussion. First, categories of people who have most likely suffered violence are often still not in positions of power following Asian regime transitions—they remain as underrepresented in formally democratic regimes as they were under dictatorships. Philippine Muslims, for instance, are every bit as marginal in current Philippine politics as they were under Marcos, and very much the same can be said about Acehnese in Indonesia or Thai Muslims. Indeed, in some ways, the Indonesian strategy to decentralize power and authority can serve to insulate the center from charges of violence perpetrated at the national periphery. To take another, more prospective example, the Burmese democracy movement shows few inclinations to do more than the junta to fully incorporate and empower ethnic minorities in the national community. East Timor's reconciliation process has been largely defanged by its leaders' desire to maintain good relations with Indonesia. While former members of the Indonesian PKI survive, few acknowledge that history as their own, and to all intents and purposes, Marxists do not exist as a political or social force in Indonesia. Efforts at justice or reconciliation in such cases simply do not have significant backing from empowered constituencies. In fact, efforts at reconciliation for past violence (apart from internationally backed tribunals in Cambodia) more typically involve one set of citizens bringing suit against the government of another country—as in efforts to find justice for former "comfort women" in Korea.[36] In this respect, efforts to punish those involved in the Kwangju incident should probably be looked at to discover if any extraordinary conditions made the effort possible.

NOTES

1. For the passage from tradition to modernity, see Barrington Moore, *Social Origins of Dictatorship and Democracy: Lord and Peasant in the Making of the Modern World* (London: Penguin, 1967). For state-building accounts, see Otto Hintze, *The Historical Essays of Otto Hintze* (New York: Oxford University Press, 1975); Hendrik Spruyt, *The Sovereign State and Its Competitors: An Analysis of Systems Change* (Princeton: Princeton University Press, 1994); Charles Tilly and

Arthur L. Stinchcombe, *Roads from Past to Future* (Lanham, MD: Rowman and Littlefield, 1997). For the struggle for democracy, see Martin Legassick, *Armed Struggle and Democracy: The Case of South Africa* (Uppsala: Nordiska Afrikain-stitutet, 2002); Elisabeth Jean Wood, *Forging Democracy from Below: Insurgent Transitions in South Africa and El Salvador* (Cambridge: Cambridge University Press, 2000). For the struggle for enfranchisement and representation, see N. Chabini Manganyi, *On Becoming a Democracy: Transition and Transformation in South African Society* (Pretoria Leiden: University of South Africa Press, 2004). For the defense of authoritarian orders, see Vincent Boudreau, *Resisting Dictatorship: Repression and Protest in Southeast Asia* (New York: Cambridge University Press, 2004); Jennifer Earl, "Tanks, Tear Gas, and Taxes: Toward a Theory of Movement Repression," *Sociological Theory* 21, no. 1 (2003): 44–68.

2. Karen Barkey and Sunita Parikh, "Comparative Perspectives on the State," *Annual Review of Sociology* 17 (1991): 523–49; Michael Mann, *The Sources of Social Power* (Cambridge and New York: Cambridge University Press, 1986).

3. Charles Tilly and Gabriel Ardant, *The Formation of National States in Western Europe* (Princeton: Princeton University Press, 1975).

4. Joel S. Migdal, Atul Kohli, and Vivienne Shue, *State Power and Social Forces: Domination and Transformation in the Third World* (New York: Cambridge University Press, 1994); R. B. J. Walker, *Inside/Outside: International Relations as Political Theory* (New York: Cambridge University Press, 1992).

5. Kiyoteru Tsutsui, "Redressing Past Human Rights Violations: Global Dimensions of Contemporary Social Movements," *Social Forces* 85, no. 1 (2006): 331–54.

6. David Beetham, *The Legitimation of Power* (Atlantic Heights, NJ: Humanities Press International, 1991); Bruce Gilley, "The Determinants of State Legitimacy: Results for 72 Countries," *International Political Science Review/Revue internationale de science politique* 27, no. 1 (2006): 47–71.

7. This may also explain the positive correlation that some researchers find between semidemocracies and repression: the association may have more to do with unsettled regime rules than with a settled point between autocracy and democracy. See Helen Fein, "More Murder in the Middle: Life-Integrity Violations and Democracy in the World, 1987," *Human Rights Quarterly* 17, no. 1 (1995): 170–91; Patrick M. Regan and Errol A. Henderson, "Democracy, Threats and Political Repression in Developing Countries: Are Democracies Internally Less Violent?" *Third World Quarterly* 23, no. 1 (2002): 119–36.

8. Beetham, *Legitimation of Power.*

9. Rommel A. Curaming's contribution to this collection, "The End of an Illusion," suggests that the shooting of agrarian demonstrators at Manila's Mendiola Bridge in early 1987 was part of a struggle within the new Philippine state apparatus.

10. See "Counter-revolutionary Violence in Indonesia," by Douglas Kammen, in this volume. In arguing that Indonesian violence in 1965–66 was counterrevo-

lutionary, Kammen essentially makes the point that it was aimed at dismantling Sukarno's regime of mass mobilization.

11. This conceptual distinction was originally worked out in Vincent Boudreau, "Repression and the Making of Underground Resistance," in *Brokering a Revolution: Cadres in a Philippine Insurgency*, ed. R. Rutten (Quezon City, Philippines: Ateneo de Manila University Press, 2009).

12. Kammen's discussion of Indonesian counterrevolutionary violence in this collection is a good case in point. While, as Kammen argues, the violence was aimed at eradicating a kind of politics central to Sukarno's regime (mass mobilization), it demonstrated state hostility to those practices in ways that eliminated an estimated five hundred thousand practitioners. Clearly these attacks operated both instrumentally and in exemplary fashion.

13. Boudreau, *Resisting Dictatorship.*

14. Beetham, *Legitimation of Power.*

15. See Sorpong Peou, "Mass Atrocities in Cambodia under the Khmer Rouge Reign of Terror," in this collection.

16. See Tyrell Haberkorn's "Getting Away with Murder in Thailand: State Violence and Impunity in Phatthalung," in this collection.

17. James L. Gibson, "Understandings of Justice: Institutional Legitimacy, Procedural Justice, and Political Tolerance," *Law and Society Review* 23, no. 3 (1989): 469–96.

18. Charles Tilly, "War Making and State Making as Organized Crime," in *Bringing the State Back In,* ed. P. Evans, Dietrich Rueschemeyer, and Theda Skocpol (New York: Cambridge University Press, 1985).

19. Roland Axtmann, "The State of the State: The Model of the Modern State and Its Contemporary Transformation," *International Political Science Review/ Revue internationale de science politique* 25, no. 3 (2004): 259–79; Linda Buckley Green, "Consensus and Coercion: Primary Health Care and the Guatemalan State," *Medical Anthropology Quarterly* 3, no. 3 (1989): 246–57.

20. Mann, *Sources of Social Power.*

21. Nicholas Blomley, "Law, Property, and the Geography of Violence: The Frontier, the Survey, and the Grid," *Annals of the Association of American Geographers* 93, no. 1 (2003): 121–41; Gregory M. Luebbert, "Social Foundations of Political Order in Interwar Europe," *World Politics* 39, no. 4 (1987): 449–78.

22. Ali Kazancigil, ed., *The State in Global Perspective* (Brookfield, VT: Gower Publishing Co., 1986); Joel S. Migdal, *Strong Societies and Weak States: State-Society Relations and State Capabilities in the Third World* (Princeton: Princeton University Press, 1988); Migdal, Kohli, and Shue, *State Power and Social Forces.*

23. Boudreau, *Resisting Dictatorship.*

24. Migdal, *Strong Societies and Weak States.*

25. Mary P. Callahan, *Making Enemies: War and State Building in Burma* (Ithaca: Cornell University Press, 2003); Thongchai Winichakul, *Siam Mapped: A History of the Geo-body of a Nation* (Honolulu: University of Hawaii Press, 1994).

26. For members of the nobility, see Hari Singh, "Tradition, UMNO and Political Succession in Malaysia," *Third World Quarterly* 19, no. 2 (1998): 241–54.

27. Benedict Anderson, "Murder and Progress in Modern Siam," *New Left Review* 181, no. 1 (1990): 33–48.

28. For a different conceptualization of the variety of state-building situations, consult Barkey and Parikh, "Comparative Perspectives on the State."

29. Todd A. Henry, "Sanitizing Empire: Japanese Articulations of Korean Otherness and the Construction of Early Colonial Seoul, 1905–1919," *Journal of Asian Studies* 64, no. 3 (2005): 639–75.

30. Elizabeth J. Perry, *Challenging the Mandate of Heaven: Social Protest and State Power in China* (Armonk, NY: M. E. Sharpe, 2002).

31. Benedict Anderson, "Old State, New Society: Indonesia's New Order in Comparative Historical Perspective," *Journal of Asian Studies* 42, no. 3 (1983): 477–96.

32. Hyug Baeg Im, "The Rise of Bureaucratic Authoritarianism in South Korea," *World Politics* 39, no. 2 (1987): 231–57; Richard Stubbs, "War and Economic Development: Export-Oriented Industrialization in East and Southeast Asia," *Comparative Politics* 31, no. 3 (1999): 337–55.

33. Nigel Biggar, *Burying the Past: Making Peace and Doing Justice after Civil Conflict* (Washington, DC: Georgetown University Press, 2001); Wendy Hunter, "Negotiating Civil-Military Relations in Post-Authoritarian Argentina and Chile," *International Studies Quarterly* 4, no. 2 (1998): 295–317.

34. Peter Burnell, "Autocratic Opening to Democracy: Why Legitimacy Matters," *Third World Quarterly* 27, no. 4 (2006): 545–62.

35. Valerie Bunce, "Rethinking Recent Democratization: Lessons from the Postcommunist Experience," *World Politics* 55, no. 2 (2003): 167–92.

36. Tsutsui, "Redressing Past Human Rights Violations."

2

From the Streets to the National Assembly

Democratic Transition and Demands for Truth about Kwangju in South Korea

Namhee Lee

This chapter examines the political and social process of enacting special laws to compensate victims of the Kwangju massacre of 1980 in South Korea and to bring the military junta leaders to justice more than fifteen years after the atrocities were committed. The substantive part of this chapter centers on a set of questions that are informed by the larger theoretical and analytical concerns laid out in the introduction and chapter 1 of this volume, such as: Why was Kwangju targeted by the new military? What were the political processes that started the violence, and what was its main political role; was it for the purpose of state building or regime construction? What was the logic behind and rationalization of the violence? That is, of the two topologies of violence characterized as either "instrumental" or "exemplary," which would better fit the case of Kwangju? What were the processes of resolving the question of the responsibility for and the legacies of the Kwangju massacre? More specifically, between the two different approaches to the issue of transitional justice, retributive and restorative, which approach does the trajectory of South Korea's case follow? What was the relationship between transitional justice and democratization in the case of South Korea?

In what follows, I argue that the extremely brutal and massive repression in Kwangju was a case of exemplary violence by the new military for the purpose of regime construction—that is, to preempt any future opposition and to force the people to submit to its rule. Further, South Korea's geopolitical location in the Cold War world and its pervasive and virulent anticommunist ideology made state violence a routine and effective mechanism to control and discipline the public. I also argue that the resolution of the past violence in the 1990s was made possible by South Korea's transition to democracy, which itself was spurred in part by persistent demands for the truth about Kwangju and the subsequent empowerment of civil society. While the process of transitional justice followed the model of retributive justice—the perpetrators were put on trial, and the victims regained their lost honor and human rights—the people of Kwangju and civil society in South Korea have strived to turn the brutal legacy of Kwangju into a transformative experience, with their continuous endeavors to commemorate and revive the "Kwangju spirit" in the present context of South Korea and beyond.

The Kwangju Uprising

The 1980 Kwangju Uprising represents a paradigmatic moment in South Korea; the military leaders' indiscriminate and brutal killing and maiming of the people of Kwangju constituted an immense tragedy, leading to the suffering of thousands in Kwangju and leaving a deep scar on the rest of the country. The people of Kwangju and the ongoing democratization movement turned pain and anger into collective energy and spearheaded demands for the truth about the Kwangju massacre and justice for its victims. These demands became an integral and constitutive part of the democratization movement in the 1980s that culminated in the 1987 June Struggle, which ushered in a gradual process of political democracy in South Korea.

Establishing the truth about the Kwangju massacre and rendering justice to the victims of the violence were crucial to breaking away from the legacy of military authoritarianism and allowing the transition to democracy to take root. After numerous setbacks and disappointments for the people of Kwangju and the public at large, not least because the main leaders of the Kwangju massacre had remained in power, the South Korean government was pressured into opening up the investigation and carrying out prosecutions against the military leaders involved in the massacre. In the historic trial of 1996, two former presidents were convicted, along with those who had played a major role in the December 12 coup in 1979 and in the 1980 Kwangju massacre.

As is well known, the Kwangju Uprising began as an ordinary student protest against military leaders' declaration of nationwide martial law and their closing of universities on May 18, 1980. However, the protest turned into a citywide popular rebellion that lasted ten days as citizens of Kwangju began to join the students in massive numbers, angered by the paratroopers' brutal and indiscriminate killing and maiming of demonstrators and innocent bystanders. Taking up arms to defend the city and themselves, they had pushed the paratroopers out of the city by May 21. For five days the people of Kwangju governed themselves autonomously and peacefully. The city's provincial building served as the center of various citizen activities from the first day of the uprising. About 150 people staying in the provincial building met their deaths on May 27 when special airborne commandos and twenty thousand martial law troops reoccupied the city with a massive array of equipment and weapons, including eighteen tanks and helicopters. Martial law forces cut off telephone lines within the city, as well as between the city and the rest of the province; thus, Kwangju was completely isolated when the troops began their carnage. During the ten-day uprising, more than two hundred individuals were killed, hundreds went missing, and thousands were injured.

Despite many uncertainties still surrounding the Kwangju massacre, certain key facts are now established beyond serious dispute. First, the new military leaders (sin'gunbu), headed by Chun Doo Hwan, who had masterminded the December 12, 1979, coup and had risen to the nation's highest military position by 1980, deliberately sent the elite "black beret" troops of the Special Warfare Command (SWC) into Kwangju on May 18. These SWC forces were trained for urban guerrilla warfare in the event of a North Korean invasion. Second, the military junta told the SWC as well as the South Korean public that Kwangju demonstrations had been instigated by North Korean agents in order to destabilize society and spearhead a communist revolution. Third, both eyewitnesses and foreign reporters gave ample evidence of egregiously excessive force used by the SWC against unarmed demonstrators, as well as random attacks on innocent civilians who were not participating in the demonstrations. Paratroopers terrorized the citizens of Kwangju, carrying out door-to-door searches, brutally beating anyone they found, and killing innocent victims including women and young girls. Many of those attacked became permanently incapacitated due to severe injuries.[1] The excessive brutality of the paratroopers caused Kwangju citizens to rise up and take up arms to defend themselves.

WHY KWANGJU?

The brutal violence committed against innocent citizens by soldiers of their own country left the people of Korea, and particularly the people of Kwangju, unable to utter the question that was nevertheless on everyone's mind: why Kwangju? But this question needs to be considered along with the question of why the people of Kwangju rose up at a time when people in other cities did not. By the early 1980s, Kwangju had become a site where the general contradictions of Korea's post-1945 pursuit of foreign-dependent capitalistic development and anticommunist ideology were enmeshed with the long history of the central power discriminating against its people and local culture, the phenomenon now known as "regionalism."[2]

South Korea's much-touted economic development, known as the "Miracle of Han," accompanied an uneven and discriminatory industrial policy that left the Chŏlla region severely underdeveloped, while the Kyŏngsang region dominated development in terms of both ownership and the location of industrial facilities and infrastructures. Only one large-scale industrial complex had been built in the Chŏlla region, compared to eight in the Kyŏngsang region; more than half of the country's fifty largest conglomerates (*chaebŏl*) were owned by those born in the Kyŏngsang region; corporations owned by individuals born in the Kyŏngsang region with one thousand or more employees accounted for 61.3 percent of the nation's total sales. Those from the Kyŏngsang region also dominated society's elite positions, from military generals to bankers and educators.[3]

The economic discrimination against the Chŏlla region reinforced the already existing social prejudice against its people, much as Italy's historically differentiated regional development accompanied negative images of southerners. The Park regime's unequal industrialization policy also left Chŏlla people comprising the lowest strata of society, constituting most of the migrant population. The mass media reproduced and amplified this negative image in their portrayal of the lower class. True to Antonio Gramsci's observation that language is not only class related but also space related, the Chŏlla dialect has long been associated with backwardness and boorishness.[4]

Long discriminated against and alienated politically, economically, socially, and psychologically, the people of Kwangju had been carrying within themselves deep-seated resentment, resignation, and frustration; they had also come to identify the political suppression of Kim Dae Jung with their own plight, and he became the symbol of their accumulated and collective suffering. Their yearning for democracy following the 1979 assassination of Park Chung Hee, which opened the possibilities for political reform and liberalization, was perhaps stronger than in any other place in South Korea; this yearning was also expressed in their high hopes for Kim Dae Jung. To the people of Kwangju, the military junta's expansion of the martial law regime on May 17 and arrest of Kim Dae Jung were all the more egregious.[5]

Kwangju was also the only place where university students continued street demonstrations immediately after the new military declared the expansion of martial law on May 17. University students nationwide had carried out massive demonstrations prior to May 17 but by then had decided to disband and lay low, having shown their displeasure toward the military and also feeling intimidated by rumors of impending military intervention. Unlike students elsewhere, where protests drew lukewarm responses from ordinary citizens, students in Kwangju received warm support from the people. They were initially galvanized by earlier protests in other cities and initiated their own demonstrations spontaneously on May 18 because they were angry at the closing of their universities and the expansion of martial law; the citizens' active and enthusiastic response contributed greatly to their continuing protests.[6]

But ultimately it was the paratroopers' indiscriminate and brutal killings of innocent people in the first few days of the protest that made the citizens of Kwangju rise up in arms, a response that the military used as a justification for their continuing systematic violence. The paratroopers' random violence over the first two days created a widely shared sentiment among the people of Kwangju that no one would be spared; the fear of violence led them to overcome the fear of the soldiers and fear itself—they "had to fight in order to survive."[7]

The violence of the paratroopers was certainly random and indiscriminate, but it had a clear aim: "making an example" of the people of Kwangju—what Vince Boudreau characterizes as "exemplary" violence.[8] Having emerged at the top of the military through the December 12 military coup (known as "12.12 incident") in 1979, Chun Doo Hwan had taken a position as head of the Korean Central Intelligence Agency (KCIA), thereby paving the way for his eventual seizure of power as head of the country. The declaration of nationwide martial law was only the final step toward this goal, and Chun had every reason to believe that the people of Korea would challenge his illegitimate seizure of power, given their history of resistance and defiance. As James West writes: "The random violence unleashed by the Special Forces evidently was calculated to terrorize the populace into immediate submission and, moreover, to deter similar outbreaks of protest elsewhere in the future. . . . By demonstrating his preparedness to kill protestors, Chun may have hoped to preempt popular opposition to his rule, in effect aggravating an atmosphere of crisis so that further draconian measures would appear inevitable when carried out in the name of smashing ostensible North Korean provocations."[9]

If the killings in Kwangju were spurred by Chun's ambitions to ascend to power at all costs and to make an example of Kwangju, then the way Chun was able to silence the people of Korea immediately after the massacre needs to be put in the historical context of the Cold War partition of the nation and the emergence of anticommunism as a state ideology. As I argue elsewhere, anticommunism in South Korea, from the moment of its inception, was directed not only toward the "real communist" North Korea and its followers but even more toward the domestic political opposition.[10] North Korea's close proximity to South Korea, the fratricidal Korean War, and the continuing confrontation between the two Koreas made anticommunism in South Korea a particularly virulent form of social control, as well as an effective conduit for state power. Relegating critical elements of society to the category of the "other," South Korea's anticommunism constituted the national identity of South Korea.

Anticommunism in South Korea was equated with national security and public safety. The regime, in other words, equated resistance to itself with a threat to the security of state, a case of what N. Ganesan and Sung Chull Kim term "conflation" of state and regime security.[11] Anticommunism in South Korea was also a deeply and thoroughly internalized experience for many, rather than just a state-imposed doctrine or policy. It had been promoted and sustained not only by the state but also by the mass media, Christian and veterans' organizations, and various civic groups. The interlocking relationship among anticommunism, national security, and the technology of state discipline provided justifications for the violence committed against the citizens of Kwangju.

One of the principal mechanisms through which authoritarian regimes controlled and disciplined society was the indiscriminate application of the National Security Law (NSL) and the Anticommunist Law. First enacted in 1948 and revised several times since, the NSL mandated harsh felony punishments for "any person who has organized an association or group for the purpose of . . . disturbing the state or who prepared or conspired to do so."[12] In reality, the NSL was applied broadly to those who expressed views on inequalities in a capitalist economy, the lack of political freedom in South Korea, South Korea's relations with the United States, Korean reunification, and so forth. Throughout the post-1945 period, the number of individuals who were tried for violation of the NSL would increase with political tension, testifying to the intimate relationship between the rise of criticisms against the regime and the rise of NSL-related cases.

Despite the failure of the state to produce any credible evidence to substantiate its allegation that North Korean agents instigated the Kwangju demonstrations, and despite the gradual filtering out of news about the atrocities of the Kwangju massacre, the public by and large remained silent for the first few years after the uprising, due to the severity of the disciplinary mechanism of anticommunist ideology in general and the indiscriminate application of the NSL in particular. This is not surprising, given that many of the individuals arrested during and after the Kwangju Uprising were convicted of high treason, sedition, and violation of NSL, among other charges, and received heavy sentences, including death.[13]

THE STRUGGLE FOR THE RESTORATION OF HONOR
AND DEMANDS FOR TRUTH

By the late 1980s, however, what had initially been denounced by the state as "the armed violence of mobs" had become "a part of the democratic movement of the students and citizens of Kwangju," and the demand to investigate the truth of Kwangju and to deliver justice to its people had become a major agenda item in public discourse. As I show below, the process by which the erstwhile "mobs" transformed into "democratiza-tion forces" cannot be considered separately from the larger process of how the South Korean democratization movement (the *minjung* move-ment) challenged the state-established public agenda and redefined the grounds of social and political discourse. As I argue elsewhere, the min-jung movement constructed what I call a "counterpublic sphere" by artic-ulating, publicizing, and legitimizing many of the major issues the state deemed unsuitable for public debate—from reunification to the regime's political legitimacy, questions of distributive justice, and the truth about the Kwangju Uprising.[14] The rise of counterdiscourses on the Kwangju Uprising was also part and parcel of the rising anti-American sentiment that became one of the defining features of the democratization move-ment of the 1980s, which I discuss in the following section. In fact, the demands for truth-finding about Kwangju and rising anti-Americanism reinforced each other and became mutually interdependent in the 1980s.

In the immediate aftermath of Kwangju, the state of terror contin-ued in society as the military junta sought to eradicate what it considered "undesirable elements": teachers and journalists who were sympathetic to the democratization movement were purged; politicians were banned from political activities; and labor and student activists were rounded up and sent to military camps to be "reeducated," a project known as the "Reeducation Corps to Purify Three Ills" (*samchŏng kyoyuktae*). More than 60,000 individuals, including participants in the Kwangju Uprising, doctors, professors, and high school students, as well as gang members, drug dealers, and smugglers, were convicted of violating "public peace and order" and sent to the camps. Subjected to hard labor and physical abuse under subhuman conditions, 50 people died during "reeducation," while 397 died due to the "aftereffects of reeducation."[15]

Soon after it was over, despite the fear of arrest and imprisonment, those who had participated in or witnessed the uprising, and the families of those who had been killed or injured or were missing, along with the minjung movement activists, put forth their demands for an investiga-tion into the truth about the Kwangju massacre. The demands took many forms and many sacrifices. Beginning in 1984, Kwangju citizens, univer-sity students, and dissidents began to stage commemoration ceremonies at the Mangwŏltong cemetery, where the dead were buried. This annual pilgrimage to the burial site became a battle between the state and the citizens, with the state trying to prevent visits by various means—making visits illegal, rendering access to the burial site difficult by leaving the road unpaved, and dispersing gatherings by force.

As the state insisted on calling the uprising a *sat'ae* (literally a "situation," as in the state of things), thereby displacing the agency of the people involved, the battle over terminology grew equally fierce and became a constitutive part of the demands for truth-finding. The people of Kwangju and the activists in the democratization movement insisted on naming the uprising the "Kwangju Minjung Hangjaeng" (Kwangju People's Uprising), identifying the citizens of Kwangju as peace-loving, democratic citizens who "courageously and resolutely rose up to defend themselves" against indiscriminate killings. Through the process of persistent demands for the truth and efforts to keep the memories of Kwangju alive, Kwangju gained its status as "morally superior," a critical weapon against the ruling regime as well as an effective basis on which to build consensus within the minjung movement and society at large.

In Kwangju, the families of those who had been were killed or injured, and who had gone missing, organized into what became known as "5.18 organizations." The movements demanding truth-finding and the various social forces centering around the Kwangju Uprising also became known as the "May Movement," which gave rise to the concept of the "Kwangju spirit"—keeping alive the memory of the Kwangju Uprising in the present political context and into the future. Beginning in the mid-1980s, various May Movement groups, along with other social-movement organizations, have come together to put forth principles for confronting past human rights abuses such as the Kwangju massacre, known as the "five principles": investigation into the truth, punishment of the guilty, compensation, restoration of honor, and commemoration and succession of the Kwangju spirit.[16]

University students in particular paid a high price for the lead they took in demanding the truth; many of them threw themselves off buildings or burned themselves to death to inspire their fellow students to rise up against the Chun regime and to alert the public to the urgency related to Kwangju. It is believed that thirty-seven students, farmers, and workers either immolated themselves or were killed while demanding the truth about Kwangju.[17] In Kwangju, the 5.18 organizations carried out various commemorative activities and sought to pressure the government into an investigation; one group sent a letter to US president Ronald Reagan asking for an investigation into the matter.[18]

Democratic Transition and Demands for the Truth about Kwangju

How did the demands for truth-finding and justice for victims, initially a voice crying in the wilderness, become a legitimate political issue and a major agenda item in public discourse in Korean society by the late 1980s and early 1990s? As is well known, South Korea's transition from authoritarian rule to parliamentary democracy came about as the ruling party declared a promise to reform on June 29, 1987, after a month-long, nationwide protest waged by people from all walks of life and after a decades-long minjung movement. In the subsequent presidential election in December 1987, Roh Tae Woo, Chun Doo Hwan's party-mate and coconspirator in the 1979 coup, became the president of the Sixth Republic by narrowly defeating two opposition candidates who had failed to form a united front. The transition to parliamentary democracy also gave rise to shifting strategies and tactics in the demands for the truth about Kwangju.

Roh Tae Woo's government, born of the "original sin" and sharing the roots of the Fifth Republic, was beset with charges of political illegitimacy from the beginning.[19] Resolving the "Kwangju problem" was, therefore, an urgent task for Roh Tae Woo, and it became critical that he distance himself from the Fifth Republic of Chun Doo Hwan. In January 1988, as a first step toward this goal, he organized an ad hoc committee called the Committee for the Promotion of Democratic Reconciliation.

Composed of former high officials of the previous republic and representatives of the government-friendly 5.18 organizations, the committee made recommendations that indicated the parameters within which the Kwangju issue would be resolved under the Roh government. Two widely divergent views were presented to the committee: one was that the state's violence had been necessary in the process of exercising its power to protect the lives and property of civilians under the extremely chaotic situation of martial law; the other was that the excessive brutality of the martial law troops in the initial phase of the demonstrations had provoked the anger of the citizens of Kwangju, which led to the eventual massacre. The committee took the position that the excessive brutality of the martial law troops had been unavoidable and that the demonstrating students with their radical slogans had brought upon themselves the harsh suppression of the martial law troops, which caused the resentment of the citizens, who were also aggravated by the groundless rumors circulating at the time.[20]

The committee also responded negatively to the most urgent demand of the people: that those responsible for the massacre be investigated and punished. The committee argued that the investigation could be used politically and that a long time had passed since the event took place (in fact, only eight years).[21] The committee instead recommended national reconciliation, providing the basis for the Compensation Act, which was eventually enacted in August 1990.

In April 1988, as recommended by the committee, Roh Tae Woo officially renamed the Kwangju Uprising "part of the democratic movement of the students and citizens of Kwangju" and promised to offer financial support and medical services to the victims of Kwangju and to construct a monument and memorial park.[22] However, Roh opposed official investigation into the Kwangju massacre. Given this situation, the committee's recommendation of national reconciliation merely confirmed the Roh government's lack of will to deal with the issues of Kwangju.[23]

AT THE NATIONAL ASSEMBLY: THE PUBLIC HEARING AND THE COMPENSATION ACT

In the initial period of the Roh government, opposition parties held the majority in the National Assembly (as a result of the April 1988 general election), forcing the ruling party to accommodate, even in limited ways, opposition demands that the government address Kwangju and other wrongs committed by the state during the Fifth Republic. After a few months of intense maneuvering among the political parties, the "Special Committee on Investigation of the May 18th Kwangju Democratization Movement" was created.[24] From November 1988 to February 1989, the special committee conducted a public hearing on the Kwangju Democratization Movement, during which sixty-seven witnesses, including former president Chun Doo Hwan, were brought in to testify.

The creation of the special committee was possible largely because of the political alignment in the National Assembly, where opposition parties held the majority. The hearing was televised and became one of the most widely watched media events in recent Korean history. Despite the evasive and self-serving testimony of Chun Doo Hwan and others during the hearing, the hearing nevertheless provided some new facts and confirmed some long-held public suspicions related to the Kwangju massacre. For many in South Korea, the hearing also provided their first opportunity to hear and see evidence of the massacre and the extent of the random violence and excessive use of force unleashed by SWC forces.[25]

The hearing revealed that both the December 12 coup of 1979 and the Kwangju massacre of 1980 were carried out by members of a secret private club within the military called "Hanahoe" (Group of One), which was composed of the eleventh and twelfth classes of the Military Academy. Following the coup, Chun Doo Hwan and Roh Tae Woo, the leaders of this club, occupied key positions in the military and were in positions of command during the Kwangju massacre—Chun Doo Hwan as the head of the Defense Security Command, as well as the director of the Korean Central Intelligence Agency (KCIA), and Roh Tae Woo as the commander of the Capital Security Command, one of the country's key military security positions. The hearing also brought to public attention the hitherto unspoken link between the South Korean military and the United States. While the question of who was ultimately responsible for the deployment of troops into Kwangju was never settled, charges of US complicity in the Kwangju massacre persisted throughout the 1980s and 1990s.[26]

The hearing also demonstrated both the remarkable degree of unity and solidarity among the citizens of Kwangju and the dignity with which they conducted themselves during the five days when the city was left completely isolated (the martial law troops retreated from the city on May 21 and retook it in the morning on May 27). In what political scientist Jung-woon Choi called an "absolute community," the people of Kwangju regarded the lives and property of other people as their own, overcoming "all distinctions between humans . . . as disparate individuals joined together as one" and risking their lives to recover their dignity as human beings.[27] During the ten days of demonstrations, not one incident of looting or robbery was seen or reported.[28] More than anything else, the hearing established the moral authority of the Kwangju Uprising and took away any basis for the regime's claim that the Kwangju demonstrations were caused by ruthless mobs on North Korean provocation.[29]

As the hearing proceeded, Roh Tae Woo, on November 26, 1988, announced a plan to enact a special law to provide measures to heal the wounds of the victims of Kwangju. In December 1988, the ruling party and the opposition party introduced separate bills to the National Assembly; while the ruling party focused mainly on monetary compensation for those killed and injured, the opposition party focused on the priority of the investigation of the facts.

The enactment of the Compensation Act in 1990 was a contentious process. For months fierce debates were waged on what the act should be named, a point that was considered important in conferring the status of either legality or illegality to the acts of the state during the Kwangju massacre. The opposition party and the 5.18 organizations demanded that the term "reparation" (*paesang*) be used in the act's title, since this implied that the damage was caused by illegal acts of the state; the ruling party instead insisted on using the term "compensation" (*posang*), implying that individuals were inadvertently sacrificed in the process of legal dispensation of a state act.[30] The Compensation Act was also ambiguous on the issue of the responsibility of the military junta: while the uprising was now considered part of the democratization movement and therefore justifiable, no legal determination was made regarding the coup's unlawfulness or the military's role in the massacre.[31]

By the time the act was finally adopted and promulgated in August 1990, the South Korean political landscape had turned yet another dramatic corner: the merger of Roh Tae Woo's ruling party with two smaller opposition parties in January 1990 had given the ruling party the majority in the National Assembly, leaving the Chŏlla-based Peace Democratic Party (headed by Kim Dae Jung) the only opposition party. Bolstered by this political reconfiguration, the ruling party reneged on its previous promise to work closely with the opposition party on the Compensation Act and unilaterally passed its own version, which was promulgated on August 6, 1990, and became effective on August 17, 1990.

Many of the citizens of the Kwangju and May Movement organizations criticized the act as a political maneuver to placate victims without solving any fundamental issues related to Kwangju. The 5.18 organizations were also split about the act. Some moderate or progovernment elements among the 5.18 organizations (such as the Association of 5.18 Bereaved Families) had appealed to the ruling party for quick passage of the act, even demanding that it be passed without the consent of the opposition party if differences persisted.[32] Some groups declared that they would not recognize the act, since it had been passed unilaterally by the ruling party, and insisted that the government enact a special law that would realize the five principles for solving the problem of Kwangju.[33] However, close

to 90 percent of those who were eligible to receive compensation ultimately accepted the money; this number included many who belonged to
5.18 organizations that officially opposed the act.[34] This is not surprising,
given that most of the victims were from the lower classes and suffered
from unemployment and poverty. According to the 5.18 Kinyŏm Chae-
dan (the 5.18 Memorial Foundation), compensation was distributed at
five different times; the last payment was made in March 2004. The number of total applications for compensation for the dead was 240; for missing persons 409; and for the injured 5,019. Of these, 154, 70, and 3,028
cases, respectively, were compensated.[35]

Looking at the process of compensation over the past fifteen years,
it is undeniable that the compensation provided much-needed financial
relief for many of the victims, along with a sense of "justice" and a certain "recovery" from gross human rights violations. But it also prioritized
serving the political purpose of stabilizing the regime over investigation
into the truth of Kwangju and punishing those responsible. Payments to
individual victims prior to any official acknowledgment of the participation and sacrifices of the citizens of Kwangju also gave rise to tension
between the victims of the massacre and the citizens of Kwangju, as well as
causing divisions among the 5.18 organizations. The mass media's sensa-
tional coverage of the unusually large amounts of compensation (relative
to other cases) also attracted some unethical individuals who fabricated
records in order to receive money, further causing dispiritedness among
the people in Kwangju.[36] Many victims who received compensation felt
that they should have a sense of closure and felt uneasy about continuing
to demand an investigation.

THE RISE OF THE CIVILIAN GOVERNMENT AND THE "RECTIFICATION OF HISTORY"

Regardless of where they stood on the issue of compensation, the majority of South Koreans have consistently opposed impunity for the former
military junta for its role in the Kwangju massacre. During the Fifth and
Sixth Republics (1979–1993), when those responsible for the massacre
were in power, there were limits to solving the issues of Kwangju; for this
reason, 5.18 organizations and activists in the democratization movement
greeted Kim Young Sam's civilian government in 1993 with renewed hope
and enthusiasm. Despite the initial promising start for political reforms

early in his presidency, Kim Young Sam persisted for more than two years in opposing prosecution of his predecessors. The Kim government was born with "congenital defects"; Kim had merged his oppositional political faction with the ruling party of Roh Tae Woo and the right-wing faction led by Kim Jong-pil, creating the Democratic Liberal Party (DLP) to achieve victory against Kim Dae-Jung in the 1992 presidential election.[37] Although the details of the merger have not been disclosed, it was widely speculated that Kim made a political bargain to grant impunity to Chun and Roh in return for their support.[38]

Beginning in the early 1990s, the vocal and mounting pressure from the public to punish those responsible for the Kwangju massacre also included legal actions through criminal complaints. In July 1993, a group of thirty-eight military officers who had been arrested by the military junta in the course of the December 1979 coup filed criminal complaints that Chun, Roh, and others be indicted for military mutiny and treason before the fifteen-year statute of limitations lapsed.[39] On May 13, 1994, a group of 322 citizens, including one of the leading figures of the Kwangju demonstration, filed criminal complaints against Chun, Roh, and fifty-six others, urging their punishment. They argued that the victims of the massacre were "patriots rightfully opposing patently unconstitutional measures ordered by Chun on May 17–18, including his declaration of nationwide martial law, dissolution of the National Assembly, banning of assemblies and demonstrations, and preventive detention of opposition political figures and student leaders."[40]

The prosecutors' response to these demands once again proved to be disappointing. On October 29, 1994, after sixteen months of investigation, the prosecutors declared that Chun and Roh would not be prosecuted for insurrection despite finding that they had engaged in illegal troop movements, insubordination, desertion of martial law posts, homicides, and other acts constituting mutiny under the Military Penal Code. In what became one of the most convoluted legal arguments produced by the court, the prosecutors concluded that "an effective coup legitimized the regime and rendered it non-justiciable by law."[41] In other words, "despite committing the acts of treason the new government had succeeded in coming to power and enacted a series of legal and administrative measures. Any judicial ruling of treason would invalidate all subsequent governmental measures and undermine the successive republic's legal foundation."[42] The court also argued that the indictment of military leaders would "revive national divisiveness and confrontation over the past" and that "they [had] already been judged by the people through parliamentary hearings on the Fifth Republic."[43]

Kim Young Sam also continued to evade indictment of the military junta leaders, even as he tried to distance himself from the previous regimes of Chun and Roh, declaring his own government to be an extension of the Kwangju democratization movements and calling for an honest evaluation of the Kwangju Uprising. He also echoed the court's ruling, saying that the truth of the Kwangju massacre, along with the military junta's guilt, should be reserved for the "judgment of history."[44] He suggested that punishment could lead to renewed conflict through the public retelling of "the shameful story of the darkest age."[45] It was widely believed that Kim Young Sam himself was responsible for the prosecutorial decisions against prosecution. It became obvious to the public that the transition to a civilian government had not brought about an end to presidential control over criminal law enforcement.[46] Throughout his tenure in office, Kim Young Sam was beleaguered by widespread criticism that his decisions were governed by the logic of realpolitik, not by principle.[47]

By this time many ordinary citizens, regardless of their political allegiance, generally accepted the view that the Kwangju massacre was a treasonous act. As pointed out by legal scholar Pak Un-chŏng, this view would not have been acceptable even five years before; many more people then had probably thought that even if there were a law governing treason, there was no use in applying the law as no one would actually be prosecuted. But only a few years later, ordinary citizens' thinking and views had changed, an indication, scholars pointed out, that the general public had come to view South Korea as a law-governed, democratic society, where law should take precedence over political power.[48]

The public demand that the former dictators be punished and that a special law be enacted began immediately after the prosecutor's announcement. In August and September 1994, over 200 professors of Seoul National University issued a statement arguing that "the prosecution's logic runs counter to . . . the people's hope . . . to clear up the vestiges of past military regimes and to construct a true democracy."[49] Nearly 7,000 professors from fifty-four universities signed the petition, calling for the enactment of a special law. By August 25, 3,560 professors from seventy-eight universities had signed the petition. A total of 8,344 elementary and secondary teachers from 1,378 schools also signed. In Kwangju about 50 university professors took to the streets. Tens of thousands of students from over one hundred universities boycotted classes and joined in campus protests. A public forum focusing on the prosecution's decision was held, and lawyers also took to the streets for the first time in South Korea's history.[50] Although the street protests and petition drives were led mainly by professionals who had influence on public opinion, it is important to point out that participants were not limited to professionals, university students, or members of civic organizations, but included people from all walks of life and of various political allegiances.[51]

Amid the growing and massive protests, in late 1995 Kim Young Sam suddenly reversed his decision and agreed to "rectify" the wrongs of history, allowing indictments to proceed and pushing for the enactment of a special law. Kim was facing a myriad of problems at the time; his popularity was waning, partly due to his failure to support prosecution of the former junta, as indicated by the dismal performance of the ruling party in the June 1995 local elections. In November Roh Tae Woo was found to have a secret slush fund of "astronomical sums"—over 500 billion won (US$650 million), of which 170 billion (US$215 million) had been retained when Roh left office in February 1993. It was widely speculated that Kim Young Sam had benefited from this money as the successor of Roh's political party.[52]

Kim Young Sam's volte-face was thus designed to serve many purposes: to regain political legitimacy for Kim's own government after his "Faustian bargain" with the former dictators; to break through the crisis caused by the revelation of Roh's secret slush fund and the allegation that Kim partook of these funds; to appease the general public, which was growing weary of his moderate stance on many reforms, and to gain support in the upcoming April 1996 general election; to mollify the people of Chŏlla Province, who were disappointed by Kim's unwillingness to solve the 5.18 problem; and to upend Kim Dae Jung's leadership by solving the 5.18 problem and thus undermine the opposition party's attack on his previous decisions on the issues of Kwangju.[53] But the most critical factor in Kim's turnaround, more than thirty-two months after his inauguration, was the pressure from the people through mass movements, including demonstrations, petition drives, and other modes of direct political pressure. These moral pressures from civil society also caused prosecutors in charge of the investigation to reverse their position, as well as that of the Constitutional Court. As James West remarked, "They ultimately took a position consistent with popular sentiment, even when this entailed abandoning ostensibly 'principled' prior decisions declining prosecution."[54]

THE SPECIAL ACTS CONCERNING THE MAY 18 DEMOCRATIZATION MOVEMENT

Soon after Kim Young Sam's announcement, the National Assembly began to discuss legislative measures. Negotiations among the political parties on the content of the special legislation now revolved around the opposition parties' demand that a special prosecutor be appointed rather than entrusting the case to the same prosecutorial apparatus that had previously declined to indict Chun and Roh.[55] After much debate and political wrangling, the National Assembly enacted two special laws on December 19, 1995, which were promulgated and became effective on December 21, 1995.

The first law is titled "Act on Non-Applicability of Statutes of Limitations to Crimes Destructive of the Constitutional Order." This act defined treason and insurrection as "crimes destructive of the constitutional order" and abolished the statute of limitations for prosecutions of the designated crimes. The second law, titled "Special Act on the May 18 Democratization Movement" (hereafter the 5.18 Special Act), directly addressed the events of 1979 and 1980 and was designed to deal with the conduct of Chun's military junta during these events; it suspended the statute of limitations until February 24, 1993, when Roh Tae Woo left office.

The investigation into the 1979 coup d'état and the 1980 Kwangju massacre led to the indictment of sixteen former military officers, including Chun and Roh, for military mutiny, treason, and massive corruption. Heads of large business conglomerates were also charged with providing these defendants with a secret slush fund. The mutiny charges were related to the forcible arrest of senior martial law commanders on and after December 12, 1979, while the treason charges focused on the military junta's declaration of nationwide martial law; the dissolution of the National Assembly; the arrest of opposition politicians; and the murder of Kwangju citizens by military commandos between May 17 and 27, 1980.

"The Trial of the Century"

Widely dubbed "the trial of the century" (also called "the trial of the stars," since many of the defendants were former generals), the trial was momentous in the history of South Korea; the nation confronted its past authoritarian regimes and their "original sin" for the first time.[56] What was more, the first two South Korean presidents to ever voluntarily step down from power faced charges of insurrection, treason, and murder.[57] As historian An Pyŏng-uk noted, opportunities to judge and punish authoritarian dictators occur usually during a time of revolution. That South Korea brought former rulers to face judgment in court not in a time of revolution but of parliamentary democracy, that these rulers would be judged according to the rule of law, that South Korea had an opportunity to investigate these rulers and assign responsibility for their wrongdoings, and that South Korea had "overcome" what was widely perceived to be "disgraced history"—all of these were considered by many to be a momentous event and an experiment that had wider meanings not only for South Korea but also globally.[58]

The trial also symbolized not only the end of the military authoritarianism that had dominated South Korea for over thirty years but also the end of the military culture associated with it, such as the hitherto prevailing tendency to regard only end results while ignoring process, to consider only state-dictated standardized views while ignoring diversity of views and values, and to disregard individual sacrifice for the purpose of achieving state goals, all of which characterized the state-oriented thinking and policies under previous regimes. It was also thought that the people of South Korea, by exercising their rights as democratic citizens, had finally become "owners of the constitution and guardians of constitutional order" and had helped to restore the country's historical and political legitimacy.[59] The trial also showed that South Koreans were determined not to carry over their mistakes to future generations, resolved instead to wipe the slate clean.[60]

Without going into the court's detailed and torturous, not to mention quirky, legal proceedings and arguments, it suffices to note that ultimately the court responded by presenting a popular belief that "the defendants were responsible for creating a legitimacy crisis that they aggravated by their overreaction at Kwangju in May 1980 and then used as a pretext for expanding their power from the sphere of military command to the sphere of politics."[61] The defendants were convicted of treason, homicide for the purposes of treason, mutiny (for their illegal seizure of power in the December 1979 coup and in May 1980), and corruption. In 1980, the same defendants had claimed that their actions were taken to save a country in danger and had declared the protestors in Kwangju guilty of treason.[62] In the final decision of the Supreme Court on April 17, 1997, Chun was sentenced to life imprisonment and Roh to seventeen years. The others received prison sentences ranging from three and a half to eight years. Chun and Roh were pardoned by Kim Young Sam immediately prior to his leaving office, with the approval of then president-elect Kim Dae Jung.

The defendants vociferously claimed their innocence and the non-justiciablity of the trial, pointing out "inconsistencies" in the legal proceedings and the "political nature" of the trial. They argued that the 5.18 Special Act violated the due process of law and should not be retroactively applied since the statute of limitations had already expired. They also argued that the case had already been politically resolved. That is, if the defendants were to be punished, then the current government should also share accountability because it owed its existence to the previous government, which had originated in the military coup in 1979. Chun Doo Hwan denied any intent to seize political power in carrying out the coup and claimed that his arrests of senior commanders were justified because they were conducted in the course of his investigation into Park Chung Hee's assassination.[63] Records of prosecutorial interrogations were not released to the public to satisfy its right to learn the facts about the massacre and to clear up misconceptions about the Kwangju Uprising.[64]

The court also did not have the will or wherewithal to deal with the murder charges arising from the Kwangju massacre and instead focused on the less flagrant charges such as treason and insurrection, giving priority to investigating the illegality of arresting senior military officers in the December 1979 coup and the declaration of nationwide martial law in May 1980. Chun and Roh were not convicted for the mass killing in Kwangju. In the end, the trial failed to establish a record or authoritative facts regarding the Kwangju massacre; defendants were evasive or disingenuous about their roles; no testimony was given by Choi Kyu-ha, who served as president from 1979 until August 1980; no consensus was possible on the scale of casualties.[65]

Chun Doo Hwan, who in 1980 headed both the Defense Security Command and the Korean Central Intelligence Agency, claimed that no killing had been, or could have been, carried out under his authority. Both the then–martial law commander and the minister of defense also denied any responsibility for the order to shoot the demonstrators. The generals who were in Kwangju at the time claimed that they had acted only under given orders, and low-ranking officers and soldiers maintained that they had merely followed their superiors' orders. They did acknowledge that killings occurred but insisted that they acted in self-defense against violent demonstrators. They also denied any role in the killings that resulted from the military operations of May 27, 1980, the day when martial law troops retook the city.[66] With no one issuing the order to shoot, with no known incident of disciplining the soldiers for acting on their own without an order, how was it that so many people were killed and injured? Who should ultimately be held responsible for the killings? These questions were not answered at the trial.

Furthermore, Kim Young Sam's pardon of Chun and Roh discredited any claims of accountability, leaving the public suspicious that the motives and outcome of the trial were political and preordained. The court's shifting of its position, initially declining to indict the defendants and then reversing its position only under public pressure, also gave the public pause about its will or capacity to uncover the whole truth.[67]

In the historical context of a divided Korea and of the Cold War structure in East Asia, however, legal processes for settling the issues of the Kwangju Uprising, however problematic, should be recognized for their contribution to "a greater consolidation of democracy," firmly bringing to a close the legacy of military rule and state violence.[68] The enactment of the special laws and the judicial process are also considered to be successful cases of the rectification of history and have become models for articulating legal and judicial remedies for other past wrongs committed by the state. Under past authoritarian regimes, numerous democratization movement activists were expelled from their schools or jobs, arrested, detained, tortured, and imprisoned, and many died under suspicious circumstances. In 2000, the government promulgated the "Act Related to Restoring Honor and Compensation for Those Involved with the Democratization Movement," with the aim of providing compensation to and restoring the honor of those wronged by the state because of their involvement in the democratization movement.[69] In 2005, the "Basic Act for Coping with Past History for Truth and Reconciliation" was enacted, calling for an inquiry into past military and police atrocities committed from August 15, 1945, through authoritarian rule and also during the Korean War (1950–1953).[70] The act was intended to broaden the investigative scope into human rights violations committed by the state, which until now had been considered a constitutive part of state building and beyond the scope of legal and judicial remedies. The act suggests that it is no longer possible for the state to act with impunity "in the name of tradition, culture, development, or sovereignty."[71]

The Institutionalization of the Kwangju Uprising and the Limits of the Discourse of Democracy

In 1997, May 18 was declared an official Memorial Day. In 2002 Mangwŏltong cemetery was relocated to the city and consecrated as "the National May 18 Cemetery." Various 5.18 organizations, citizens' groups, and the local government joined to erect a memorial hall and monument in the city. The military camp that had held the armed forces during the massacre was redesigned and transformed into the May 18 Memorial Park. One hundred places in Kwangju and neighboring South Chŏlla Province were designated historical sites. Provincial Hall Plaza, the epicenter of the ten-day struggle, will be turned into the May 18 Memorial Plaza.

These various memorial projects and the government's official designation of the Kwangju Uprising as a democratization event—what one might call the institutionalization of the May 18 movement—illustrate both the promise and the limits of the discourse of democracy in circulation in South Korea. The institutionalization of May 18 is clearly a product of democratization in South Korea and has opened up possibilities for more thorough investigation and opportunities to envision new prospects for continuing and reviving the 5.18 spirit.

At the same time, institutionalization also holds the possibility of erasing the memory of state violence and of long-term regional discrimination against and suffering of the people of Chŏlla, along with suppressing its revolutionary character and potential. As the Kwangju Uprising has been incorporated into the dominant national discourse, its commemoration events have been conducted in accordance with fixed meanings.[72] Since 1998 local government and civic leaders have led events commemorating the Kwangju Uprising; anyone criticizing these events or raising issues that are not officially sanctioned has been excluded. In some years participants have been selectively invited.[73]

The new cemetery that replaced the old cemetery, Mangwŏltong, is another example of the institutionalization of the memory of the Kwangju Uprising, which speaks more about "official" memory than about efforts to revitalize the spirit of Kwangju. As the representative case of the memorial projects, the new cemetery was designed as a space for commemoration, education, and tourist visits. Visually dominating the entire landscape in the center of the cemetery is the Commemoration Tower, which is forty meters (about 131 feet) tall and looks down on visitors.[74] Jong-Heon Jin observes that the place is strikingly similar to many of the national monuments built during the authoritarian regime of Park Chung Hee, which, with their "authoritative and hierarchical structure," manifested Park's "exclusionary politics of national identity."[75]

It was in the process of remembering Kwangju as a people's uprising for democracy and justice, against the official narrative of Kwangju as a rebellion of violent mobs, that the Kwangju Uprising came to acquire its revolutionary possibilities and paradigmatic potency in the 1980s democratization movement, which gave birth to the 1987 transition to democracy. While the institutionalization of Kwangju goes on at the level of the state and in the official arena, with the participation of some citizens of Kwangju, others in Kwangju and across the country have continued to strive to revive the "spirit of 5.18" in the context of a contemporary South Korea that has been deeply transformed. For example, the May Movement organizations have spearheaded human rights and peace movements in solidarity with other Asian human rights and democracy movements. The representative case of this is the Asian Charter on Human Rights, adopted by the Conference of Asian Human Rights Groups in 1998, which was initiated by Kwangju Citizens' Solidarity, a group based in Kwangju. The conference was launched to facilitate and promote debates on human rights and in particular to present the people's views on human rights in the face of some Asian leaders' claim that "human rights were alien to Asia."[76] To keep the memory of Kwangju alive is to continue to rearticulate the spirit of Kwangju in the changed global context, to open up the "unexpected field of possibilities" and potential of the Kwangju Uprising. In this regard those involved in preserving the memory of the Kwangju Uprising seek inspiration from developments within their country to inspire broader regional movements and developments.

Notes

1. Kim Chae-gyun, *5.18 kwa Han'guk chŏngch'i: Kwangju posangpŏp kwa 5.18 t'ŭkbyŏlpŏp kyŏlchŏng kwajŏng yŏn'gu* [May 18th and Korean politics: A study of the process of the enactment of the Compensation Act for the Kwangju democratic movement and the special acts concerning the May 18th democratization movement] (Seoul: Hanul ak'ademi, 2000), 15; James M. West, "Martial Lawlessness: The Legal Aftermath of Kwangju," *Pacific Rim Law and Policy Journal* 6, no. 1 (1997): 93–94.

2. Kim Chae-gyun, *5.18 kwa Han'guk chŏngch'i*, 16.

3. See Kim Hang-min and Yi Tu-yŏp, eds., *Chiyŏk kamjŏng yŏn'gu* [Studies on regionalism] (Seoul: Hangminsa, 1991); Hwang T'aeyŏn, *Chiyŏk p'aegwŏn ŭi nara* [A country of regional domination] (Seoul: Mudan Midio, 1997), 9.

4. Antonio Gramsci, *Modern Prince*, 29–51, quoted in Renate Holub, *Antonio Gramsci: Beyond Marxism and Postmodernism* (London: Routledge, 1992), 139–40; Kim Manhŭm, *Han'guk chŏngch'i ŭi chae insik* [Rethinking Korean politics] (Seoul: P'ulpit, 1997), 164–65.

5. Kim Chun, "1980 nyŏn ŭi chŏngse paljŏn kwa taerip kujo" [The development of the confrontational structure of the 1980], in *Kwangju minju hangjaeng yŏn'gu* [Kwangju people's uprising], ed. Chŏng Hae-gu et al. (Seoul: Sagyejŏl, 1990), 159–60.

6. Ibid., 159.

7. Ibid., 160.

8. See Vince Boudreau, "Interpreting State Violence in Asian Settings," in this collection.

9. West, "Martial Lawlessness," 96–97.

10. Namhee Lee, *The Making of Minjung: Democracy and the Politics of Representation in South Korea* (Ithaca: Cornell University Press, 2007), esp. chap. 2, "Anticommunism and North Korea."

11. See N. Ganesan's and Sung Chull Kim's conclusion to this collection.

12. Quoted in William Shaw, ed., *Human Rights in Korea: Historical and Policy Perspectives* (Cambridge: Council on East Asian Studies, Harvard University, 1991), 184.

13. Kim Chae-gyun, *5.18 kwa Han'guk chŏngch'i*, 16–17.

14. See Lee, *Making of Minjung*, esp. chap. 4, for further discussion of the "counterpublic sphere."

15. See Samch'ŏng Kyoyuktae In'gwŏn Undong Yŏnhap, *Samch'ŏng kyoyuktae paeksŏ* [White paper on the Reeducation Corps to Purify Three Ills] (Seoul: Hanaro, 2003).

16. Keun-Sik Jung, "Kwangju Revived? Past, Present, and Future," in *Memories of May 1980: A Documentary History of the Kwangju Uprising in Korea*, ed. Chung Sangyong and Rhyu Simin, trans. Park Hye-Jin (Seoul: Korea Democracy Foundation, 2003), 410–21.

17. Ibid., 421.

18. Kim Chae-gyun, *5.18 kwa Han'guk chŏngch'i*, 88–89.

19. Sin Il-sŏp, "Kwangju Minjuhwa undong posangpŏp ŭi chŏngch'i, sahoejŏk ŭimi" [The political and social meaning of the Compensation Act for the Kwangju democratic movement], *Minjujuŭi wa inkwŏn* 5, no. 2 (2005): 177. "Original sin" in the South Korean political context refers to the military takeover by Chun Doo Hwan and his cronies in the Dec. 12 military coup.

20. Ibid., 178; Kim Chae-gyun, *5.18 kwa Han'guk chŏngch'i*, 121–22.

21. Sin Il-sŏp, "Kwangju Minjuhwa undong posangpŏp," 179; quoted in In Sup Han, "Kwangju and Beyond: Coping with Past State Atrocities in South Korea," *Human Rights Quarterly* 27, no. 3 (2005): 1004.

22. In Sup Han, "Kwangju and Beyond," 1004.

23. Yi Yong-jae, "Kwagŏ chŏngsan kwa minjujuŭi: 5.18 sabŏp chŏriŭi ŭiŭi rŭl chungsim ŭro" [Rectification of history and democracy: Focusing on the juridical meaning of 5.18], *Minjujuŭi wa inkwŏn* 4, no. 2 (2004): 249; Sin Il-sŏp, "Kwangju Minjuhwa undong posangpŏp," 179.

24. Sin Il-sŏp, "Kwangju Minjuhwa undong posangpŏp", 18; In Sup Han, "Kwangju and Beyond," 1003–5.

25. Kim Chae-gyun, *5.18 kwa Han'guk chŏngchi*, 137.

26. Ibid., 128–31.

27. Jung-woon Choi, "The Formation of an 'Absolute Community,'" quoted in *Contentious Kwangju: The May 18 Uprising in Korea's Past and Present*, ed. Gi-Wook Shin and Kyung Moon Hwang (Lanham: Rowman & Littlefield, 2003), 4, 8.

28. Kim Chae-gyun, *5.18 kwa Han'guk chŏngchi*, 128–31.

29. Ibid., 19.

30. Sin Il-sŏp, "Kwangju Minjuhwa undong posangpŏp," 182–85; Kim Chae-gyun, *5.18 kwa Han'guk chŏngch'i*, 143.

31. In Sup Han, "Kwangju and Beyond," 1031.

32. Sin Il-sŏp, "Kwangju Minjuhwa undong posangpŏp," 187.

33. Kim Chae-gyun, *5.18 kwa Han'guk chŏngch'i*, 171.

34. Ibid., 140.

35. Lee, *Making of Minjung*, 46.

36. Sin Il-sŏp, "Kwangju Minjuhwa undong posangpŏp," 197–99.

37. Kim Chae-gyun, *5.18 kwa Han'guk chŏngch'i*, 20.

38. Geoff Gentilucci, "Truth-Telling and Accountability in Democratizing Nations: The Cases against Chile's Augusto Pinochet and South Korea's Chun Doo-Hwan and Roh Tae-Woo," *Connecticut Public Interest Law Journal* 5, no. 1 (2005): 89–90.

39. West, "Martial Lawlessness," 104.

40. Quoted in West, "Martial Lawlessness," 106.

41. Quoted in Gentilucci, "Truth-Telling and Accountability," 80–81.

42. In Sup Han, "Kwangju and Beyond," 1006.

43. Quoted in West, "Martial Lawlessness," 104.

44. Gentilucci, "Truth-Telling and Accountability," 89; In Sup Han, "Kwangju and Beyond," 1005.

45. In Sup Han, "Kwangju and Beyond," 1005.

46. West, "Martial Lawlessness," 163.

47. Keun-Sik Jung, "Kwangju Revived?" 423.

48. Pak Ŭn-chŏng, "Pŏp, him, chŏhang: 5.18 ŏttaŏkke haesŏkhal kŏtinga," [Law, power, and resistance: How should one interpret 5.18], in *5.18 pŏpjŏk ch'aegim kwa yŏksajŏk ch'aegim* [Legal and historical responsibility for 5.18], ed. Pak Ŭn-chŏng and Han In-sŏp (Seoul: Ewah Yŏja Taehakkyo Ch'ulp'anbu, 1995), 16–17. Pak also notes that in a 1990 scholarly publication on the topic of historical responses to Kwangju, various responses, including literary and psychological, were discussed, but there was no mention of legal responses such as the application of the charge of treason to the military leaders, which came to dominate the public debate only five years later.

49. West, "Martial Lawlessness," 108.

50. Kim Chae-gyun, *5.18 kwa Han'guk chŏngch'i*, 189–90; Yi Yong-jae, "Kwagŏ chŏngsan kwa minjujuŭi," 251, 253.

51. Pak Ŭn-chŏng, "Pŏp, him, chŏhang," 21.

52. Kim Chae-gyun, *5.18 kwa Han'guk chŏngch'i*, 179; Gentilucci, "Truth-Telling and Accountability," 90; In Sup Han, "Kwangju and Beyond," 1006.

53. Kim Chae-gyun, *5.18 kwa Han'guk chŏngch'i*, 179–80.

54. West, "Martial Lawlessness," 149.

55. For this and the following two paragraphs, I have relied extensively on West, "Martial Lawlessness," 98–128.

56. In Sup Han, "Kwangju and Beyond," 1008.

57. Ibid., 1009; Kim Chae-gyun, *5.18 kwa Han'guk chŏngch'i*, 103–37.

58. An Pyŏng-uk, "Chŏn, Noh chaep'an e taehan yŏksajŏk p'yŏngga" [Historical interpretation of the trial of Chun Doo Hwan and Roh Tae Woo], *Yŏksa pipyŏng* 37 (Fall 1996): 122.

59. Ch'oe Chae-chŏn, *Kkŭnaji annŭn 5.18* [5.18 is not over] (Seoul: Justinianus, 1999), 106–7.

60. An Pyŏng-uk, "Chŏn, Noh chaep'an e taehan yŏksajŏk p'yŏngga," 130.

61. West, "Martial Lawlessness," 145.

62. In Sup Han, "Kwangju and Beyond," 1013.

63. Ibid., 1009.

64. Yi Yong-jae, "Kwagŏ chŏngsan kwa minjujuŭi," 257; An Pyŏng-uk, "Chŏn, Noh chaep'an e taehan yŏksajok p'yŏngga," 130.

65. According to the 5.18 Memorial Foundation, close to 140 incidents and questions integral to discovering the truth of the Kwangju Uprising were not investigated by the court, such as who ordered the shooting of protestors on May 21, what happened to those who were secretly buried, what happened on the final day at the provincial building, and who started the fire at the Kwangju Munhwa Broadcasting (MBC) building. See Ch'oe Chae-chŏn, *Kkŭnaji annŭn 5.18,* 114.

66. In Sup Han, "Kwangju and Beyond," 1017.

67. West, "Martial Lawlessness," 152; Gentilucci, "Truth-Telling and Account-ability," 84–85; Yi Yong-jae, "Kwagŏ chŏngsan kwa minjujuŭi," 257.

68. Jung-kwan Cho, "The Kwangju Uprising as a Vehicle of Democratization: A Comparative Perspective," in Shin and Hwang, *Contentious Kwangju*, 79; In Sup Han, "Kwangju and Beyond;" Yi Yong-jae, "Kwagŏ chŏngsan kwa minjujuŭi," 244.

69. Kuk Cho, "Transitional Justice in Korea: Legally Coping with Past Wrongs after Democratization," *Pacific Rim Law and Policy Journal* 16, no. 3 (2007): 590. The passage of this act was also propelled by the persistent efforts of human rights organizations and the families of victims, who had carried out a 422-day nonstop sit-in in front of the National Assembly (ibid.).

70. Cho, "Transitional Justice in Korea," 607–8.

71. In Sup Han, "Kwangju and Beyond," 1044–45.

72. Jong-Heon Jin, "The Role of Symbolic Landscape in the Construction of National Identity in Modern Korea" (PhD diss., University of California, Los Angeles, 2004), 101.

73. Ibid., 109.

74. Ibid., 108.

75. Ibid., 105–7.

76. In Sup Han, "Kwangju and Beyond," 1045; Jung, "Kwangju Revived?" 423.

3

Unsettled State Violence in Japan

The Okinawa Incident

Hayashi Hirofumi

Although Japan's aggression in Asia is well known, less attention has been given to cases of state violence that have taken place on Japanese soil since the modern period began with the Meiji Restoration in 1868. The case of Okinawa is one of the most notorious, even considering that it occurred during wartime. During the Battle of Okinawa, the last ground battle between the United States and Japan, a great number of Okinawan people suffered violence or death at the hands of the Japanese military.

Okinawa was sacrificed by the Japanese military and government in order to defend the mainland. Under US military tyranny Okinawans tried to come back to Japan in a quest for a peaceful Okinawa without military bases. During that time, the memory of Japanese military cruelty was subconsciously repressed as Okinawans tried to identify themselves as Japanese, not Okinawans. However, after reversion to Japan in 1972 Okinawans came to realize they had been betrayed once again by the mainland, because US bases still remained. This caused Okinawans to remember how they had suffered at the hand of the Japanese military, and they began to positively reevaluate Okinawan culture and identify themselves as Okinawan. As the Japanese government continually tries to deny Japanese military atrocities against Okinawans, the understanding of the

Battle of Okinawa is still a contemporary issue that is closely related to the US base issue. I will deal here with the Battle of Okinawa in 1945 as a case study of state violence in Japan.

THE BATTLE OF OKINAWA

Okinawa is the largest island in the Ryukyu Archipelago. It is located 350 miles south of Kyushu, one of the main Japanese islands. Okinawa was considered a vital air and supply base for the US invasion of mainland Japan during the final phase of the Pacific War.[1] The Battle of Okinawa began with air and sea bombardments on March 23, 1945, with US forces landing in the Kerama Islands (Kerama Retto) on March 26. A few days later, on April 1, US forces landed on the main island. After a fierce battle lasting three months, on June 22, the commander of the Thirty-second Army committed suicide. With the final US mopping-up operations completed on June 30, the Ryukyu campaign was declared over on July 2.

US forces lost 12,500 troops, including both ground and sea forces. This number was the highest of any operation in the Pacific theater. Japanese forces lost 94,000, including civilian employees. Among these, Okinawans accounted for 28,000; in addition, about 120,000 Okinawan civilians perished. The total number of Okinawan victims is estimated at about 150,000. The total human cost of the battle was more than 200,000. According to the G2 Report of the US Tenth Army, estimated enemy casualties, including prisoners, as of June 30, 1945, were as follows.[2]

Killed in action (counted)	107,539
Killed in action (estimated)	23,764
POWs (military)	7,401 (7,654 as of July 15, 1945)
POWs (unarmed laborers)	3,339 (3,581 as of July 15, 1945)
POWs (combat civilians)	15

The number killed in action is overestimated, while the number of POWs (unarmed laborers) may include Korean forced laborers. The total number of POWs is 10,755 (11,250 as of July 15), giving a ratio of about 10 percent (10.5 percent as of July 15) to the number killed in action (counted). If the number killed is actually taken to be the more realistic estimate of 94,000, this ratio would be 11.4 percent (12.0 percent as of July 15).

Not only did the Japanese military fail to provide protection to Okinawan civilians, but in many cases soldiers actually placed civilians in the line of fire in order to protect themselves. The purpose of this chapter is to consider this issue.

State Violence against the Okinawans

Although the large number of civilian victims can be attributed mainly to US bombardment, which came to be known as the "Typhoon of Steel," the Japanese themselves also massacred many civilians or drove them to their deaths. I will now discuss the types of suffering brought on the Okinawan people during the Battle of Okinawa.

Japanese Strategy and the Okinawans

Okinawa was sacrificed to defend the mainland and the emperor; for this purpose, both the Okinawa defense forces and the local Okinawan population were destined to suffer heavy losses. The Thirty-second Army mobilized everyone and everything in Okinawa. Male adults between the ages of seventeen and forty-five were drafted into the defense forces; others, both male and female, were mobilized as volunteer corps or labor forces. Even boys under seventeen and young girls were issued hand grenades and compelled to take part in night suicide attacks. Provisions and other goods were collected and delivered to the military by priority. Children and the elderly were advised to evacuate to Kyushu or Taiwan and later to the northern area of Okinawa Island. The military purpose of this evacuation, however, was to remove useless people who might prove an obstacle to the Japanese military. The chief of staff for the Thirty-second Army declared in a newspaper article that the Japanese military would not share its provisions with civilians even if they were starving, as the Japanese army could not under any circumstances risk defeat in order to save civilian lives.[3] The leaders of the Japanese military, both the Okinawa defense forces and Imperial Headquarters, clearly had no intention of protecting civilian lives or security; on the contrary, they thought only of making the maximum use of the local people.

Retreat to the South and Neglect of the Local People

At the end of May, the headquarters of the Thirty-second Army ordered a retreat to the south edge of Okinawa in order to continue resistance for as long as possible. However, by this time a great number of people had already fled and found refuge in the south. On Okinawa Island there are numerous natural caves, which the local people call *gama*. These stalactite caves held strong against bombardment and therefore made good shelters.

In the wake of the order to retreat, an avalanche of tens of thousands of troops and civilians streamed southward. As I will explain later, this order created a terrible tragedy. In addition, three days before committing suicide on June 22, the commander of the Thirty-second Army issued an order to troops not to surrender but to fight to the death. People were thrown out onto the battlefield without any protection. As the Japanese Army never surrendered or conducted an all-out suicide attack, the fighting continued indefinitely, greatly prolonging the suffering of both civilians and soldiers.[4]

In Itoman, a city in the south, 70 percent of all fatalities during the Battle of Okinawa came after the retreat.[5] Over half, or 54 percent, of fatalities for Urazoe, a city in the midland area that was the site of the bloodiest fighting in April and May, came after the retreat.[6] In the north, where many civilians from the midland and southern areas escaped to the mountains, most deaths were from starvation or malaria due to prolonged fighting. In all areas, if the Thirty-second Army had not decided to withdraw, the number of Okinawan dead would probably have decreased by one-third, perhaps by as much as one-half. Needless to say, even without the retreat, the Okinawan people would still have suffered greatly. However, it is no exaggeration to say that Japanese military strategy caused thousands of deaths.

The Killing of Local People by the Japanese Military

Numerous civilians were killed by the Japanese military throughout the Okinawan Islands during and even after the Battle of Okinawa. These killings can be divided into a variety of categories.[7]

When the Japanese military came to a cave where civilians had taken refuge, they ordered the civilians to leave the cave. Those who refused were cut down by sword on the spot.[8] Those who refused to submit provisions because their families were starving were also often killed.[9]

Even when civilians were allowed to stay in a cave, the military seized the deepest and therefore relatively safest area, forcing civilians forward to the most dangerous spot, near the cave entrance, where guards were stationed. When the US military reached a given cave, American interpreters tried to persuade the people inside it to come out, promising that the Americans would protect and feed them. Many Nisei interpreters, Okinawan Nisei among them, had been dispatched to Okinawa as staff of the military government.[10] They would call to the people inside in Japanese or often in the Okinawan local language. Babies or small children who cried from hunger or for other reasons were choked to death, as they might draw the attention of American soldiers. Mothers were forced to murder their own children; if they refused, a Japanese soldier would sometimes do it instead.[11] Those who answered the American calls and tried to leave the cave were bayoneted, killed by a sword, or sometimes shot from behind.[12]

In those caves the Japanese military failed to reach, on the other hand, civilians who responded to the American voices by venturing outside were in fact given protection by American troops. Brainwashed and repeatedly taught that Americans were so cruel and merciless that anyone they captured was sure to be humiliated and then brutally murdered, the Okinawans were initially terrified of Americans. Young women in particular had had this message drummed into their heads: if captured they would be molested, raped, and ultimately killed. Frightened as they were of the Americans, however, the kind treatment they received after capture changed their minds. They were provided with food and drink, and the wounded were given medical treatment.[13] One of the main factors that had kept people from surrendering was fear of brutal American atrocities. However, they eventually realized that the Japanese authorities had lied to them.[14] Some of the bravest offered to lead Americans to caves where their family, relatives, or neighbors were still hiding and help persuade them to come out. In some cases such actions were purely voluntary; in others Okinawans were requested to do so by American soldiers.

It is almost impossible to estimate the number of Okinawans killed by the Japanese. At least several hundred deaths can be confirmed, but an exact figure cannot be provided. According to Okinawan testimony, a significant number of male captives were shot on the spot by US soldiers.[15] Testimony by American soldiers, as presented by Gerald Astor, indicates that they were told to take prisoners for intelligence purposes but that they took very few and killed civilians on occasion.[16] If US troops had been taking prisoners from the beginning of the Battle of Okinawa, we could expect a far greater number of Japanese POWs to have been taken in Okinawa and other places. It is not far from the truth to say that Japanese propaganda, which held that US forces would brutally mutilate and kill Japanese captives, did have some basis in fact. However, we must not forget that many Okinawans described American soldiers as being much kinder than their Japanese counterparts. In spite of these qualifications, however, it is clear that the number of POWs taken during the Okinawan campaign was still quite high when compared with other battlefields in the Pacific.

Indirect Killing of Civilians by the Japanese Military

There were also numerous indirect killings by the Japanese military or cases in which people were forced or urged to die. Many of the civilians who took refuge in caves or other shelters were driven out by the Japanese military, leaving them exposed to American bombardment. The number of civilians thus indirectly killed must number into the tens of thousands. In numerous other cases, people were robbed of food by Japanese soldiers and as a result starved to death or died of malaria and other diseases. Refusal to submit food could also have fatal consequences. For example, in one case a little boy of school age who tried to get his sugar cube back from a soldier was stabbed to death in a cave.[17]

The situation in other islands of the Ryukyu Archipelago where the American forces did not land was almost the same as in Okinawa.[18] Miyako Shoto and Yaeyama Shoto, which lie to the south of Okinawa Island, were raided by air, but there was no ground battle. The main causes of civilian deaths in these islands were starvation and malaria. After the Japanese troops came, the food situation grew rapidly worse, as the troops required the local people to provide them with provisions. Furthermore, inhabitants of some areas and islands were forced to move, relocating to places allocated by the Japanese military, most of them potentially malarial areas where people had avoided living. In Yaeyama Shoto about sixteen thousand local people were infected with malaria, and more than thirty-six hundred died, only a small number of them killed by air raids. This was also the case on Miyako Shoto. According to a telegram dispatched to Tokyo by a navy unit in Miyako Shoto, the navy had a store of provisions that would last them six months, while the local population starved.[19] The Japanese military did not once share their provisions with the local population. When the chief of staff for the Thirty-second Army stated that the

military would not share its provisions with civilians, this was not simply a moral lecture.[20] It was rather a statement of policy describing actual
Japanese military practice.

Mass Suicide: Forced Death by the Japanese Military

During the battle, there were several cases of Okinawa civilians committing mass suicide, urged on by Japanese soldiers. Cases in the Kerama
Island Group are representative examples, with victims of mass suicide
on the three islands of the group estimated at 559.[21] According to my
estimation, at least half or perhaps more of the victims of mass suicide in
Okinawa died in the Kerama Retto. Besides these cases in Kerama, there
were several cases in which the victims numbered several dozen.

Two major arguments have been put forth to explain why local people committed mass suicide. One commonly accepted theory is that
"Kominka Kyoiku"—wartime education indoctrinating people as imperial subjects during the 1930s and 1940s—was the most important factor.
Various methods were used to indoctrinate civilians so that they would
be willing to fight and die for the emperor, including school education,
directives from local and central governments, and the mass media. Capture by the enemy was regarded as extreme disgrace, even for civilians.
The importance of Kominka Kyoiku in this regard is demonstrated by
the testimony of many Okinawans, such as Kinjo Shigeaki, whom I will
introduce later.

On the other hand, it has also been claimed that Okinawans died
for the emperor and the nation of their own free will—that they were
not victims but honorable heroes. This argument is based mainly on the
testimony of cadres of Japanese troops stationed in the Kerama Island
group, ignoring the testimony of islanders. The officers in the Kerama
Island group in fact tried to evade their responsibility in local people's
deaths. Ironically, although the Japanese military killed many islanders as
spies and ordered civilians not to surrender, the commander of Zamami
Island was himself captured by the US military before the end of the war.
The "honorable heroes" argument has not been acknowledged in Okinawa or in academic circles, but it is supported by mainland rightists and
the Japanese government.

While the Kominka Kyoiku theory has been widely accepted, as I point
out in my book *Okinawasen to Minshu* (2001), I investigated numerous

cases throughout the Okinawa islands and discovered that the influence of Kominka Kyoiku was in fact limited. Indeed, the presence of the Japanese military was the most crucial factor here: most cases of mass suicide happened where the Japanese military was stationed with civilians. If Japanese troops had not been present, the civilians could have surrendered and would have been protected by the US military. In addition, while the younger generation had been educated under the Kominka Kyoiku system, older people were not so indoctrinated. The Kominka Kyoiku theory, mainly based on the testimony of people who were teenagers during the war, might thus explain the behavior of young people, but not that of the older generation. Further, among local populations, young people had no power of self-determination.[22]

It is well known that the Japanese military and government strictly prohibited officers and soldiers from being taken prisoner. Surprisingly, this policy was also applied to civilians. Even children, women, and elderly persons were thus forced to die rather than surrender. This message was repeated at every possible opportunity—in the mass media, in the schools, by the public administration. The slogan of the Thirty-second Army, in fact, was "Gun-Kan-Min Kyosei Kyoshi," which literally means "military-officialdom-civilians live together and die together." In short, when soldiers died, officials and civilians should die a hero's death along with them. People were indoctrinated at every opportunity: they must die rather than be captured.

Further, the campaign to depict Americans as being unspeakably cruel was unrelenting. Propaganda asserting that Americans were so brutal that they would surely, rape, humiliate, and finally kill every Japanese was pounded into civilians' heads. In addition, Japanese soldiers and veterans who had been to the front in China privately and repeatedly told the Okinawan people about what they had done there—that they had killed Chinese captives with the sword or bayonet and casually raped Chinese girls.[23] Civilians thought that if even the Japanese, supposed to be decent and trustworthy, had committed such bloodthirsty atrocities, the American devils would surely be capable of far more brutal acts.

My third point is that the military delivered hand grenades to officials and civilians in advance. Young or adult men were often given two grenades. One was to use against the enemy, and the other was for suicide, to avoid capture. Most cases of mass suicide started with the exploding of grenades.

We must therefore conclude that mass suicide was not voluntary but was *forced* or *induced* by the military and the government. In fact, the term "mass suicide" may not even be entirely accurate. However, this term has been used since the 1950s to show that people were driven into a corner, led to believe they had no choice but to kill themselves. This is why we use the phrase "forced mass suicide." Although many similar situations may be found, mass suicide was in fact not prevalent. In places where there were no Japanese soldiers, people chose to surrender or escape whenever possible. It was not easy for civilians to kill themselves. Although the Kominka Kyoiku theory remains prevalent, my contention that civilians were in fact forced or induced to suicide by the military or government presence seems to be gradually gaining support.

On the whole, it is clear the Japanese military did not provide protection to Okinawan civilians and in many cases even victimized them. It is common knowledge in Okinawa that such events took place during the Battle of Okinawa: the islands as a whole were victimized to protect the mainland, Okinawan civilians were ill treated, and civilians were killed by the Japanese military. Their inhumane treatment at the hands of the Japanese military is seared in the Okinawan memory and will continue to be commonly acknowledged by all Okinawans, regardless of their political affiliation.

WHY THE JAPANESE MILITARY REGARDED CIVILIANS AS TARGETS

Mistrust and Discrimination against Okinawans

The Japanese military's mistrust of Okinawans did not suddenly surface during the early stages of the Battle of Okinawa. Until the mid-nineteenth century, Okinawa was not part of Japan, but an independent country, the Ryukyu Kingdom. Ryukyu was formally annexed to Japan as Okinawa prefecture in 1879. Okinawan prefectural officials were dispatched to the island from the mainland because ex-officials of the Ryukyu Kingdom refused to be subjugated to the Japanese government. Some actually worked to regain Ryukyu's independence, with the assistance of the Qing Dynasty of China. These activities came to an end with Japan's victory over China in the Sino-Japanese War of 1894–1895. After this war the Japanese government began to gear up its policy of assimilation in

Okinawa—in other words, Japanization. The original Okinawan language, for example, was now regarded as uncivilized, and education in standard Japanese was strictly enforced. This policy was connected to the conscription ordinance that was put into effect in Okinawa in 1898, twenty-five years later than on the main islands of Japan. At the time not many young Okinawans were able to speak or understand standard Japanese well.

A 1910 report prepared by the Okinawa Garrison Headquarters, which was in charge of conscription, demonstrates Japanese mistrust of Okinawans, claiming that Okinawan military thought was infantile and that the people's national consciousness was very low. The report also notes that there were many Okinawan draft dodgers.[24] In 1922, the Okinawa Conscription Area Headquarters drew up a report on public morals in Okinawa, pointing out that Okinawan loyalty toward the imperial family and the national polity was weak and that military consciousness among Okinawan men was so weak that they had no desire to be soldiers.[25] Such mistrust continued in succeeding years. In 1934 a commander of the Okinawa Conscription Area Headquarters submitted a report in which he criticized Okinawans for not caring whether or not the nation progressed.[26]

Okinawans had always been discriminated against by the people of mainland Japan, and such discrimination was common among officers and soldiers of the Thirty-second Army. The headquarters of the Thirty-second Army, for example, issued an order prohibiting Okinawans from speaking their native dialect. The order stated that those caught speaking the Okinawan dialect would be "disposed of" as spies. The military term *shobun* (literally "to dispose of") routinely meant execution.[27] A considerable number of such cases were reported in the testimony of Okinawans. As the military situation in Okinawa grew worse for the Japanese, rumors that Okinawans were acting as spies for the Americans began to circulate. Spokesmen for the Thirty-second Army headquarters often openly accused Okinawans of spying to newspaper reporters and the Okinawan police.[28] Those who could not accept Japan's impending defeat tried to attribute their heavy losses to the activities of Okinawan spies. When American bombardment was accurate, Japanese troops suspected that some native spy in the vicinity had given signs to American forces. Without such betrayal, they believed, the Imperial Japanese Army could not possibly lose a battle.

Suspicion toward Okinawans

The Japanese military made maximum use of the local population for military purposes. Military outposts were set up near residential areas, and the local people were mobilized as laborers to dig trenches and construct other military facilities. In addition, officers and soldiers were lodged at local private houses, because schools and other communal facilities were not able to furnish ample accommodations. Thus, civilians were in the position of knowing or having access to military secrets. The military authorities therefore looked upon the local population with suspicion, afraid that they would reveal military secrets if they fell into enemy hands.[29]

From the preparation stage, the Japanese military and government had suspected civilians of spying or of being potential spies. A high priority was placed on counterintelligence activities. Speech and behavior were carefully watched for signs of subversive thought, and antimilitary or antiwar sentiment was closely monitored by the *kempei,* or police. In particular, people who had returned to Okinawa after emigrating to Hawaii or continental America were kept under strict surveillance as dangerous elements, regarded as potential spies for America.[30] The Japanese military had a high level of mistrust toward Okinawans. However, we should not overlook the fact that this was also the case with the Chinese and other local peoples under Japanese occupation. In other words, the Japanese military's suspicion of the Okinawan people was consistent with the view it held regarding all peoples under Japanese occupation.

Prohibition against Being Captured

It is well known that the Japanese military strictly prohibited officers and soldiers from being taken prisoner. The problem here is that this rule also applied to civilians. It was in June–July 1944 that Imperial Headquarters first discussed its policy regarding civilians, during the Battle of Saipan, when the Japanese military was totally annihilated. This was the first battle in which the Japanese military fought alongside many Japanese civilians, more than twenty thousand of them involved in the fighting.

According to the minutes of a conference of bureau and section chiefs of the Ministry of War, held on July 2, 1944, the chief of the Military Affairs Bureau referred to the opinion of the Office of the Army General

Staff (Imperial General Headquarters—Army Section) that women and children should die honorably on the battlefield along with soldiers.[31] The chief stated that although it might be desirable for women and children to so die honorably, the problem was whether the army should issue such an order. If the Imperial Headquarters or the Ministry of War issued such an order, the emperor would inevitably be involved. The leaders of the army therefore decided to avoid issuing such an order, instead keeping their conclusions a secret among the conference participants.

Surprisingly, the leaders of the army did in fact want civilians, including women and children, to die for the nation's honor even if the Japanese military were totally annihilated. At the same time, however, they worried about the emperor's responsibility in such a case. Thereafter, they began to implement a variety of measures to encourage civilians to choose death for the emperor over survival through capture.

As noted earlier, one aspect of the campaign to encourage civilians to choose death was the campaign to publicize American brutality, beginning in August 1944. After this point, such campaigns were conducted not on the initiative of journalists and the mass media, but through cabinet decisions and under the guidance of the Home Ministry. The Home Ministry was in charge of censorship and guiding public opinion. It is entirely fair to say that the Japanese military either forced or induced people, both military and civilians, to die.[32] Those without the courage to die for the emperor, or who tried to survive by being captured by the enemy, were regarded as traitors destined to die.

The Japanese government and military leaders expected Okinawans to show their loyalty to the state and the emperor. Although some did as expected, the majority did not. For this reason the Japanese military grew more irritated with Okinawans and behaved more cruelly toward them.

Postwar Okinawa and the Narrative of the Battle of Okinawa

Relief for the War Dead

The issue of relief for the war dead is still a problematic one, relating not only to Okinawa's case but also to compensation for victims of the Japanese military in Asia. Except during the occupation, when US forces placed a ban on military pensions, soldiers wounded in the war and survivors of military war dead have been issued pensions. Since Japan recovered its independence in 1952, however, the issue of civilian war dead and casualties other than military personnel or civilian employees has come into question. During the war, between 1931 and 1945, the number of Japanese dead was about 3,100,000, including 2,300,000 military personnel and civilian employees and 800,000 civilians. The demand for relief has increased among the families of civilians who were killed or wounded during the war. In 1952, the Law for Relief of the War Wounded and for Survivors of the War Dead (hereafter the Relief Law) was enacted. According to this law, civilians who died or were injured during the execution of their duties at the behest of the Japanese military were issued relief funds as combat cooperators or participants.[33] Those sanctioned as combat cooperators or participants were enshrined in the Yasukuni Shrine as Spirits of the War Dead. The Yasukuni Shrine, which formerly belonged to the military, was privatized after the war. Nevertheless, the Japanese government continues to secretly provide the shrine with assistance and with lists of war dead for enshrinement.

The Relief Law was based on the principle that the government should provide relief to those who fought and died for the nation. This principle is premised on the assumption that the war Japan waged and its conduct during that time were just and proper. Relief funds are issued according to the degree to which the recipient contributed to the war. Recipients are regarded not as victims of a war of aggression or of Japanese militarism, but as loyalists and heroes who fought for the nation.

Since the 1950s the Japanese government has been using a double standard in this regard. Although to Allied nations the Japanese government often expresses regret over the last war, in other venues it usually takes the stance that Japan conducted a just war or that it had no choice but to carry on fighting due to the pressure of the Allied encirclement, or the so-called ABCD encirclement.[34] The Japanese government's viewpoint is in fact revealed in the Relief Law and in its attitude toward the Yasukuni Shrine, which honors only war dead who fought to the death for the emperor. At the time of the war, it was officially believed that the emperor was absolutely sacred and that wars conducted under the name and by the order of the emperor were always righteous. Japanese soldiers under the emperor's command, therefore, could not possibly have committed any atrocities. Needless to say, no allowance is made for admission that Japan was the aggressor. This mode of thinking underpins the Relief Law.

Under the American military occupation, Okinawans struggled under difficult living conditions; the Relief Law would provide them with much-needed financial assistance. Okinawans did eventually begin to appeal to the Japanese government, and in 1957, the Relief Law was finally applied to Okinawan civilians.[35] However, if a claimant applied on the grounds that his father had been killed by Japanese soldiers, his claim was rejected, because the father was not a combat cooperator. The claims of applicants disabled by injuries received during American bombardment as a result of having been forced out of caves by Japanese troops were rejected for the same reason. Yet their applications were accepted if they claimed to have left the cave voluntarily in order to cooperate with Japanese troops. In the case of people who starved to death because their food was confiscated by Japanese troops, applications were only accepted when surviving family members stated that they had voluntarily given their food to Japanese soldiers in hopes of victory. Examining the vast number of application forms for relief funds that have accumulated so far, we discover that everyone, without exception, not only in Okinawa but throughout Japan, enthusiastically cooperated with the Japanese military and the nation on their own initiative and that not a single Japanese opposed the war or the Japanese military.

If the Japanese government persists in this line of thought, compensating Asian victims will be a logical impossibility, because they rebelled rather than cooperated with the Japanese war effort. The Relief Law clearly shows that the government still believes that Japan waged a righteous war, rather than a war of aggression.[36]

The Struggle for Remembering

Soon after US troops landed on Okinawa Island on April 1, 1945, the Ryukyu Islands were placed under the jurisdiction of the US military administration. Although this military administration was abolished and the US Civil Administration of the Ryukyu Islands (USCAR) was set up in December 1950, this was in reality an extension of the military government. Japan regained sovereignty over most of the country by agreeing to sever the Okinawa Islands from the rest of the nation in 1952, and the US military continued to rule Okinawa until 1972.

After the Battle of Okinawa, people had to collect the remains of the dead and put them to rest, because they could not work in the fields without doing so. Several modest monuments were set up for the dead. In the early 1950s local news reporters and survivors published several books. One of these, *Tetsu no bofu* (Typhoon of steel), written by local news reporters, dealt with cases of mass suicide.[37] This was the first book that introduced such events to the public. Even after its publication, however, an overwhelming majority of Okinawan people kept silent, because recalling their experiences during the war was too bitter an experience. As for mass suicide cases, silence was kept until the 1970s.

At the same time, under US military rule, the human rights of Okinawans were systematically violated. In the 1950s, a broad area of Okinawan land was forcibly taken for use for US bases. Numerous military-related incidents and crimes against local residents occurred. The island-wide struggle against the US bases expanded in the 1950s. In an effort to defend Okinawan human dignity, a movement to return the island to Japan and end the US presence gained momentum in the 1950s and 1960s.[38]

During the period of US rule, Okinawans made every effort to identify themselves as Japanese because they wanted to return to Japan in order to realize a peaceful Okinawa without bases. They harbored the illusion that Japan had denounced all war and military activity in accordance with Article 9 of the Japanese Constitution and believed that reversion to Japan would mean the removal of all US bases from Okinawa. The Okinawan memory of suffering at the hands of the Japanese military had been overwritten by anger at tyrannical American rule.

In 1969, the US and Japanese governments signed an agreement that provided for the reversion of Okinawa to Japan. However, the Okinawan people felt betrayed once again by the Japanese government, for most of the US bases remained in Okinawa, and the clause concerning the removal of atomic weapons was ambiguous. When Okinawa was finally returned to Japan in 1972, of the US bases in Japan, 75 percent were still concentrated in Okinawa, which accounts for just 0.6 percent of the total land area of Japan. In addition, the Self-Defense Forces were deployed to Okinawa, forces that, in the minds of many Okinawans, overlapped with the former Imperial Japanese Army.

In the 1960s mainland Japan began to pay attention to Okinawa, as the issue of Okinawa's reversion to Japan became a political issue. At this time, many veterans from the mainland published their war chronicles on the Battle of Okinawa, and each prefecture set up its own monument for the war dead who had been drafted from that prefecture. Utterly oblivious to what the Japanese military had done during the battle of Okinawa, however, these mainlanders were not interested in the victimization of Okinawans at the hands of Japanese soldiers.[39] They thought only of regaining lost territory, which they considered essential to bringing an end to the postwar period. Under such circumstances, Okinawans recalled old memories of ill treatment and atrocities at the hands of the Japanese military during the Battle of Okinawa.

The memory and understanding of the Battle of Okinawa among Okinawans are therefore closely related to the postwar history of the islands. Until 1972, most literature concerning the battle was written by mainland writers and veterans. There were few works that considered the experiences of the Okinawan people themselves. The struggle against the US military and for return to Japan left them with little energy to spare for recollecting the past. Even more important, they unconsciously suppressed memories of the Battle of Okinawa because they tried to identify themselves as Japanese. At the end of the 1960s, when the reversion of Okinawa to Japan was agreed upon, memories of the Battle of Okinawa and of the betrayal and cruel treatment of Okinawans by the Japanese military came to the surface. Before and after 1972, several publications in Okinawa accused the Japanese military of brutality during the Battle of Okinawa. Among them, the most important was *Okinawa kenshi* (Okinawa prefectural history), volume 9, *Okinawasen kiroku* (Documents of the Battle of Okinawa), *Part 1* (1971), and volume 10, *Okinawasen kiroku* (Documents of the Battle of Okinawa), *Part 2* (1974). These two books of more than a thousand pages each contained the edited testimony of several hundred Okinawans. The editors criticized former works on the Battle of Okinawa because they concentrated on military action, while paying little attention to the suffering of the Okinawan people. These two books were the first to deal with the Okinawan war experience and became the model for later literature on the Battle of Okinawa. Many cases of Okinawans being massacred, ill treated, robbed of food, driven out of shelters by Japanese forces, and other events were vividly described and proven to have taken place. As for mass suicide cases in Kerama Islands, the testimony of those concerned was included in volume 10. Unfortunately, the great majority of those involved still kept silent, especially women. In addition, all this documentary evidence was scarcely introduced to the mainland.

While they hoped for help with economic and social-welfare development from the Japanese government in the 1970s, people came to regret the dilution of Okinawan culture that had accompanied Japanization and developed a tendency to emphasize their own distinctiveness and identity. In the 1980s, Okinawans began to regain pride in their own culture and history, and they relearned the history of the Ryukyu Dynasty, during which they had flourished through peaceful trade with other Asian countries.[40] They again began to demand an independent future without US bases. Their struggle for Okinawan identity has been repeatedly obstructed by both the US and the Japanese governments, but efforts still continue.

In the 1980s, an understanding of the Battle of Okinawa became one of the most important building blocks for the construction of an Okinawan identity. Each local government in Okinawa began producing its own municipal history in one or more volumes, dealing with the experiences of local people during the battle. Many residents and students participated in collecting and editing people's testimonies. Newspapers and television broadcasts repeatedly featured these themes. The experiences of Okinawans during the Battle of Okinawa, including their suffering at the hands of the Japanese military, have become common knowledge since the 1980s.[41] The saying "Inochi koso Takara" (life is precious) became popular in Okinawa, directly opposed to the Japanese notion of fighting to the death and/or suicide attack: survival by being captured, even as a POW, is much better than dying in battle.[42]

Since the 1980s, Okinawans have realized that it was the *hi-kokumin* (traitors) who saved people's lives, that the lives of these people who were never Japanized and what they did during the war should be valued as a part of Okinawan heritage. While Japanese militarism led to suicide attacks and the coercion of both soldiers and civilians to fight to the death rather than becoming POWs, Okinawans rediscovered in their sufferings during the Battle of Okinawa their tradition of valuing life above all else. In this context, the experiences of deserters and POWs in the Battle of Okinawa can be viewed in a positive light.

The Textbook Dispute in the 1980s

The Japanese government responded by attacking Okinawa's view of its own history. First, in 1982 the Ministry of Education attempted to have a passage deleted from a high school history textbook that stated that the Japanese military had killed many Okinawans during the Battle of Okinawa.[43] As part of the same program of textbook censorship, the Ministry of Education ordered that numerous descriptions of Japanese atrocities in Asia, including the Nanjing atrocities and Unit 731, also be deleted. On the whole, the Ministry of Education is reluctant to have anything relating to Japanese military atrocities taught in the schools.

The Okinawa Prefectural Assembly, including Liberal Democratic Party members, unanimously carried a resolution of protest against the Ministry of Education and demanded that the passages be restored. This 1982 textbook dispute caused great anger against the Japanese government among Okinawans and indeed helped to promote a better understanding of the Battle of Okinawa among Okinawans. The Japanese government finally gave in to Okinawa's protests and conceded that textbook passages concerning the killing of Okinawan civilians by the Japanese military might be restored.

However, in the following year, 1983, the ministry caused a new problem. While permitting descriptions of Japanese military atrocities to remain in history textbooks, ministry officials ordered that the words "mass suicide" be inserted into any textbook passages concerning the deaths of Okinawan civilians, its intention to show that these civilians were not victims but honorable citizens who voluntarily gave up their lives for the nation. Ienaga Saburo, one author of a history textbook, filed a lawsuit against this censorship. The Supreme Court accepted the censorship but admitted the findings behind Ienaga's contention: "mass suicide" was not an honorable and voluntary form of death for the nation. As a result, most textbooks began to describe mass suicide as having been coerced by the Japanese military.[44]

In the wake of this lawsuit, rightist writers and those involved with the Japanese Self-Defense Forces claimed that Okinawans had not been forced to die but voluntarily chose to die for the nation, that they were not victims of the Japanese military but honored war dead. In 1985, when the lawsuit was still pending in court, Prime Minister Nakasone Yasuhiro made an official visit to Yasukuni Shrine, where he praised the Spirits of the War Dead enshrined there. The campaign to deny Japan's aggression or atrocities and to justify Japan's conduct during the war intensified, a form of backlash against the movement I outlined in the previous section of this chapter.

To support Ienaga's lawsuit, one man who had testified as a witness in court gave his account of the mass suicide on Tokashiki Island, one of the Kerama Islands. Kinjo Shigeaki, who was then seventeen years old, bashed his family to death together with his elder brother, because a hand grenade had failed to explode. In court, he recounted his experience with deep regret, explaining how people had in fact been forced to die by the Japanese Army. His courageous testimony made an impact on many conscientious people on the mainland. Later he wrote about his experiences in a book.[45]

In the first half of the 1980s another mass suicide case came to light. In a cave called Chibichiri-gama, in Yomitan village, where US forces landed on April 1, 1945, eighty-three villagers had died. Most of them are thought to have suffocated after a veteran set fire to blankets. Among the victims, just over half were children under fifteen years old. After the war, many of the victims' bodies were collected, but this case was kept secret until a man from the mainland tried to find out what had happened. The writer Shimojima Tetsuro had learned about the incident through an interview with a former villager who had immigrated to Ishigaki Island, one of the Okinawa Islands group. Shimojima had then gone to Yomitan village and found two persons who would corroborate the man's story. Due to these efforts, those involved began to break their silence. The first report on this mass suicide was published in 1984.[46] A monument to the victims was set up in front of the cave in 1987. During this process many women involved testified, providing a better understanding of their emotional trauma after the war. The case of mass suicide at Chibichiri-gama thus became known to the public. Other mass suicide cases also came to light in the 1980s, although many survivors of mass suicide still kept their silence.

The 1980s was also an epoch-making decade in mainland Japan regarding historical awareness of the Battle of Okinawa in general. In particular, the 1982 textbook dispute had left a great impact on historians and other intellectuals, and the Chinese, South Korean, and other Asian governments severely criticized the Japanese government for trying to whitewash history. Under this extended barrage of harsh criticism, the Japanese for the first time realized how terribly Asian people had suffered at the hand of the Japanese military and accepted that the issue of Japan's war responsibility was not yet settled. Thereafter, historians began to research various atrocities and war crimes committed by the Japanese military during the Pacific War. Particularly noteworthy is the fact that veterans began to speak out about their own inhumane conduct against Asian people during the war. Some confessed that they had bayoneted local Chinese in training sessions as fresh recruits, while others narrated mass killings of villagers. Although they had kept silent just after the war, they now realized that historical truth might be lost if they did not speak out. This led them to tell their stories and openly express their regret to their Asian victims. In 1986, for the first time, several scholars from the mainland organized a research group on the Battle of Okinawa. The outcome of their research was published in the form of two books in 1987, the first fruits of collaborative research by mainland scholars.[47]

Simultaneously, Okinawa had begun to attract tourists beginning in the 1970s, the number of visitors increasing every year. In Japan every school makes a yearly excursion, and in the 1980s Okinawa became a main attraction for high schools. Okinawa is appealing to schoolteachers, not only because Okinawan culture is striking for mainland students but also because Okinawa offers good opportunities to study peace and war, including the Battle of Okinawa and present-day US base problems. Students and teachers typically visit various war sites and listen to the narratives of survivors. Introductory books and guidebooks for visitors, not only teachers and students but other tourists, have been published since the 1980s, usually addressing the suffering of Okinawans during the Battle of Okinawa.[48] In the 1980s, therefore, both Okinawans and mainlanders became aware of the importance of the Battle of Okinawa, and the Okinawan view of the Battle of Okinawa became widespread. This historical perception is closely related to the US base issues, as in this way the victimization of Okinawans by mainland Japan that began in the past continues today.

From the 1990s to the Present

In the first half of the 1990s research on Japanese atrocities and war crimes made great progress, in particular the issue of the Japanese military's "comfort women." As a result, people came to think of Japan's war not as a justified military action, but rather a war of aggression. School textbooks began to deal with Japanese war crimes, such as Unit 731, the Rape of Nanjing, comfort women, and so on. An opinion poll taken in 1994, conducted by Japan Broadcasting Corporation (NHK), showed that about half of the Japanese now believed that Japan's war was a war of aggression. This percentage was the highest since the war had ended.[49]

However, a strong and systematic backlash to this new openness, supported by many members of the Liberal Democratic Party, began in the mid-1990s.[50] Objectors attacked textbooks that dealt with various Japanese atrocities, including the comfort women system, demanding that such material be deleted in order for citizens to recover a sense of national pride. Under political pressure, publishers of textbooks began to tone down the descriptions of atrocities, the minister of education stating in 2004 that it was desirable for such references to Japanese atrocities to be deleted.

A description of Korean forced labor was virtually deleted from junior high history textbooks that were approved by the Ministry of Education in April 2005 for use beginning in 2006. Furthermore, the term "comfort women" can no longer be found in textbooks. As a whole, any mention of Japanese aggression and atrocities has been drastically cut under pressure from the Ministry of Education, the Liberal Democratic Party, and the right-leaning mass media.

It is well known that former prime minister Abe Shinzo and key persons in his cabinet have acted as core members of these textbook campaigns. When Abe attained the post of prime minister in 2007, the Ministry of Education launched a new attack to take advantage of the circumstances, now ordering that the word "coerced" be deleted from descriptions of mass suicide. As a result of this revived censorship, readers of history textbooks now again get the impression that mass suicide took place without military involvement or coercion.[51]

Once again, however, censorship provoked Okinawans' anger. Survivors who had witnessed mass suicide broke their sixty years' silence, although most had kept quiet until then. Most of these survivors had been children or teenagers in 1945; they are the last generation that clearly remembers the events of the war. Sharing a sense of crisis that historical truth might be obliterated by the Japanese government, they acted in the belief that this was their last chance to hand down their experiences to future generations.[52] Two local newspapers, *Okinawa Times* and *Ryukyu Shimpo,* carried their testimonies almost daily; local television broadcasts also featured their narratives. All forty-one municipal and town councils in Okinawa soon passed resolutions demanding repeal of the censorship and the restoration of clear statements regarding the Japanese military's coercion. The Okinawan Prefectural Assembly unanimously passed two such resolutions within three weeks, and more than 110,000 people gathered at a prefectural residents' assembly on September 29, 2007, demanding the repeal of the censorship. Okinawan anger had exploded.

Meanwhile, those on the right wing, including members of Parliament from the Liberal Democratic Party, mounted a counterattack. Late in December 2007 the Ministry of Education relented to a certain extent but continued to demand that the term "military coercion" be deleted: Japanese military "involvement" could be admitted, but not Japanese "military coercion." This problem remains unsolved.[53]

The issue of censorship is also connected to a political movement. In 2005 a right-wing group filed a lawsuit charging slander against Oe Kenzaburo, the 1994 Nobel laureate for literature, and his publisher, Iwanami Shoten. The intention of the lawsuit, obviously supported by important members of former prime minister Abe Shinzo's cabinet, including Abe himself, was to restore the honor of the Imperial Army and military personnel.[54] Asserting that, contrary to a statement in one of Oe's books, there had been no order to commit mass suicide, the claimants demanded that Iwanami cease publication of the book. However, in 2008, both the district and high courts rejected the claimants' demands.

Textbook censorship has also been supported by other right-wing politicians, such as Abe Shinzo, Nakagawa Shoichi, Aso Taro, and Machimura Nobutaka, who claim that Japan waged a righteous war and that therefore it need not apologize for Japanese military conduct. Even in the Liberal Democratic Party a number of politicians take this stance. Their aim is to revise the Japanese Constitution, particularly Article 9, which renounces war, so that Japanese Self-Defense Forces can officially participate in wars abroad. In support of this aim, they refuse to acknowledge atrocities committed by the Japanese military in former wars. The Battle of Okinawa will therefore remain an important point of contention for some time. The general election of August 2009, which resulted in the change of government to the Liberal Democratic Party, has shifted the political situation to a certain extent. Nevertheless, on this issue, the new government is taking the same stance as the former government, its minister of education so far showing no intention of changing the education policy. This means that the possibility of reconciliation between Okinawans' interpretations and official acknowledgment of their view is lost for the time being.

A Path to Resolution

Acknowledgment of the Facts

What can be done to resolve the issues I have outlined here? First, the Japanese government should formally acknowledge the fact that the Japanese military and government victimized Okinawa in various ways, causing the deaths of many innocent Okinawans, both directly and indirectly. At the same time, government officials, including cabinet members, should stop denying the facts concerning other Japanese military atrocities.

The Japanese government has never conducted a survey of civilian war dead in Okinawa. The exact number of dead is still unknown, although most municipalities in Okinawa have conducted detailed surveys of their own. In addition, it is supposed that ten thousand or more Koreans, including male forced laborers and "comfort women," perished in Okinawa, although it is difficult to determine the exact number due to a lack of data. The Japanese government has some lists of Korean men who were civilian employees but has not disclosed them to the public.

Although successive prime ministers have attended the annual memorial ceremony commemorating the end of the Battle of Okinawa on June 23, none has made an official apology for Japanese conduct during the battle. The Japanese government, including the Ministry of Education, should cease its censorship regarding "mass suicide" and restore former descriptions clarifying the coercion by the Japanese military. Although Japanese military conduct is examined to a certain extent in the Okinawa Prefectural Peace Memorial Museum, no national museum or monument commemorates what really happened during the Battle of Okinawa.

Compensation for War Victims

The Law for Relief of the War Wounded and for Survivors of the War Dead is fundamentally problematic. Okinawans who were killed or forced to die by the Japanese military should be compensated as victims of state violence, not as war collaborators. Such a change in the Relief Law would open up new possibilities for a solution to the problem of compensation for Asian victims of the Japanese military.

Recently, communication in the private sector between South Korea and Okinawa is becoming more active. Both peoples were suppressed and discriminated against by Japan, and both suffered war damage. During the Battle of Okinawa not only Okinawans but Koreans suffered greatly. In 2006 a monument for Korean victims of the Battle of Okinawa was erected in Yomitan village; a monument for "comfort women" was established on Miyako Island in 2008. Korean survivors were invited to the unveiling ceremonies for both these monuments. Both Korea and Okinawa are still confronted with problems caused by the presence of US bases on their soil. Sharing a common view of history and a common contemporary situation, Okinawa and South Korea are now cooperating in anti–military base campaigns. Greater communication between Taiwan and Okinawa is also beginning, little by little.

Linking Past and Present: The US Military Base Issue and the Battle of Okinawa

The source of Okinawan discontentment with the government lies not only in history but also in the present issue of US military bases. Of the US bases in Japan, 75 percent are concentrated in Okinawa, which makes up just 0.6 percent of the total land area of Japan. The government has tried to appease Okinawan anger and frustration regarding US bases with financial aid. The construction industry has traditionally backed the Liberal Democratic Party because it enjoys the benefit of public works. Nevertheless, a plan to construct a new airfield on the beautiful Okinawan coral reef sea has been at a standstill for more than a decade.

The lessons Okinawans learned from their experience during the Battle of Okinawa are that "life is precious" and that the military never protects civilians. They have learned that the presence of military bases exposes the local population to danger and can involve them in warfare. Their goal is an Okinawa without military bases. For Okinawans, the war is still not over. Only when the last military base has been removed will the war in Okinawa finally come to an end.

Japan's state violence against Okinawans was conducted during the collapsing stages of the imperial government. Military domination in Okinawa had been collapsing due to US aggression, and the awareness of crisis among the military cadre surely accelerated its violence against the local population. This violence was instrumental: ideology and education were rapidly losing influence over Okinawans, who had come to realize that military propaganda was deceitful in the wake of the US landing. Consequently, violence became the only method to enforce military mastery over Okinawans. At the same time, it can be said that this violence was exemplary: it was delivered as a warning to others, mainly abettors or leaders who guided local people to act against military orders.

One of the origins of this violence was the ideology of the emperor system, from the Meiji period. Members of the state had been required to devote themselves without conditions to the emperor; those who would not die for him were regarded as traitors. This notion developed to distorted extremes during the Pacific War. Another origin was Japan's successive aggression against East Asian countries, such as Korea and China, since the end of the nineteenth century. Violence against local populations who did not obey military orders was routine. Most Japanese troops in Okinawa had previously been stationed and fought in China; procedures applied to Chinese people were also employed in Okinawa.

The recognition of Okinawan suffering during the battle of Okinawa is shared among Okinawans but not among people on the mainland. The Japanese government can no longer deny the fact that the Japanese military killed many Okinawans. However, the issue of the treatment of mass suicide in textbooks has not yet been solved. Both the Japanese government and individuals on the right wing refuse to admit that mass suicide was forced or induced by the Japanese military. They still adhere to a narrative according to which Okinawans voluntarily sacrificed their lives to the nation and were therefore not victims of the Japanese military, but loyalists.

The issue of Okinawa is deeply interlinked with national identity. We may say that Okinawans do not think of themselves as merely Japanese, but as both Japanese and Okinawan, maintaining that "life is precious" in opposition to mainland military philosophy. Most tend to see Okinawa's suffering as having come from mainland Japan, which even now burdens Okinawa with US bases against its will. For Okinawans, the past and present are inseparable. The issue of the recognition of Okinawan suffering remains unresolved.

NOTES

1. On the progress of the Battle of Okinawa, see Roy E. Appleman, *The War in the Pacific: Okinawa: The Last Battle* (Washington, DC: Center of Military

History, United States Army, 1984); George Feifer, *Tennozan: The Battle of Okinawa and the Atomic Bomb* (New York: Houghton Mifflin, 1992). In addition there are several hundred books in Japanese on the Battle of Okinawa. For a general description of the Battle of Okinawa, see Fujiwara Akira, ed., *Okinawasen: Kokudo ga senjo ni natta toki* [The Battle of Okinawa: When the homeland became a battlefield] (Tokyo: Aoki Shoten, 1987); Hayashi Hirofumi, *Okinawasen to minshu* [The Battle of Okinawa and the people] (Tokyo: Otsuki Shoten, 2001); and Hayashi Hirofumi, *Okinawasen ga toumono* [Questions from the Battle of Okinawa] (Tokyo: Otsuki Shoten, 2010).

2. HQ Tenth Army, *G2 Report,* Mar. 26, 1945–June 30, 1945 (RG407/2948, National Archives and Records Administration [NARA], US); Tenth Army, *Tenth Army Action Report: Report of Operations in the Ryukyus Campaign, 26 March 1945 to 30 June 1945.* See also Hayashi, *Okinawasen to minshu,* 336–39.

3. *Okinawa Shimpo,* Jan. 27, 1945.

4. Akira, *Okinawasen: Kokudo ga senjo ni natta toki,* 94–95.

5. Itoman City, *Itoman shishi* [Municipal history of Itoman], vol. 7, part 2 (1998), 29.

6. Urazoe City, *Urazoe shishi* [Municipal history of Urazoe], vol. 5 (1984), 316.

7. See Hayashi Hirofumi, *Okinawasen: Kyosei sareta "Shudan jiketsu"* [The Battle of Okinawa: Forced "mass suicide"] (Tokyo: Yoshikawa Kobunkan, 2009), 91–92; Hayashi, *Okinawasen ga toumono,* 120–32.

8. See Itoman City, *Itoman shishi,* vol. 7, part 2, 630.

9. See Naha City, *Naha shishi* [Municipal history of Naha], vol. 2-B-6 (1974), 130.

10. Regarding Nisei interpreters and US psychological warfare, see G2 Tenth Army, *Intelligence Monograph: Ryukyu Campaign,* date unknown (just after the battle for Okinawa ended) (Okinawa Prefectural Archives). The original document is preserved in the NARA, Archives II.

11. See Okinawa Prefecture, *Okinawa kenshi* [Okinawa prefectural history], vol. 9, *Okinawasen kiroku* [Documents of the Battle of Okinawa], *Part 1* (1971), 250, 375, 410.

12. See Sakakibara Shoji, *Okinawa: Hachiju yokka no tatakai* [Okinawa: Eighty-four days of battle] (Tokyo: Shincho-sha, 1983), 189; Ginowan City, *Ginowan shishi* [Municipal history of Ginowan], vol. 3, 217.

13. There are many testimonies detailing the atrocities. See Miyagi Harumi, *Haha no nokoshitamono* [Legacy of my mother] (Tokyo: Kobunken, 2008), 36, 78.

14. Unfortunately, this was not the only attitude the Americans showed toward the Okinawans. Later, as women began to suffer from severe sexual violence at the hands of American soldiers, favorable feelings toward Americans diminished. See Miyagi Harumi, "Okinawa no Beigun to Seiboryoku" [The US military and sexual violence in Okinawa], *Senso Sekinin Kenkyu* [The report on Japan's war responsibility], no. 24 (June 1999).

15. I deal with more than ten such cases in Hayashi, *Okinawasen to minshu,* 356–59.

16. Gerald Aster, *Operation Iceberg* (New York: Donald I. Fine, 1995), 211. See also E. B. Sledge, *With the Old Breed* (Oxford: Oxford University Press, 1990); Yoshida Kensei, *Okinawasen: Beihei ha naniwo mitaka* [The Battle of Okinawa: What did US soldiers see?] (Tokyo: Sairyu-sha, 1996).

17. Ishihara Masaie, *Okinawa no tabi* [Traveling Okinawa] (Tokyo: Shuie-sha, 2000), 175–77.

18. Hayashi, *Okinawasen ga toumono,* 164–70.

19. Hayashi Hirofumi, "Ango Shiryo ni miru Okinawasen no Shoso" [Some aspects of the Battle of Okinawa: A study of the magic documents], *Shiryo henshu shitsu kiyo* [Bulletin of the historiographical institute] (Okinawa Prefectural Board of Education), no. 28 (Mar. 2003): 10.

20. *Okinawa Shimpo,* Jan. 27, 1945.

21. For the details of each case of mass suicide, see Hayashi, *Okinawasen: Kyosei sareta "Shudan jiketsu,"* 18–59.

22. Hayashi, *Okinawasen: Kyosei sareta "Shudan jiketsu."*

23. Okinawa Prefecture, *Okinawa kenshi* [Okinawa prefectural history], vol. 10, *Okinawasen kiroku* [Documents of the Battle of Okinawa], *Part 2* (1974), 649, 848.

24. Urazoe City, *Urazoe shishi,* 299.

25. Ibid., 300–303.

26. Ishii Torao, Commander of Okinawa Conscription Area, "Okinawa bobi taisaku" [Okinawa defense plan], 1934, submitted to the Minister of War, Library of the National Institute for Defense Studies (hereafter LNIDS), Ministry of National Defense.

27. See Otani Keijiro, *Kempei* [Military police] (Tokyo: Shin-Jinbutsu Orai-sha, 1973).

28. Yamakawa Taiho, *Hiroku Okinawasen* [Secret memoir: The Battle of Okinawa] (Tokyo: Yomiuri Shinbunnsha, 1969), 296–97.

29. Oshiro Shoho, *Okinawasen no shinjitsu to waikyoku* [The truth of the Battle of Okinawa and its distortion] (Tokyo: Kobunken, 2007), 75–76.

30. Direction by the Fifteenth Independent Mixed Regiment, Aug. 30, 1944, LNIDS.

31. Ootsuka Fumio, Chief of Medical Section, Ministry of War, memorandum, LNIDS.

32. Hayashi, *Okinawasen: Kyosei sareta "Shudan jiketsu,"* 152–61.

33. On the Japanese government's policy of war dead relief, see Utsumi Aiko et al., eds., *Handbook sengo hosho* [Handbook on postwar reparations] (Tokyo: Nashinokisha, 1992), 10–22.

34. A is America, B is Britain, C is China, and D is Dutch.

35. Ryukyu Seifu Shakai-kyoku [Social Department, Ryukyu Government], *Engo no ayumi* [History of War Relief Fund] (Naha: 1958).

36. Hayashi, *Okinawasen: Kyosei sareta "Shudan jiketsu,"* 222–28.

37. Okinawa Taimusu-sha, *Tetsu no bofu* [Typhoon of steel] (Tokyo: Asahi Shinbunsha, 1950).

38. As for the postwar history of Okinawa, see Okinawa-ken, *Okinawa: Kunan no gendaishi* [Okinawa: Modern history of hardship] (Tokyo: Iwanami Shoten, 1996).

39. Yakabi Osamu, *Okinawasen, Beigun senryoshi wo manabinaosu* [Restudying the Battle of Okinawa and the American military occupation] (Tokyo: Seori Shobo, 2009), 131–33.

40. See Hayashi Hirofumi, "Ryukyu no kaze ko" [Thinking Ryukyu wind], http://www32.ocn.ne.jp/~modernh/hobess01.htm.

41. For main publications in the 1980s, see Yoshihama Shinobu, "Okinawa sengoshi ni miru Okinawasen kankei kankobutsu no keiko" [Trends in publications on the Battle of Okinawa: Perspectives in postwar historical studies], *Shiryo henshu shitsu kiyo*, no. 25 (Mar. 2000).

42. On the origin of the phrase "life is precious," see Yakabi Osamu, "Rekishi wo mezasu ichi: Inochi koso takara toiu kotoba no hakken" [Life is precious: An Okinawan perspective on history], *Quadrante* (Institute of Foreign Affairs, Tokyo University of Foreign Studies), no. 4 (Mar. 2002); Shima Tsuyoshi (pseud., Oshiro Masayasu), *Okinawasen wo kangaeru* [Considering the Battle of Okinawa] (Naha: Hirugi-sha, 1983).

43. Eguchi Keiichi, "Kyokasho mondai to Okinawasen" [The textbook dispute and the Battle of Okinawa], in *Okinawasen to tennosei* [The Battle of Okinawa and the emperor system], ed. Fujiwara Akira (Tokyo: Rippu Shobo, 1987).

44. Hayashi Hirofumi, "Okinawasen 'Shudan jiketsu' eno kyokasho kentei" [Textbook censorship on "mass suicide" in the Battle of Okinawa], *Rekishigaku Kenkyu* [Journal of historical studies], no. 831 (2007).

45. Kinjo Shigeaki, *Shudan Jiketsu wo kokoro ni kizande* [Mass suicide: Carved in my heart] (Tokyo: Kobunken, 1995).

46. Shimojima Tetsuro, *Minamikaze no fuku hi: Okinawa Yomitan-son shudan jiketsu* [A day of south wind: Mass suicide in Yomitan Village, Okinawa] (Tokyo: Doshinsha, 1984).

47. Akira, *Okinawasen: Kokudo ga senjo ni natta toki;* Akira, *Okinawasen to tennosei.* These two books are the result of the collaboration of the same six researchers, including the author.

48. One of the most popular guidebooks is Arasaki Moriteru et al., *Kanko kosu de nai Okinawa* [Okinawa off the regular tourist route], 4th ed. (1983; Tokyo: Kobunken, 1983, 2008).

49. For research on the issue of the Japanese military's "comfort women," see Hayashi Hirofumi, "The Japanese Movement to Protest Wartime Sexual Violence: A Survey of Japanese and International Literature," *Critical Asian Studies* 33, no. 4 (2001): 572–80.

50. For the backlash since the mid-1990s, see Hayashi Hirofumi, "Disputes

in Japan over the Japanese Military 'Comfort Women' System and Its Perception in History," *Annals of the American Academy of Political and Social Science* 617, no. 1 (2008): 123–32.

51. Ishiyama Hisao, *Kyokasho kentei* [Textbook censorship] (Tokyo: Iwanami Shoten, 2008).

52. For achievements of Okinawan journalists, see Jahana Naomi, *Shogen Okinawa shudan jiketsu* [Testimonies of Okinawa mass suicide] (Tokyo: Iwanami Shoten, 2008); Okinawa Taimususha, ed., *Idomareru Okinawasen* [The Battle of Okinawa challenged] (Naha: Okinawa Taimususha, 2008).

53. See Hisao, *Kyokasho kentei.*

54. Tawara Yoshifumi and Uozumi Akira, *Abe Shinzo no Honsho* [The real character of Abe Shinzo] (Tokyo: Kinyobi, 2006).

4

Popular Views of State Violence in China

The Tiananmen Incident

Jeffrey N. Wasserstrom
and Kate Merkel-Hess

Over the last twenty years, the story of what happened in China in 1989 has been reduced to an increasingly simple set of events: students stood off against soldiers in Beijing in order to champion democratizing reforms, and the international media watched helplessly on June 4 as hundreds were slaughtered in Tiananmen Square. This narrative gets some key details wrong: for example, it is likely that very few people died right in Tiananmen Square itself in early June (it is possible that none did, and in any case, the main killing fields were on nearby streets, not on the plaza). In addition, the conventional version of the story is often backed up by misleading bits of information, such as references to the man who stood before a line of tanks on June 5 (in the most iconic photograph from the time) being a student (he was probably a worker) or statements that imply that the most commonly waved banners referred to democracy (they often simply had the names of universities on them, and if they had political slogans, these were likely to refer to anger over corruption). More generally, this narrative, while much closer to the truth than the "Big Lie" promoted by the Chinese government (based on the delusional notion that there were no innocent victims of a massacre, just some thugs and "counterrevolutionary" rioters who faced off against soldiers who showed great restraint), diminishes the complexity of protestors' demands and the scope of the protests and underplays the significance of patriotism as a motivating force in the protests. Moreover, when it comes to how the protests are memorialized and discussed in China, most foreigners are under the impression that the country has experienced a forced amnesia, a belief that ignores the widespread, complex—if often sub rosa—debates and discussions of "6/4" (*liusi*), the most common term there for the 1989 conflict.

In this chapter, we explore how differing memories of the events of 1989 have shaped expectations for reconciliation (or not) inside and outside China. This consideration leads us to the conclusion that, unlike some of the other instances of state violence considered in this volume, calls for "reconciliation" regarding the events of 1989 are often not focused solely on the event itself but instead have been incorporated into a broader Internet culture in China that pits citizen efforts to openly discuss historical and contemporary events against the government's goal of maintaining stability through the suppression of potentially inflammatory speech—and, more broadly, promulgating information about history that legitimates the Communist Party's position and limiting open reassessment of troubling periods in this organization's post-1949 history.[1] In this way, while 1989 remains a compelling shorthand (if a fading one) for China's human rights abuses abroad, in the People's Republic of China (PRC) itself the events of 1989 have been subsumed into a debate in emerging media on who controls the memory and memorializing of the country's past.

DIFFERING ACCOUNTS: HOW THE EVENTS OF 1989 HAVE BEEN TOLD AND NOT TOLD

We will not recount here all the events that took place in Beijing (and other cities at the same time) in April, May, and June 1989, as reliable and detailed accounts of these occurrences (some written by people who were on the spot, as we were not) already exist.[2] However, we would like to draw attention to some key characteristics of the movement that must be understood fully in order to comprehend the government's use of violence to respond to the protests and the lasting importance of 1989 in the

Chinese and global consciousness. We would also argue that a more complex view of 1989's events is, indeed, critical to explaining China's political and social path in the intervening twenty years and that any discussions of increasing rights or citizen participation in contemporary China must be framed by the tensions between society and government that emerged in spring 1989.

First, we should begin with the setting and the main protagonists. Beijing was the epicenter for the student protests that started events in motion. It was in Beijing that students first began to memorialize Hu Yaobang, who died on April 15, 1989, and who had been punished by the Chinese Communist Party for his failure to crack down on a series of student protests in 1986 and 1987 (whose centers were Hefei, a city in Anhui province, and Shanghai). Students from Beijing (Peking) University organized students from campuses around the capital to hold a demonstration on April 17—a demonstration that grew into successive days of protest marches and then into the famous student hunger strike.[3] While students remain at the center of accounts of 1989, in fact the students were quickly encompassed by a much broader group of supportive citizens drawn from workers' unions across Beijing.[4] Workers and other Beijing residents marched with the students; provided the necessary medical, logistical, and sanitary support for the crowds in Tiananmen Square; and kept military forces at bay, blocking roads when convoys eventually attempted to enter the city.

We know the most about the Beijing protests because they were the largest and, most important, because the international media, in town to cover talks between Deng Xiaoping and Mikhail Gorbachev, was on hand to beam images to the world of the events that took place in China's capital. But demonstrations (some very large in size) took place in other cities around the country, and as the weeks of protest went by, demonstrators from the provinces trickled into Beijing, reinforcing the lagging crowds of hunger strikers and their supporters. In a volume edited by Jonathan Unger, scholars recount protests of tens of thousands in cities across the country—including Shanghai, Changchun, Shenyang, Xian, Changsha, and other locations.[5] Other accounts of 1989, such as writer Lijia Zhang's memoir about her leadership role in worker protests in Nanjing and government reports that detail the formation of student organizations in Tianjin and Hunan, fill us in on what happened in additional locations in the Chinese spring of discontent.[6]

Given the cross-class makeup of the crowds at the biggest marches—tens or hundreds of thousands of people, some of them students or intellectuals but many of them workers, took to the streets and central squares of cities such as Shanghai and Guangzhou, while a million did so in Beijing—it should not come as a shock to learn that the majority of the hundreds of people killed in early June (there is no official death toll, but based on the most reliable firsthand accounts that seems the likely general size of it) were not educated youths. Some students died, to be sure. However, the majority of those slain, both in Beijing and in the western city of Chengdu, a Sichuan locale, where a massacre also took place in early June, were laboring men and women and other ordinary city-dwellers.[7]

Second, in clarifying the story of what occurred in 1989, it is important to fully understand the message protestors carried into the streets. In popular Western accounts of the movement, protesting students called for "democracy," and many observers speculated that a "revolution" was under way in China. In reality there was much more emphasis at the time on the evils of corruption in general and on the selfishness and nepotistic tendencies of particular leaders than on a desire for elections. Anger over government malfeasance and a poor economy was the driving force behind the protests, and protestors wanted change on these matters and framed their struggle as one to save the nation (a time-honored theme in student-led struggles from early in the twentieth century). Student leaders, some of them privileged children of high-ranking party members, did not want to overthrow the government and reiterated this in their publications, as they knew they had to in order to maintain the movement's legitimacy and minimize the chances for harsh reprisals, something that the strategy did not prevent from coming but may well have delayed.

Students and intellectuals, while stopping short of calling for revolution, did express support for Hu Yaobang's calls for "democratization and reform of the political system" and demanded a political system that would live up to international ideals as well as the rights enshrined in the Chinese Constitution. As one handbill from Beijing Normal University professors stated, "The citizens' basic civil rights . . . must be protected. . . . Efforts opposing political democratization under the pretext of 'not being suitable to China's conditions' enjoy no popular support and are extremely harmful."[8] But document after document from 1989 reinforces that protestors were calling on the government to change, not demanding its removal, making it in some ways, as one of us has argued elsewhere, much more like Prague 1968 than Prague 1989.[9] The reason understanding this fine distinction matters is because it changes how we evaluate the aftermath of 1989's events. This will be discussed further below, but the government has in the intervening twenty years addressed the two primary drivers of the 1989 protests, if sometimes in a limited way (and with occasional backsliding). First, the government recognized that economic conditions exacerbated popular unrest and implemented an ambitious project of economic growth. Second, in the past ten years, the government has slowly taken steps toward increased local self-governance. We do not wish to overstate these efforts, as they are still a far cry from popular rule, and they are not rights universally enjoyed in China. Some China watchers feel these efforts are just window dressing. What implications these localized changes might have for broader civil rights remains uncertain. Even so, it is important to acknowledge the power of the 1989 protestors' demands, resonating through the decades as the government formulates policies to maintain its control.

Finally, in discussing misconceptions about 1989, we should note that the details of the government's violent response are often muddled. A major source of confusion concerns who exactly died in the June 4th Massacre, how these victims were killed (the assumption is often made that most were crushed by tanks, but automatic weapons caused many more deaths), and where they were slain (not in Tiananmen Square, but in the streets near that giant plaza).

The Chinese government continues to insist that there was no massacre at all. It maintains instead that the event was simply an effort by soldiers—who showed great restraint when dealing with crowds and sometimes lost their lives in the process—to put an end to a "counterrevolutionary riot" that had disrupted life in China's capital, threatened the stability of the nation, and if left unchecked could have sent the country spiraling back into the kind of disorder that had characterized the Cultural Revolution era.

As we have already noted, that view of events has been labeled, quite appropriately in our view, the "Big Lie" about 1989. A few soldiers were killed (in some cases burned alive in their vehicles by crowds), but they were not the only and certainly not the main victims of the violence of early June. The government exaggerated greatly when raising the bogeyman of the Cultural Revolution (something it had also done in 1986, in posters that referred to that year's protesters as "New Red Guards"), since the protests of 1989 were largely nonviolent.[10] And so on. The Big Lie is not, however, the only widely but incorrectly disseminated version of key events. For example, as we noted above, many in the West continue to believe, erroneously, that most or all of those killed during the June 4th Massacre were students. In fact, most were members of other classes.

Who has shaped views on 1989 inside and outside China? This is a critical question in understanding the formation of the beliefs about 1989 that we have just sketched. For those outside China, the answer is a wide variety of sources. However, as detailed above, the dominant narrative of 1989's events continues to be shaped by popular coverage at the time, which emphasized the role of students and the demands for democracy above equally important (if less compelling for the media) participants and motivations. The assumption is that inside China, where the government has put in place wide-ranging suppression techniques to prevent discussion of "6/4," even less is known about 1989, particularly among generations who came of age in the 1990s and early 2000s. This assumption is somewhat misleading.

While it is true that government censors have been effective at curtailing discussions of 1989—and most media-savvy Chinese citizens are aware of the blockade—the Internet has made it impossible for the government to completely suppress discussion. Naturally, discussions of the events have been occurring informally among families and friends since 1989, but the Internet has brought those discussions into the public domain and has increased calls for acknowledgment by the government of June 1989's violence. For instance, in June 2008 the English-language patriotic blog "Fool's Mountain" (started in the wake of the Tibetan riots and the torch-relay protests to provide Chinese voices in English) ran an extensive series of translated accounts and reminisces from 1989 participants.[11] The accounts, as the editors wrote, were an attempt "to capture our conflicted feelings towards that violent summer."[12]

This small English-language entry point leads the way to an extensive underground of online information about 1989 that, despite their best efforts, the censors are never able to shut down entirely. As Guobin Yang notes in his recent book on speech on the Chinese Web, *The Power of the Internet in China*, Chinese "netizens," as online participants have come to be called (in Chinese, *wangmin*), creatively subvert and circumvent the well-understood limitations on online speech. But Yang argues that, as students did in 1989, netizens insist that their circumventions are "spontaneous," which helps them to side-step official wrath against calculating rule-breakers.[13] One such "spontaneous" act of dissent during 2009's twentieth anniversary occurred when a number of Chinese Web sites went offline around June 4, replacing regular content with an announcement that their Web sites would be down for "Chinese Internet Maintenance Day."[14] While it is unclear whether these Web sites closed out of protest or because Web administrators feared they would easily run afoul of the strict limits on speech during early June, many Web users in China and abroad read the closures as a commentary on government speech policies. Another example is the increasing use of a new term, "May 35th," to describe the June 4 anniversary. As censors have become adept at censoring the term "6/4," Internet users have begun to write instead about "535," in what writer Yu Hua has described as a "cat-and-mouse game" of Internet politics, always attempting to stay one clever step ahead of the censors. At a basic level, such actions belie any notion that 1989 is a completely "unknown" and "undiscussed" issue on the mainland.

The possible effects of such "underground" online speech should be neither overstated nor underestimated. Both the government's censorship measures and a broad sense among the Chinese public that many of the demands of 1989 are now moot (and the protestors themselves naive, if well-intentioned) seem likely to curtail any social explosions over 1989's legacy. What we believe these postings point to, however, is a continued desire among some Chinese citizens for public acknowledgment of the 1989 violence. Such a desire will likely continue until either enough time passes that the government feels safe in admitting that mistakes were made in its handling of the incident (as happened in the late twentieth century with some crises of the Mao years) or those who advocate for government acknowledgment (such as Ding Zilin, head of the organization "Tiananmen Mothers," formed by parents of students who died on June 4) pass away.

More Than Students: The National and International Context for the Tiananmen Crackdown

Students did take the lead in the initial protests, and one of their goals was to push for political reform. The Tiananmen Uprising was a sequel of sorts to an earlier wave of campus protests, which were, like those of

1989, rooted in a complex mix of frustrations and desires. The youths involved wanted more personal freedom and were frustrated with various aspects of university life, from compulsory calisthenics to the low quality of cafeteria food, and they wanted campus leaders to be chosen via open elections rather than being handpicked by the party. These protests swept through several Chinese cities in December 1986 (the biggest demonstrations took place in Shanghai) and ended at the start of 1987 (with a New Year's Day march to Tiananmen Square by Beijing students).

There were some scattered protests in 1988, but the resurgence of a true movement did not come until mid-April of 1989. There were plans in the works for a demonstration on May 4 of that year, when the eightieth anniversary of China's greatest student movement (the May Fourth Reform Movement) arrived, but a fluke event jump-started the struggle ahead of time. This was the mid-April death of Hu Yaobang, who had become a hero to the students when he was criticized and demoted for taking a soft line on the protests in 1986 and 1987. Hu's death opened a window of opportunity for the students, since when he died he was still an official, just not one with a top position, so the state could hardly prevent people from gathering to mourn his passing. The students turned the occasion into an act of protest, as well as a simple expression of sadness, when they began saying things like what a shame it was when good men died, while bad ones lived on and stayed in control.

One key difference from the protests in 1986 and 1987 was that, by the time the Tiananmen Uprising peaked in May 1989, it was much more than just a student movement. By then, the most important demonstrations involved members of many different social groups. Workers were particularly numerous in marches, drawn to the cause in part by the fact that, though students made democracy one of their watchwords, they spent as much energy attacking the leadership for growing corruption and for failing to spread the fruits of economic development broadly enough, something that echoed powerfully throughout Chinese society at a time when inflation was rampant and when it often seemed that the only people growing rich were the children of top leaders and those with high-level official connections. Journalists in state media were another more surprising group to join in some protests, while schoolteachers and professors took part as well.

Support from other classes peaked after students staged a hunger strike, an act that had special potency since lavish banquets had become a symbol of the selfish behavior of officials. Tapping into a longstanding Chinese tradition of educated youths laying their bodies on the line to protect the nation, the hunger strikers were seen by many as having proved that they were far more deeply committed to the good of the country than were Deng Xiaoping and other party oligarchs. This was the beginning of cross-class support for the student movement. As many other scholars and journalists have written, workers from many backgrounds, from journalists to members of the military, marched on the streets of Beijing in support of the students.

The mid-May swing of popular sentiment to the students is obvious, as one scholar points out, in a shocking shift in domestic press coverage. Usually tightly controlled by the government and generally hewing to the government line, journalists were broadly supportive of the student movement, marching with their work units throughout April and May 1989. As Zhou He notes in his analysis of press coverage of the movement from May to June, positive coverage peaked from May 17 to May 19, days that his interviewees called "the three days of press freedom."[15] During these days, Zhou argues, the stories on the movement in the *People's Daily* portrayed the government negatively 70 percent of the time, compared to 0-percent negative coverage during the preceding month and just over 1-percent negative coverage in the weeks that followed (during which the government declared martial law, and orders were issued to journalists to stop inflammatory reporting).[16] Other scholars writing about the press have also noted its critical role in signaling to society that controls were briefly loosened—and noting that the subsequent crackdown also foretold for readers the government's move toward increased control and threat.[17]

This mid-May moment was a critical turning point for the movement and part of what made it nationally resonant. Broad support for the students among workers, the party's traditional power base, was key in further mainstreaming student demands and also marked a challenge to government rule. It is likely that this shift, when a broad cross-class coalition took up the students' demands, led those within the party leadership to realize that this protest was unlike those of 1986 and 1987, though an appropriate response seemed yet unclear. The national economic situation was also extremely important in creating conditions for protest. The late 1980s marked the end of a decade of economic reform, but for many people—and particularly young people—the greatest impact of the reforms at this time had been greater insecurity, as the government closed government-run businesses, phased out guaranteed jobs for college graduates, and began to curtail the basic social security and social services that had sustained families during the Mao years. By 1989, some of the inequities of China's marketization were also increasingly apparent. For instance, though beginning in the mid-1980s many cities had adopted new regulations to govern migrant *hukou* status (and expand migrant legal status in the cities), migrant access to social services was limited.[18] However, while in the late 1980s growing urban-rural divides had in fact been reversed and, as Deborah Davis observed at the time, while many rural residents were doing better economically than poor urban dwellers, a yawning gap opened between rural and urban access to social services like education and health care. Moreover, she wrote, "the Chinese education system was more fragmented, less egalitarian and more stratified than it had been since the late 1950s."[19] For Chinese of all backgrounds, the late 1980s were thus a moment of increasing insecurity as the economic system and social safety nets were renegotiated and reshaped.

While many Chinese had yet to feel the impact of the economic changes happening in major coastal cities and the handful of special economic zones, they were getting increasing glimpses of the world beyond China and coming face-to-face with the material and cultural discrepancies between China and more developed countries. As one of us has written about in another context, student leader Wuer Kaixi reflected later that students wanted Nike shoes—and that this desire to participate in the increasingly global material youth culture was a strong motivator for students.[20] And, in fact, the student movement itself became a consolidator of a new Chinese youth culture, highlighting for youth across the country, for instance, the music of singer Cui Jian, whose ballad "Nothing to My Name" became the unofficial theme song of the movement.

Despite all these factors that explain urban youth engagement with the movement, they are still insufficient to explain the broad resonance of the 1989 movement domestically or, particularly, abroad, where it had implications far beyond the local issues of government corruption and limitations on speech and behavior. The iconic images from Tiananmen, for instance, of the Goddess of Democracy statue (which looked exactly like the Statue of Liberty) or of the Beijing citizen standing in front of a line of tanks, inspired action and response worldwide. In Eastern Europe, the man in front of the tanks became a symbol of government resistance for protestors calling for the end of Communist governance there. The international response to the movement—as well as the international context of growing attacks on Communism's strongholds—may have shaped the Chinese government's violent response, and we will speculate on this further in the next section. However, it is important to note the strong domestic context for protestor's demands, as well as for the government's response. In this regard, a brief analysis of the underlying nationalism of the 1989 movement is critical.

The international context for the movement is well known and often overemphasized. The world community became widely aware of the protests when Mikhail Gorbachev arrived in Beijing in mid-May for a historic summit with Deng Xiaoping. The visit's plans were disrupted by the protestors: Gorbachev was greeted at the airport, rather than at the planned reception in Tiananmen Square (where more than a hundred thousand protestors had gathered), and other activities in the square were canceled. The presence of the reform-minded Gorbachev emboldened protestors. As reporter Nicholas Kristof wrote at the time for the *New York Times*:

> The demonstrations were doubly embarrassing for the Chinese leaders because of the obvious enthusiasm that many of the protesters felt for Mr. Gorbachev. Several had prepared banners in Russian hailing him as a great reformer, and a crowd of workers and bicyclists applauded when he drove past them on his way to the Great Hall of the People.[21]

Protestors' accolades for Gorbachev, the repeated singing of the Internationale, and the Goddess of Democracy, among other signals, led commentators to frame the movement as part of a worldwide call for the end of Communism. While reading the movement in this way can have comparative value, as we have sketched above, the motivations for change were internal, and protestors were calling not for the overthrow of the Chinese Communist Party but for the party to live up to its own ideals and laws in the governance of China.

As a result, the crowds were not always welcoming to foreign reporters attempting to convey information about the protests to overseas audiences. As Philip J. Cunningham relates in his memoir of the protests, in the highly charged atmosphere of the square, antigovernment sentiment could quickly turn to antiforeign rhetoric, old grievances overlapping with new.[22] At no time did protestors call for international assistance that exceeded global attention to their cause to get the party leadership to respond to their calls for greater transparency and greater rights for the Chinese people. Students perceived themselves as acting on behalf of the nation—a belief reinforced by their adoption of Hou Dejian's patriotic song "Heirs of the Dragon" as one of the theme songs of the movement. Even so, in the end, having misread cues from protestors for months— misreadings that arguably caused the protests to quickly balloon in size and scope as popular sympathy turned to the students, who were portrayed as patriots whose overtures had been spurned by the corrupt and cloistered old party leaders—the government once again misread the protests as a referendum on their control over China (rather than, say, as a referendum on their style of governance and their recent policies). The role of the international community in this relationship was critical, at least symbolically. For the party, the protests that curtailed Gorbachev's visit were an international humiliation and an attack on its legitimacy in front of the international community. Protestors, on the other hand, saw themselves as patriotic voices, speaking out in the hope of strengthening their nation. This mismatch in perspective may help to explain the government's violent response, as well as the fact that this response was unexpected among Beijing's population. The Chinese government clearly felt a "loss of face" during an internationally symbolic occasion, to borrow a common Chinese expression, and this perception in turn conditioned the nature of its response toward the protestors.

VIOLENCE AND THE CHINESE STATE IN HISTORICAL PERSPECTIVE[23]

China's image abroad is often that of a thuggish state readily willing to take harsh measures to silence those who disagree with it—an image for which a key reference remains June 4 but that has been reinforced powerfully by later events, from the campaign against Falun Gong that began in 1999 to the 2008 crackdown in Tibet and the 2009 crackdown in Xinjiang. The authorities have used harsh measures to suppress some kinds of unrest, especially when it involves sophisticated levels of organization (the case with Falun Gong) and border regions (the case with Tibet and Xinjiang), and has gone to extraordinary lengths to limit awareness of these actions. But it has taken a less draconian stance toward other sorts of resistance, at times even punishing local officials who have been criticized by protesters.[24] This point deserves close scrutiny, since the Western press gives so much attention to patterns of dissent and moments of upheaval in the PRC and since the mix of factors that determines exactly how the government responds to a particular protest is far from straightforward. And in the post-1989 period, the state's toolbox of suppression techniques has broadened considerably, particularly its deployment of soft-power methods that prevent the necessity of force.

The calculus that tips the official response toward or away from outright repression is complex. Equally complicated is the decision about whether there will be a complete or merely a partial effort to block information. Because of what happened during the Tiananmen Uprising and the awareness of the importance of cross-class protests in places like Poland in the 1980s, movements involving members of more than one occupational or economic group are seen as particularly dangerous. Before moving on to the additional factors that draw high-level attention to protest, we wish to stress the critical importance of this cross-class coalition in analysis of the 1989 events. While the spread of protests from city to city was worrying, it appears that the leadership felt particularly threatened—and the tone of government rhetoric toward and official tolerance of the protests correspondingly changed in response—as the makeup of the crowds shifted in mid-May 1989 from primarily students and other intellectuals (in China, college students are considered *zhishifenzi*, that is, part of the intelligentsia, simply its youngest members) to a coalition of workers, urban residents, and young activists. Not only did this mark 1989's events as distinct from the protests of 1986 and 1987, but it signaled to the party the social spread of the students' circumscribed demands to a wider expression of dissatisfaction with the party's leadership on economic and social matters.

Another key factor is how geographically dispersed dissenters are: tightly localized events—ranging from small-scale tax strikes to neighborhood discussions of new chemical plants—tend to be treated more leniently. A third factor that influences the severity of regime response, both toward protesters and toward the ability of domestic and foreign journalists to cover events, is how well organized the participants in an outburst seem to be. The less evident careful coordination is, the more likely the response will be to mollify crowds, rather than strike terror into them—and the more likely that reporters will be able to cover the event.

Two additional things are worth noting about protest. First, as already flagged above in our comments on Tibet and Xinjiang, geography helps determine whether a hard or soft line will be taken. Force tends to be used much more swiftly when unrest occurs in frontier zones, where large percentages of the population do not belong to the majority "Han" group and where economic grievances and anger associated with ethnic and religious divides make for a particularly volatile combination. Recent protests in these regions, such as the Tibetan uprisings in February and March 2008 and the Urumqi riots of July 2009, drew swift, harsh responses.

Second, the regime's relatively lenient treatment of some protests could be interpreted as a sign of self-confidence. Political scientist Kevin O'Brien has made a strong case that it is a mistake to treat reports that many protests occur as indicators of weakness. It may be a sign of regime strength that the government is ready not just to admit that protests are occurring but sometimes even to allow people to let off steam without responding harshly.[25]

One of the regime's campaigns of repression that has most baffled foreign observers is the quick moves it took to crush the Falun Gong sect just over a decade ago and the resoluteness of its policy toward the group ever since. When the crackdown began, the group in question had never engaged in a violent protest and seemed—to outsiders at least—to be simply a spiritual movement. Led by a man named Li Hongzhi, whose admittedly unusual ideas include claims to powers that many Westerners would consider akin to magical and whose version of "scientific facts" many would dub superstitions, it nonetheless did not have a political agenda. The fact that the Chinese government viewed Falun Gong as a threat is easy to understand, however, using the rubric outlined above. This is because its adherents came from all walks of life (even some party officials had joined it); were spread throughout the country (cells formed in many cities); and showed a capability for coordinated action (evidenced by ten thousand protesters appearing, seemingly out of nowhere, to hold the 1999 sit-in demanding an end to official criticism of the group).

Other reasons have been given for the ruthless campaign against Falun Gong. For example, a leading scholar on the subject, historian David Ownby, stresses the ideological challenge that Falun Gong posed to the Chinese Communist Party (CCP) even before it began to present the party as an evil organization (something that took place after the crackdown against its members began). Ownby convincingly argues that the CCP was threatened by Hongzhi's novel fusion of Chinese traditions and modern "science," for the party claims a monopoly on bringing together what it means to be both Chinese and modern, via the "scientific" socialism of Marx.[26]

The CCP response to Falun Gong needs to be seen as a special case for other reasons as well. For example, during imperial times, Chinese regimes were sometimes weakened or overthrown by millenarian religious movements, including some that began as quiescent self-help sects. And the party is especially concerned about protests that have ties with charismatic figures, a description that fits Li Hongzhi well. That said, the CCP response still illustrates the general pattern described above of struggles being treated most seriously when they are multiclass, multi-locale, and organized. As we have already stated, this corresponds to the response to the events in Beijing in 1989, where events that took place in multiple locales and, particularly, that spanned a broad range of actors were ultimately the catalyst for the government's violent response.

Falun Gong is important as the most widespread and major case of government suppression of a movement since the 1989 crackdown. It illustrates the lessons learned by the government from the 1989 uprising. In the decade since the suppression of Falun Gong, however, the government's most commonly used tactics have shifted once again, mutating in response to changing technologies and their impact on the ease of communication and organization. David Bandurski of "China Media Project," for instance, has identified in recent years a shift in Chinese government communication policies toward shaping rather than just responding to (or attempting to suppress) media narratives. Bandurski refers to this shift as "Control 2.0," a kind of Big Brother public relations campaign that seeks to channel and direct public opinion through the media.[27] While "Control 2.0" plays out in the media, a gentler obstructionist secret police force works to obfuscate coverage of 1989 by foreign media. For instance, reporters wishing to use Tiananmen Square as the backdrop for their reports on 1989's twentieth anniversary found their cameras blocked at every turn not by heavy-handed thugs, but by the slapstick version of the secret police: strolling undercover police who, on a bright sunny day, purposefully wandered in front of cameras with umbrellas, effectively blocking the shots (though not the audio). The goal seemed to be not preventing reporting on the event, but simply annoyance, an indication of a state so confident in its message that it no longer needed to suppress the story of 1989 (at least for a foreign audience) but instead could simply mock its efforts at reportage.

Such "soft-power" techniques may have a longer legacy than recent years, however. In a recent paper, Rob Weller writes of the "blind-eye governance" policies of post–economic reform China, by which he means that the government willingly turned a blind eye to extralegal activities that did not impede government business or cause problems for officials. Weller argues that, while the government took a harder line on even apolitical civil society activities in the years following the 1989 events, these years were an aberration in a three-decade run of laissez faire attitudes toward organizations, as long as they do not run afoul of the government.[28]

The counterpoint in Weller's argument, of course, is that it is not only the government that has learned to more smoothly navigate the management of dissent in the post-1989 period; active citizens, too, have a carefully honed sense of which activities will draw official attention and which will not (an assertion that Guobin Yang's research on citizen activism bears out). The result in recent years has been a continued tension between, on the one hand, measured growth of citizen activism and speech that falls largely within limitations set by the government and, on the other hand, government efforts to hold the line on open discussion of certain topics and events. Informed Chinese citizens are well aware that 1989 remains one of those topics, and this explains why calls for truth-finding and reconciliation remain marginal. As we will discuss further in the final section, Chinese citizens have tabled (for the time being) open discussion of 1989 and other similar events in favor of wider economic and intellectual horizons and a very slow but ultimately steady expansion of rights for the majority of people.

MAKING A CHOICE: ECONOMIC PROSPERITY AND SLOW POLITICAL REFORM

Economic prosperity and slow political reform were the government's peace offering to angry and discontented Chinese in the years following 1989. And there was widespread anger following the crackdown. As one observer wrote, "Peking is a city that has not been permitted to grieve for its dead, and the festering grief and shock have produced a lasting defiance, which is the most threatening possible force in a society based on deference."[29] But the government, in the wake of the crackdown, insisted that a strong state was critical for China. Consider, for example, how well events of the 1990s fit with the regime's assertion that China's national interest was best served by a strong state and emphasis on stability as something to be valued. For Beijing propagandists trying to argue for this point of view, the Yugoslavian descent into chaos was a godsend.

The collapse of order in that part of southeastern Europe allowed the CCP to point out, if never in these precise terms, that no matter how dissatisfied someone might be to live in a *Communist* state, there was a less appealing alternative out there: living in a *post-Communist* country like the unstable and war-torn region that Tito had once governed. Furthermore, after NATO forces intervened to protect Kosovo, the CCP was able to claim that a post-Communist era involved not just economic collapse and widespread violence but a loss of independence—an especially sore point in a nation that had long suffered from imperialist encroachments.

The year 1989 presented a major challenge to the CCP that many thought it only barely managed to withstand: the protest wave that brought a million people into the streets of Beijing and onto the capital's biggest plaza and tens or hundreds of thousands into the central districts of scores of other cities. The party survived, but only, as we have seen, after Deng Xiaoping and the other oligarchs of his generation took a series of drastic steps. They ordered the June 4th Massacre, they carried out a campaign of mass arrests, and they demoted Zhao Ziyang and placed him under house arrest. The other key event of 1989 was the rise to power of Jiang Zemin, the Shanghai leader who proved his skills to the oligarchs by taking a firm stand against the protests and restoring order in his city with a limited use of force.

The year was also a challenging one for Deng and his allies because Communist regimes fell in Budapest, Bucharest, and other European capitals. In 1989 Solidarity rose to power in Poland (winning its first election on the very day that People's Liberation Army soldiers were firing into crowds in Beijing), the Velvet Revolution took place in Prague, and the Berlin Wall crumbled. And though the Soviet Union remained intact and Communist Party–run, its days began to seem numbered.

In the wake of these developments, it became the conventional wisdom outside of China that the group responsible for the June 4 brutality could not possibly hold onto power for long. The "End of History" had arrived, the catchphrase of the time went, and soon there would be no Communist states left. Throughout the 1990s the notion that the CCP was unlikely to endure remained an article of faith for many Western journalists, academics, and policy makers, though there began to be more and more dissenting voices during the first years of the new century, as it became doubtful that the "Leninist extinction" (another phrase from the Western literature of the time) would reach Beijing.[30] The tide has shifted even more recently. Many now agree that, barring unexpected events, the CCP is likely to be with us for some time to come.

Many supporters of the movement hoped that, within a few years, the regime would reassess the protests of 1989. A similar set of 1976 demonstrations, also centered on Tiananmen Square and also triggered in part by the death of an admired official (in that case Zhou Enlai), were initially dubbed "counterrevolutionary riots" but then, after Deng's rise, reassessed as a "patriotic" struggle. Relatives of slain students and workers and human rights activists around the world have pushed for something similar to happen with 1989, but this has not come to pass.

One reason is that there has not been the kind of dramatic shift within the party leadership that took place in the aftermath of the 1976 protests. Deng's 1978 rise signaled a dramatic turnaround, and he could logically interpret the 1976 protests as a precocious signal of support for his eventual rise.

The situation relating to the June 4th Massacre is very different. There are said to be tensions within China's current leadership group, particularly between people with close ties to Jiang Zemin and his immediate successor, Hu Jintao. But all current leaders were associated with Deng and his policies and see themselves as continuing the reforms he started. They resist taking actions that could be seen as repudiating Deng's vision; they fear that doing so might, by extension, serve to undermine their own legitimacy.

One reason why Deng and Jiang were able to prove the skeptics wrong in the 1990s and why Hu's successors remain in control today has already been noted: they have been able to point to the traumas experienced by some formerly Communist countries. Here are four other factors worth stressing when seeking to understand the surprising longevity of the CCP:

First, the regime has made great and largely successful efforts to co-opt traditionally restive or particularly troublesome groups. Entrepreneurs frustrated at feeling stymied by getting too little respect from the authorities and having too little influence in how China was run were among those who supported the 1989 protests. China's leaders now welcome them into the Communist Party. Intellectuals in post-1989 China have access to a much wider array of books and journal articles and can travel abroad more easily, and this has helped minimize, though not completely eliminate, their disaffection with the party, which led so many of them to support the Tiananmen protests. And the government has stopped micromanaging student daily life on university campuses, which has similarly lessened the discontent of a group whose actions were crucial in 1989.

Second, the regime has followed a post-1989 strategy of patriotic education, emphasizing the party's historical ties to anti-imperialist movements. Like all of the other enduring Communist Party regimes—those of North Korea, Vietnam, and Cuba—and unlike many of those that fell in 1989—including those in Poland and Hungary—China's came to power via an independence struggle.

Like the heads of all the other enduring Communist Party regimes, China's leaders make overstated claims about the role their organization played in saving their countries from imperialists (underplaying the contributions of other groups), but all are justified in asserting ties to nationalist uprisings. In the Chinese case, the party's role in anti-Japanese resistance battles is celebrated whenever the regime's legitimacy needs burnishing, and China's role in the Korean War (presented as an effort to free a neighbor from foreign domination) is also commemorated.

Third, the regime has worked hard to raise dramatically the standard of living and the availability of consumer goods within its leading cities. This is something that none of the Communist Party regimes that fell late in the last century managed to do, and it helped bring about the collapse of those regimes. Purely political concerns, including frustration relating to issues of freedom of speech, contributed to dissatisfaction with the Communist regimes that fell in 1989, as did a sense, in many cases, that these governments were foreign impositions (stooges of Moscow), but so, too, did material issues. People living in East Berlin, for example, knew that on the other side of the Berlin Wall, those residing in what had formerly been part of the same city could shop at much more attractive department stores and supermarkets. Comparable things could have been said in 1989 about the contrast between Shanghai and capitalist

Taipei in Taiwan, but the difference is now gone. Europe's state socialist regimes claimed that they were not only morally superior to their capitalist rivals but could compete with them materially. They could not, and it cost them. China's regime has done a better job at quite literally delivering the goods.

Fourth, the regime has adopted a flexible strategy toward new protests that has worked well to prevent a new broad-based movement from taking shape. Mao famously said that a single spark could turn into a prairie fire. And China's leaders certainly do not govern a country where conflagrations are uncommon, since there are, by their own admission, tens of thousands of protests taking place every year, from rural outbursts related to forced relocations, to factory strikes like the highly publicized ones that swept through southern China around the time that the twenty-first anniversary of June 4 came and went in 2010. The CCP has thus far managed, however, by using different measures to deal with different sorts of unrest, to keep these many sparks from igniting another nationwide blaze.

This success points us toward the power of the Chinese case to explain, as this volume seeks to do, the relationship between violence and the state in Asia, but it also points us toward its unique characteristics. Unlike in so many of the other cases described here, the Chinese state and the Communist Party have weathered the 1989 fallout with few political ramifications. Part of this can be explained by the government's successful manipulation of 1989's violence—which was instrumental in the moment—to "exemplary" ends, as Vince Boudreau describes in this volume's introduction. The majority within China may not have believed the "Big Lie," but the government's description of events did its work in terms of acting as a cautionary tale for other potential dissenters. In this regard, the violence brought to bear on the population of Beijing and other cities was successfully deployed for regime maintenance, shoring up the CCP's hold on power, even while it subsequently made concessions (mainly economic) to ameliorate the dissatisfied.

The implications of the CCP's post-1989 successes in China for a revisiting of Tiananmen are great, and the government continues to take steps to suppress and eliminate written discussions of 1989. However, as we noted in our introduction, this does not mean that 1989 is forgotten in China. It remains a topic of discussion for those who experienced it, and, as with other repressed historical events, the Internet has provided a new venue for the sharing and collection of personal memories of these events. In this way, Chinese citizens have found a liminal space in which to challenge the government's official silence on 1989, carving out a place to preserve their memories. At the same time, the memory of 1989 is placed alongside other verboten topics of discussion in calls by intellectuals for greater government honesty and accountability, calls that are also disseminated online. For instance, in December 2008, an online petition called "Charter '08" that called for greater human and civil rights in China made both explicit and implicit reference to 1989:

> A hundred years have passed since the writing of China's first constitution. . . .We are approaching the twentieth anniversary of the 1989 Tiananmen massacre of pro-democracy student protesters. The Chinese people, who have endured human rights disasters and uncountable struggles across these same years, now include many who see clearly that freedom, equality, and human rights are universal values of humankind and that democracy and constitutional government are the fundamental framework for protecting these values.

The document also called for, among many other things, "truth in reconciliation" and the establishment of a "Truth Investigation Commission charged with finding the facts about past injustices and atrocities, determining responsibility for them, upholding justice, and, on these bases, seeking social reconciliation."[31] As a result of his involvement, Liu Xiaobo, the document's primary author and a veteran of the 1989 protests, was sentenced to eleven years in prison in late 2009, and many of its signatories have reported being under persistent surveillance. Liu has since been awarded the 2010 Nobel Peace Prize, although he and members of his family have been prevented from receiving it. Their dogged efforts to jumpstart a discussion on civil rights in China demonstrate the persistence of the desire in some quarters to continue to push for democratic change—and the continued linking of the 1989 protests to a broader agenda for civil and social rights. While there are few indications that a critical mass of Chinese citizens are concerned about reconciliation on 1989, there are more reports of local pushes for greater rights of assembly, speech, and justice. It may be that if greater openness on national wounds like 1989 is to occur, it will come as a result of small-scale increases in civil rights rather than being the catalyst for those civil rights.

NOTES

1. For a useful recent discussion of the Communist Party's ongoing concern with managing understanding of and debates about history, see Richard McGregor's *The Party: The Secret World of China's Communist Rulers* (New York: HarperCollins, 2010); this topic is also dealt with in many issues of the important online journal *China Heritage Quarterly* (http://www.chinaheritagequarterly .org/).

2. See, e.g., George Black and Robin Munro, *Black Hands of Beijing: Lives of Defiance in China's Democracy Movement* (New York: John Wiley and Sons, 1993); Craig Calhoun, *Neither Gods nor Emperors: Students and the Struggle for Democracy in China* (Berkeley: University of California Press, 1997); and, for a notable recent addition to the literature, Philip J. Cunningham, *Tiananmen Moon: Inside the Chinese Student Uprising of 1989* (Lanham, MD: Rowman and Littlefield, 2009). For participants' accounts of events, see also the award-winning, interview-based documentary *The Gate of Heavenly Peace* (Long Bow Group, 1995), shown as a *Frontline* episode and also at film festivals; details about the film and links to relevant readings can be found at http://www.tsquare.tv, a site created to accompany the documentary.

3. Jonathan Spence, *The Search for Modern China* (New York: W. W. Norton and Co., 1990), 739.

4. A good representation of this broad participation is given in *The Gates of Heavenly Peace* and in the second segment ("Tens of Millions of Protestors") of *Frontline*'s 2005 documentary *The Tank Man*.

5. See Jonathan Unger, ed., *The Pro-Democracy Protests in China: Reports from the Provinces* (Armonk, NY: M. E. Sharpe, 1991). For more on the protests in Shanghai, see Jeffrey N. Wasserstrom, "Epilogue: The May 4th Tradition in the 1980's," in *Student Protests in Twentieth-Century China: The View from Shanghai* (Stanford: Stanford University Press, 1991), 295–327.

6. Lijia Zhang, *Socialism Is Great! A Worker's Memoir of the New China* (New York: Atlas and Co., 2008); Andrew J. Nathan and Perry Link, eds., *The Tiananmen Papers: The Chinese Leadership's Decision to Use Force against Their Own People—In Their Own Words*, comp. Zhang Liang (New York: Public Affairs, 2001), 62.

7. Black and Munro, *Black Hands of Beijing*.

8. From "Open Letter to the Party Central Committee, Standing Committee of the National People's Congress, and State Council" (88–89) and "Our Views" (110), both in *China's Search for Democracy: The Student and the Mass Movement of 1989*, ed. Suzanne Ogden et al. (Armonk, NY: M. E. Sharpe, 1992).

9. See, e.g., "Let's Cry Out to Awaken the Young Republic—May Fourth Declaration of the Autonomous Student Union of Universities and Colleges in Beijing" (165–67), in Ogden et al., *China's Search for Democracy*. On the Prague 1968 analogy, see Jeffrey N. Wasserstrom, "Chinese Bridges to Post-Socialist

Europe," in *Between Past and Future: The Revolutions of 1989 and Their Aftermath*, ed. Sorin Antohi and Vladimir Tismaneanu (Budapest: CEU Press, 2000), 357–82.

10. One of the authors, Wasserstrom, saw official posters on a Shanghai campus late in 1986 that warned of the dangers of "New Red Guards"; the analogy was at least as far-fetched in 1986 as it would be in 1989.

11. "Fool's Mountain: Blogging for China" can be found at http://blog.foolsmountain.com/. It is currently blocked in China. Some of these accounts include Buxi Tang, "Six Four: The Early Morning Vus," June 4, 2008, http://blog.foolsmountain.com/2008/06/04/six-four-the-early-morning-bus/; "Six Four: He Xin's 1990 Speech at Beida," June 3, 2008, http://blog.foolsmountain.com/2008/06/03/six-four-he-xins-1990-speech-at-beida/; and "Spring 1989 in Shanghai—A Memory of the '89 Student Movement," Apr. 15, 2009, http://blog.foolsmountain.com/2009/04/15/spring-1989-in-shanghai-a-memory-of-the-89-student-movement/.

12. "Six Four: The Person I Admire Most Is Myself," June 4, 2008, http://blog.foolsmountain.com/2008/06/04/six-four-the-person-i-admire-the-most-is-myself/.

13. Guobin Yang, *The Power of the Internet in China: Citizen Activism Online* (New York: Columbia University Press, 2009), 35. On 1989, Yang is pointing to Craig Calhoun's work on the student protests, *Neither Gods nor Emperors*.

14. See, e.g., "China: Chinese Internet Maintenance Day," http://advocacy.globalvoicesonline.org/2009/06/03/china-chinese-internet-maintenance-day/; "Tiananmen Square: China Observes Internet Maintenance Day," http://www.digitalcommunities.com/blogs/international/Tiananmen-Square-China-Observes.html.

15. Zhou He, *Mass Media and Tiananamen Square* (New York: Nova Science Publishers, 1996), 102.

16. Ibid., 94, 104–6. For a further analysis of the role of the Beijing press corps, see Frank Tan, "The *People's Daily* and the Epiphany of Press Reform," in *Chinese Democracy and the Crisis of 1989: Chinese and American Reflections*, ed. Roger V. Des Forges, Luo Ning, and Wu Yen-bo (Albany: SUNY Press, 1993).

17. See, e.g., Michael J. Berlin's "The Performance of the Chinese Media during the Beijing Spring" in Des Forges, Luo, and Wu, *Chinese Democracy and the Crisis of 1989*.

18. On changes to the *hukou* system in the 1980s, see Kam Wing Chan and Li Zhang, "The Hukou System and Rural-Urban Migration in China: Processes and Changes," *China Quarterly* 160 (1999): 831–35.

19. Deborah Davis, "Chinese Social Welfare: Policies and Outcomes," *China Quarterly* 119 (1989): 577–78.

20. Jeffrey N. Wasserstrom, "Tiananmen at Twenty," *Nation*, May 27, 2009, http://www.thenation.com/doc/20090615/wasserstrom.

21. Nicholas Kristof, "Gorbachev Meets Deng in Beijing; Protest Goes On," *New York Times*, May 16, 1989.

22. See, e.g., the excerpts from Philip Cunningham's memoir at the blog "The China Beat": "Looking for Gorbachev," May 15, 2009, http://www.thechinabeat .org/?p=462; "The Night of No Moon," June 4, 2009, http://www.thechinabeat .org/?p=487.

23. The discussion in this section draws heavily upon material that appears in Jeffrey N. Wasserstrom, *China in the 21st Century: What Everyone Needs to Know* (New York: Oxford University Press, 2010).

24. For a typical recent case in point, see Associated Press, "China Dismisses Local Leaders after Angry Protest," July 25, 2009, http://news.yahoo.com/s/ap/20090725/ap_on_re_as/as_china_unrest.

25. Kevin J. O'Brien, "Rural Protest," *Journal of Democracy* 20, no. 3 (2009): 25–28.

26. See David Ownby, "China's War against Itself," *New York Times,* Feb. 15, 2001, which ends with the claim that Falun Gong's "evocation of a different vision of Chinese tradition and its contemporary value is now so threatening to the state and party because it denies them the sole right to define the meaning of Chinese nationalism, and perhaps of Chineseness." See also Ownby's book *Falun Gong and the Future of China* (New York: Oxford University Press, 2008).

27. See, e.g., pieces at "Chinese Media Project" like David Bandurski's "The Shishou Riots and the Uncertain Future of Control 2.0," June 29, 2009, http://cmp.hku.hk/2009/06/29/1673/; and Qian Gang's "Central Party Media 'Grab the Megaphone," Aug. 21, 2009, http://cmp.hku.hk/2009/08/21/1709/.

28. Robert Weller, "Globalization and Blind-Eye Governance in China" (paper presented at the conference "1989: Twenty Years After," University of California, Irvine, Nov. 5–8, 2009, http://www.democ.uci.edu/research/conferences/documents/weller.pdf [unpublished, cited with author's permission]).

29. Nicholas Jose, "And the Beat Goes On," in *New Ghosts, Old Dreams: Chinese Rebel Voices*, ed. Geremie Barmé and Linda Jaivin (New York: Random House, 1992), 316–19.

30. See, e.g., Edward Friedman and Barrett L. McCormick, eds., *What If China Doesn't Democratize?* (Armonk, NY: M. E. Sharpe, 2000); Bruce Dickson, *China's Red Capitalists: The Party, Entrepreneurs, and Prospects for Political Change* (Cambridge: Cambridge University Press, 2003).

31. This text is according to the definitive version of the charter, translated by Perry Link for the *New York Review of Books:* http://www.nybooks.com/articles/archives/2009/jan/15/chinas-charter-08/?page=1. There are, however, multiple versions of the charter available online, and not all include the explicit reference to Tiananmen.

5

Mass Atrocities in Cambodia under the Khmer Rouge Reign of Terror

Sorpong Peou

This chapter seeks to shed some light on both state violence and mass atrocities committed under the Khmer Rouge reign of terror (from April 1975 to the end of 1978) and their legacies, especially with regard to the ways in which they have been dealt with.[1]

I have argued elsewhere that the scope and gravity of violence committed by the Khmer Rouge regime were far more extensive and brutal than under any other political regime in Cambodia.[2] When assessed in terms of scale and gravity, the mass atrocities that took place under the Khmer Rouge rank first among the world's revolutionary regimes during the Cold War: the regime "engaged in the most atrocious slaughter, through torture and widespread famine of about one-fourth of the country's population."[3] Karl Jackson further asserts that "no previous revolutionary elite has moved so relentlessly to hunt down and kill as many as possible of the trained and educated manpower."[4] The number of people who perished during the three years and eight months of terror has been estimated at 1.7 million (out of a population of about 8 million).[5] The exact number will never be known, but there is no doubt that terrible mass atrocities took place. The regime possessed violent means and used them in ways that have been characterized as genocide, war crimes, and crimes against humanity. Although there is overwhelming evidence suggesting that the regime committed mass atrocities, it remains debatable whether it committed genocide (as most observers see it).

Three main arguments are advanced in this chapter. First, the Khmer Rouge regime heavily relied on violence as the main instrument in its pursuit of a utopian dream—the building of a new political order based on an ideology that has been characterized as "radical egalitarianism." This argument challenges the conventional wisdom that the Khmer Rouge leaders, especially Prime Minister Pol Pot, were solely responsible for the mass atrocities because of their racialism and personal lust for power. There is little truth to this perspective; in fact, cultural and ideological variables have greater explanatory power.

Second, it would be grossly misleading to jump to the conclusion that perceptional and structural/institutional factors did not play a much bigger role. In fact, violence associated with radical egalitarianism may also have been a byproduct of extreme insecurity as perceived by the Pol Pot leadership, which was constantly gripped by fears of state and regime collapse. The perception of extreme insecurity also resulted from the regime's serious institutional weaknesses, and there was a great and even growing gap between its utopian dreams and its institutional incapacity to govern and ensure state and regime survival.

Third, the pursuit of retributive justice as a way to deal with this tragic past has proved far from effective. If radical egalitarianism, extreme insecurity, and institutional weaknesses were the combined cause of mass atrocities, retributive justice based on the assumption that individual political criminals must be punished may not be the best way forward. In Cambodia, the peace process resulted from a series of negotiations and peace agreements (based on the norms, principles, and procedures of liberal democratic politics), as well as formal and informal amnesties granted to some Khmer Rouge leaders—a form of national reconciliation. The stable peace Cambodia has enjoyed since the late 1990s did not result from the pursuit of justice, either. Moreover, retributive justice may have contributed to the strengthening of authoritarianism rather than democracy. The Khmer Rouge trials also represent a form of victor's justice.

The overall thesis advanced is as follows: the Khmer Rouge committed mass atrocities, and no amount of punishment will ever be enough for its leaders, but by assigning all responsibility to individual Khmer Rouge leaders for everything that went wrong during their reign of terror, we may not find the best cure for such state violence. The best way to avert this type of tragedy is to prevent egalitarian diehards (especially when unprepared to govern) from coming to power and to build democratic institutions that are inclusive and that ensure credible security for all parties within a stable system of institutional checks and balances.

SOURCES OF STATE VIOLENCE: AN ANALYTICAL FRAMEWORK

The atrocities committed by the Khmer Rouge are classified at least as follows: as genocide, war crimes, and crimes against humanity. Most policy makers, journalists, lawyers, and scholars have usually described the Cambodian "killing fields" (following the Khmer Rouge's military victory) as a case of genocide. The Khmer Rouge or Pol Pot regime committed murder against entire civilian populations, especially ethnic groups. The chauvinist section of the revolutionary regime (led by Pol Pot) systemically used violence against unarmed civilians. Two dominant causal factors are racialism and power. Violence and war initiated by Pol Pot were associated with racialism (or racialist ideology) and his lust for power.[6]

This academic perspective remains extremely seductive: it has had considerable political and academic influence on those who contend that what the Khmer Rouge regime did amounted to genocide and that its leaders must be punished. They recognize that the majority of the victims were Khmer (estimated at around 1,325,000), the largest ethnic group in the country (7,100,000 in 1975), but point out that the ethnic minorities suffered disproportionately in far greater numbers. Non-Khmer ethnic minorities included the Chinese, Vietnamese, Thais, Laos, and Muslim Chams. More than 215,000 of Cambodia's 430,000 Chinese perished. The Khmer Rouge expelled some 100,000 Vietnamese from Cambodia in 1975 and then murdered 125,000 of those who remained. About 90,000 of the 250,000 Muslim Chams were also slaughtered.[7] Most recently, the judge of the Extraordinary Chambers in the Court of Cambodia (ECCC) further confirmed death tolls estimated earlier at somewhere between 1.7 and 2.2 million people, of whom some 800,000 were killed violently.[8]

Whether the Khmer Rouge killing fields represent a case of genocide remains debatable. No doubt the Khmer Rouge committed horrendous mass atrocities, and this revelation runs contrary to the early "literature of denial" (when this author was still in forced labor).[9] However, this perspective is ideologically biased: it disregards other complex causes of the atrocities, and some of its proponents have been quite intolerant of alternative views.[10] Lest we forget, the concept of genocide itself remains controversial, largely because of its ideological and political nature.[11] Edward Herman and David Peterson, for instance, remind us of the historical fact that the word "genocide" itself has been both used and abused (in my view, by all sides of the ideological spectrum). In the United States, government officials, journalists, and academics, for instance, have branded indiscriminately as evil or genocidal or genocide prone those regimes or movements that interfered in the imperial interests of capitalism. However, the word "genocide" has seldom been applied in the same way when the perpetrators were US agents and allies. American officials, journalists, and academics were not alone in this, however. Those in socialist states or scholars who advocated socialism have done the same, branding enemies of socialism as evil or genocidal. Few of those who considered themselves Stalinists attached to Communist parties with links to Moscow, for instance, questioned Soviet hegemony and repression during the Cold War. By and large, socialist thinkers and activists tend to remember the heinous crimes committed by the Nazis but "have neglected the crimes committed by the Communists. . . . As for Lenin, Mao, Ho Chi Minh, and even Stalin, they have always enjoyed a surprising reverence."[12] Mao Zedong of China (known as the Red Emperor) enjoyed just such regard among socialist activists and scholars during the Cold War, including those in the West. Before his death in 1976, the Communist Party of China still considered his repressive policies as having "great merits." But as shall be discussed later, Mao was a man of violence.

Deeply problematic in the race-based explanation is the way the conceptual issue of "Khmer chauvinism" and power is framed. The issue of Khmer chauvinism does not address the question of why the Khmer Rouge regime caused the death of not only members of ethnic minorities such as the Chinese, Vietnamese, and Muslim Chams but also Khmers (more than 1,000,000 of them!) and all religious groups. Many Khmer survivors have wondered whether Pol Pot himself was a real Khmer. The spokesperson of the hybrid ECCC, Lars Olsen, has remarked that "it is impossible to say [that there] was an intent to destroy the Khmers. The perpetrators were of the same nationalities as the victims."[13] The deaths of minority and religious group members also do not tell us how they died. Were all of them executed, or did many of them also die of starvation and disease? Unlike many ethnic Khmers, who were farmers living in rural areas and thus could endure hardships, most Sino- and Vietnamese-

Cambodians lived in towns and cities; many of them found life under the Pol Pot regime unbearable and thus perished easily. The regime targeted not only the Muslim Chams but also other religious groups, including the majority Khmer Buddhists.[14] Khmer Buddhist monks were defrocked, expelled from their pagodas, or even slaughtered. Across the country, Muslim mosques, Christian churches, and Buddhist temples alike were demolished or turned into workshops, warehouses, and prison-execution centers. Their religious faiths, not people within ethnic groups, were thus the main target of persecution. Such crimes can be better described as ones against humanity. To argue that killing the Cham was an act of genocide also overlooks the fact that members of the Muslim group were "the victims of an attempt to eradicate religion, as a matter of general policy."[15]

Culturalists have a slightly better explanation of this general policy. Their perspectives are probably the most popular among Cambodian people, scholars, and other international observers, because they profoundly touch on something obvious in Cambodian history: a persistent pattern of state violence. Cultural attitudes toward violence have been analyzed by scholars who extrapolate that in Cambodia there exists a tradition of violence, known as "warrior heritage."[16] The Khmer's tragic past is used as a key variable to explain the present tragedy.[17] Other culturalists refer to Cambodia's tradition of absolute power, its anti-democratic culture, or the "culture of disproportionate revenge" based on the notion of "a head for an eye."[18] According to one scholar, "The origins of this tradition go far back in Cambodian history to times when, after winning a war, a victorious Cambodian king would sometimes attempt to kill the opposing king and his entire family line."[19] A Chinese delegate to Cambodia named Zhou Daguan (c. 1270–1350) also described in his memoirs how Cambodians settled their disputes. The various forms of punishment inflicted on individuals considered to be criminal included physical torture. In Zhou's words, "they just dig a ditch in the ground outside the west gate of the city, put the criminal inside it, fill it up solid with earth and stones, and leave it at that. Otherwise people have their fingers or toes amputated, or their nose cut off." When thieves were caught, they were subject to "detention, torture, or beating." Those who were suspected of having stolen something could also have their own hands "tested" by the application of some oil that had been heated in a cauldron until it was extremely hot. Zhou writes, "If they are the thief, their hand turns putrid; if they are not, their skin and flesh stay the same as before."[20]

Cultural perspectives can also shed some light on contemporary Cambodian politics. As recently as in mid-1997, when Prince and First Prime Minister Norodom Ranariddh was ousted from power in a violent coup staged by Second Prime Minister Hun Sen, some members of the prince's royalist forces were subjected to torture and extrajudicial execution. Many who were arrested were handcuffed, blindfolded, and tortured. The forms of torture included beatings with a belt, the wooden leg of a table, and a wooden plank; kicking in the knees with combat boots; punching in the face and the body; and blows to the blade of the upper part of the nose. An iron vice was also used to squeeze the detainees' fingers or hands until they provided satisfactory answers to the interrogator's questions.[21] It is thus unsurprising that Cambodia continues to be regarded as having a cultural or traditional practice of violence against individuals, and the country's institutional types of punishment would be considered acts of violence today. However, culturalist perspectives overlook the fact that traditional forms of punishment excluded whipping, flogging, hanging, and beheading. More specifically, they cannot answer the question of why the Khmer Rouge leadership committed far worse violence than any other regimes in Cambodian history. Ideological factors have greater explanatory power than cultural ones.

The thesis that racialism was the cause of genocide under the Pol Pot regime is also based on the ideological implication that top Khmer Rouge leaders were anti-socialist (they did not follow in the ideological footsteps of true socialism!), but this argument has its own biases. If the Khmer Rouge crimes against religious groups were to be considered "genocide," it would be a form of "socialist genocide" because they were in line with the Marxist view that "religion is the opium of the people." The race-based thesis also overlooks the fact that Communist regimes worldwide were responsible for approximately 100 million deaths. Although the Khmer Rouge regime ranked first among the Communist regimes in the world when assessed in terms of the severity of crimes committed in just three and a half years, China was not too far behind. The number of Chinese who lost their lives under the Mao Zedong regime was estimated at 65 million, unprecedented in Chinese history. The mass murders did not result from racialism per se but from the drive for socialist purification.[22] One of the most famous dictums in Maoism is "victory comes from the barrel of a gun." Mao's anti-intellectualism was well known, but "it was not [his] intention to kill so many of his compatriots."[23] In fact, his goal was only to eliminate political rivals as part of Chinese state and regime building, and he was thus forced to take more repressive action against these rivals, especially when the goal "was slipping out of his grasp," as the struggle for power continued to intensify.[24] His Red Guards regarded intellectuals as "monsters and devils" who must be humiliated and put to death.[25] Mao apparently had not set out to murder such a large number of people, but the people his regime exterminated were Chinese accused of being revisionists or reactionaries—enemies of the socialist regime.

Insecurity—rather than power defined in terms of capability—better helps explain the outbreak and escalation of state violence. In the study of international security, states become aggressive when perceiving their vulnerability to be high, not as a result of their aggressive nature or military superiority.[26] Studies also reveal that when political regimes are insecure, they tend to become violently repressive. When trapped in a situation where their security needs are threatened, political leaders often engage in "a pathological set of relationships between state leadership and its agencies."[27] One may thus hypothesize that the higher the degree of vulnerability or insecurity state leaders experience, the higher the degree of violence.

State violence could be defined as "reactive" to threat without considerable premeditation, as Charles Tilly contends.[28] However, as will be suggested, insecurity (both actual and perceived) tends to force state leaders to use repressive violence. According to Boudreau in this volume, there are two basic types of state violence associated with insecurity: state-building violence and regime-changing violence. State-building violence is *instrumental* because it is more or less about building the state in the face of existential threats (such as chaos and anarchy). The state may seek to expand its political apparatus by making more or less direct efforts to bring people outside state authority under state control. State leaders, for instance, may use violence to expand their territorial control by targeting people in urban centers and/or national peripheries, especially when they have just come to power and find themselves unable to make effective policy decisions. In my view, this type of state-building strategy may involve dislocating populations by coercive means. Such violence is treated as instrumental because state authorities seek to shift the balance of power between their center and alternative centers in society by disrupting, undercutting, or eliminating the latter.

However, regime-changing violence is generally concerned with certain types of government (such as military or revolutionary) based on certain ideologies, norms, rules, and decision-making procedures. Efforts at constructing political regimes result from the need to change the existing forms of government or from the need to maintain or consolidate the existing regimes by taking action to pacify strong threats from opposition forces with different political visions. This form of violence is thus treated as *exemplary*. Exemplary violence has primary targets and secondary audiences who are not directly targeted but must take lessons from violence. The primary goal is to pacify challengers to state leaders' political visions.

Both forms of state violence—state-building (instrumental) and regime-changing (exemplary)—can overlap, however, and both are types of *preemptive* violence, especially when state leaders feel insecure and perceive their authority to be vulnerable. Such security-driven behavior is evident when those who come to power from limited territories, such as those involved in guerilla warfare, seek to expand territorial control in urban areas. They seek to eliminate any remaining contention for control of the state by using instrumental and exemplary violence to preempt existing and potential challenges to their authority and their political visions.

This does not mean that proactive or preemptive violence is their most preferred option, but that it is often the only option available to some leaders as they see it, especially when the state and their political regime become extremely insecure and have no institutional capacity to overcome existential threats to state and regime security. An excellent study by two scholars on the "the political economy of death squads" serves as a useful starting point. The study does not regard "repressive violence" as "largely reactive in character," but rather as "proactive or preemptive." The scholars deal with the question of why political regimes made up of "supposedly rational individuals . . . would pursue a policy of escalating repression if such measures are ultimately counterproductive."[29] Their research findings further suggest that "escalating repression is perpetuated not because it has a high probability of success but because of the weakness of the state [that] precludes its resort to less violent alternatives."[30]

REGIME-CHANGING AND STATE-BUILDING VIOLENCE IN THE KILLING FIELDS

The Khmer Rouge leadership relied on violence to build the state and a socialist regime. When its army captured power in 1975, one immediate priority was to build the state by using violence as the primary instrument to expand territorial control and eliminate all power-contending forces across the country.[31] In just a matter of days, the revolutionary forces rolled into all major cities (including Phnom Penh), quickly occupied them, and then at gunpoint begun a mass evacuation of all city dwellers across the country.[32] There may have been several reasons for this dramatic process of emptying the towns and cities, but one was to ensure complete territorial and political control of the country, especially cities where revolutionary forces had not enjoyed any territorial control prior to their military victory.

Another immediate aim of the Pol Pot group was to neutralize any espionage networks and to destroy all former government officials and foreign forces that could pose threats to the Cambodian state; it did this by emptying the cities where former government officials had lived and worked and by moving them around with the aim of dislocating them. As they were dispersed, the Khmer Rouge cadres began to round them up by promising them new positions but then taking them away for execution en masse.[33] The historic mass evacuation was thus based on the calculation that the state would be unable to control the entire country if the towns and cities were left intact. The revolutionary elites also considered cities "centers of foreign domination."[34] Their revolution was anti-imperialist and thus sought to prevent any attempts by foreign forces to threaten Cambodia's sovereignty and independence. Cambodia had been throughout history subject to seemingly endless foreign interference or intervention.

Regime-constructing violence also coincided with state-building violence. As the Khmer Rouge leadership sought to monopolize state power by force, it also began to build and defend its newly established political regime based on radical egalitarianism. It relied on violence not only as an instrument to consolidate territorial and political power but as a means to pacify Cambodians in general, including those not under their political control prior to 1975. Egalitarian thinkers tend to gloss over the fact that the Khmer Rouge ruthlessly pursued the socialist utopian goal of building a classless society; its murderous revolution was an extension of Mao's Great Leap Forward and Great Proletarian Cultural Revolution in particular and Marxism-Leninism in general.[35] Some scholars contend that the Khmer Rouge leadership justified the use of violence as an instrument to defend and build socialism based on its skewed understanding of Marxist-Leninist doctrine. According to one scholar, "the violence meted by the Khmer Rouge was deliberate."[36] As part of revolutionary regime-building efforts, the Khmer Rouge's anti-urbanization policy deliberately pursued the ultimate goal of constructing a new, pure society by central-izing authority among the highest echelons of the Communist Party.

Abolishing capitalism was one of the Khmer Rouge policy priorities. The Khmer Rouge leadership apparently did not set out to murder as many people as shown earlier, but they must have found it virtually impossible to abolish capitalism without first emptying the centers of commerce—the cities—where it would be unable to defend the new regime. One of the infamous slogans used during the reign of terror was "Destroy the old order; replace it with the new." One of the regime's ambitious ideological goals, established from early on, was to transform Cambodia into a soci-ety without private property. As early as 1973, Khmer Rouge authorities had already begun the process of collectivizing farmlands within liber-ated territories under their control. David Chandler makes the following observation: "Private property was abolished and people were organized into groups of families to perform tasks set for them by the party. There were several reasons for collectivization: to ensure that enough food was produced for rebel forces; to introduce socialist institutions; and to devel-opment an autonomous revolutionary style."[37]

Other existing social institutions, particularly civil society organiza-tions, were also demolished in the name of true socialism. Religious insti-tutions in particular, as noted, were marked for complete destruction. The regime thus did not appear to have sought to restore the past national glo-ries of the Khmer feudal empire (from the ninth to the fourteenth cen-tury) but to build a modern or highly industrialized but classless society.[38] It did not aim to build a new egalitarian agricultural society, either. This was only an initial step toward more advanced industrialization.[39] Cambo-dians (including this author) were told that they would one day be able to use machines for various purposes. For instance, a Khmer Rouge official explained that we would one day even rely on a machine to feed ourselves.

To achieve this utopian goal of radically building a perfect egalitar-ian society, regime-changing and -defending violence was directed at several targets that had first to be uprooted. The majority of those who lived in rural areas were of Khmer origin and also tended to distrust all urban dwellers, judged to be capitalist-minded and thus primarily tar-geted for elimination or pacification.[40] Most of those who lived in towns and cities included ethnic Chinese and Vietnamese with a long history of dominating commercial centers.[41] The Vietnamese had been brought by the French colonialists to serve in Cambodia as civil servants, artisans, and service personnel. The Vietnamese-Khmer or Khmer from Kampuchea Krom (in South Vietnam) and Sino-Khmer dominated administrative positions and commercial zones. The Vietnamese also managed the eastern Cambodian rubber plantations and provided labor. At war's end, the Khmer Rouge intensified its struggles against such class-based urban enemies from all ethnic and religious backgrounds and under foreign influence. Kenneth Quinn makes an important observation: "Cities were viewed as creations of Western influence, centers of decadence and conspicuous consumption, and impediments to change."[42]

This type of utopianism also seems to have been driven by a deep sense of moral purity. The following acts were considered unclean, impure, immoral, or simply criminal: gambling, drunkenness, prostitution, theft, adultery, and so on. As soon as the war was over, regime officials began to talk about how to clean up these filthy activities and imposed the death penalty for such "crimes."[43] Their sense of justice was based on a feeling of ideological and moral purity—a determination to destroy those judged to have committed any of these various crimes. There was no need to investigate any crimes: Khmer Rouge cadres just needed to hear mere allegations from those who reported to them. Many were taken away in front of their families and friends and publicly executed as a way to send the message that they must learn the lesson of the results of disobedience to the new "code of conduct."

Still, we cannot explain the Khmer Rouge's murderous revolution by focusing on its radical ideology alone. As evident in other cases, radical egalitarianism was not the only kind of ideology that may be characterized as a form of nihilistic revolutionary cleansing, which gave rise to state- and regime-building violence under the Khmer Rouge regime. The extreme right, as in the case of military authoritarian regimes, was also a source of such violence. Additional explanatory variables that help make sense of the tendency toward state violence under both socialist/communist and military authoritarian regimes need to be factored in.

EXTREME INSECURITY AND INSTITUTIONAL WEAKNESSES

In the case of state violence under the Khmer Rouge regime, it is far from clear that the Pol Pot leadership committed violence simply because of its lust for power. The lust for power may have resulted from the elite's perception of extreme insecurity and its extremely limited institutional capacity to accommodate rival forces perceived as existential threats to its fragile regime. Some scholars have made excellent contributions to the study of Khmer Rouge violence along this line of thinking by stressing the importance of how the Pol Pot leadership identified other racial or ethnic groups as different, subhuman, and dangerous enemies whose continued physical presence was regarded as posing an overwhelming threat to the state and regime.[44]

While this perspective insists that the Khmer Rouge regime committed genocide, it concedes that class politics was the main cause of violence and overemphasizes the role and the dangers of ideas and grand ideologies (such as socialism and liberalism), tending to *exclude* other views and explanatory factors. The perspective ignores the fact that radical egalitarianism and the reliance on violence may also have been the byproduct of the deeply fragmented Pol Pot leadership's perception of existing and potential threats to state and regime survival, as well as the extreme imbalance between repressive and accommodative institutional capacity.

High levels of insecurity experienced by the Pol Pot leadership can be assessed by showing that it became increasingly worried about the survival of the Cambodian state. The perception of insecurity was deepened by the fact that the regime was institutionally ill prepared to run the country. Pol Pot and his loyalists chose to destroy state institutions, rather than reform them.

The fact that the Pol Pot group primarily targeted the ethnic Vietnamese can also be explained by the fact that it perceived them as a growing threat to state security because of its deep distrust of Vietnam's political ambitions. Khmer Rouge leaders had always felt threatened by Vietnam, having learned from the failure of Sihanouk's policy of letting Vietnamese Communists dominate eastern Cambodia in the late 1960s. Early in the 1970s, the Vietnamese Communists fought the Republican government forces on behalf of the nascent Khmer Rouge movement (weak and vulnerable to Vietnamese influence). The Khmer Rouge had purged those judged as pro-Vietnam because of longtime affiliations with Hanoi and begun to reassert state sovereignty in the eastern part of the country. Fears of Vietnamese ambitions—in the form of an alleged Indochinese Federation—led the Khmer Rouge leadership to reject outright the "special relationship" demanded by Hanoi after 1975.

Threats to regime (and personal) survival also grew intense. There are a number of possible reasons for the Khmer Rouge elites' extreme obsession with regime (and personal) security. They saw an endless struggle against class enemies and could not trust any former government officials, fearing that the latter would be able to undermine the movement's revolutionary goals and thus seeking to eliminate them regardless of whether or not they were Khmer or members of ethnic or religious minorities. Even religion was regarded as an existential threat to egalitarianism. Buddhism, for instance, was regarded as a cause of Cambodia's weakness, and monks were condemned as "bloodsuckers" (oppressing the people) and "imperialists."[45]

Ethnic minorities did suffer in disproportionately greater numbers than Cambodians of Khmer origin, and racism may have played a role in this, but a far more powerful reason for their suffering appears to have had more to do with the threats that the Khmer Rouge leaders perceived to their regime (and personal) security. Cham Muslims, for instance, were forced to abandon their texts and eat pork; however, their opposition may have been perceived by the Khmer Rouge as a threat to the regime. For instance, the Khmer Rouge massacred the entire populations of several Cham villages, but they did so after a series of armed Cham rebellions between June and November 1978 (in one district of the country's Eastern Zone) and after the Cham had "slaughtered half a dozen [Khmer Rouge soldiers] with swords and knives."[46]

The Chinese and Vietnamese were not killed simply or only because they belonged to ethnic minorities, but more importantly because they were regarded as an existential threat to the socialist regime. In general, the Khmer Rouge elites and their peasant army deeply distrusted capitalists, regarded them as enemies of the revolution and potentially hostile to the regime, and thus sought to destroy them.[47]

Meanwhile, the Pol Pot group employed few peaceful institutional means to deal with threats to the state and its revolutionary regime. Having destroyed all existing institutions (such as religious ones, especially Buddhist ones, which advocated nonviolent methods like reconciliation, compromise, and accommodation), there was virtually nothing left to help the new regime rely on social consent for enhancing its political legitimacy in a peaceful way. By having destroyed all existing institutions, the Khmer Rouge leadership did not even have rudimentary institutional means to meet the basic needs of large urban populations because, clearly, they thought that they could not rely on the Khmer Republic's existing institutions, which could undermine its revolutionary causes. By forcing urban dwellers to evacuate their houses, the regime thought it would be able to consolidate state power and meet their basic needs.[48] But this turned out to be a terrible nightmare for Cambodians because even the countryside simply could not accommodate the needs of the large urban populations. Repressive violence was thus used as a way to ensure total obedience to the radical vision of the revolutionary regime.

The armed forces were extremely fragmented and unpopular and thus had to rely on violence. The armed movement did not get off to a promising start, when assessed in terms of military capability and institutional capacity. In 1970, the entire revolutionary movement had only somewhere between 3,000 and 4,000 troops; however, the real number may have been as low as 800. The number is said to have quickly increased to about 85,000 in mid-1971; to about 120,000 in mid-1972; and to around 200,000 by the end of that year. The exact number may have been much lower, given that the revolutionary movement was unpopular. This military expansion may look impressive on the surface, but it hides several serious weaknesses. Its efforts to recruit urban dwellers, including members of the working class whom the Khmer Rouge judged as unreliable, proved unsuccessful.[49] The rebels had to turn to peasants and members of ethnic minorities who came from "the backward sectors of unsophisticated land," but the majority of peasants did find the Khmer Rouge's ideological agenda appealing.[50] The Khmer Rouge leadership even avoided presenting itself as communist. Some new recruits found appealing the revolutionary promise of future material rewards (after capitalism and imperialism were destroyed), but others had their nonideological reasons, such as maintaining loyalty to Prince Norodom Sihanouk (who had been ousted in March 1970 by his own defense minister, General Lon Nol), undertaking new adventures as soldiers by getting out of their villages, and even avoiding being teased by girls who wanted to see them become "real men."[51] The Khmer Rouge rebels thus had to rely on force as a way to recruit members and retain them.

The rapid expansion of the revolutionary army further reveals that it could not have been professionally trained, sufficiently organized, or effectively coordinated and must thus have been strictly disciplined by force. During the first few years of the civil war, the revolutionary rebels had to rely on Vietnamese Communist forces in major combat (as they

developed infrastructure and trained troops who had joined the movement). The peasant army—made up of illiterate peasants unequipped to
take control of the administrative structure and run a civilian government—was built in a short period of time to win the war, not to govern
the country. Its military victory was also premature because of unexpected events, such as the enemy's military and political weaknesses (the
Lon Nol regime's rampant corruption and political and military incom-
petence) and the 1975 US withdrawal of massive assistance to the Khmer
Republic. The regime's most developed institution was apparently the
Communist Party of Kampuchea (CPK), which appeared to have been
still highly under-institutionalized. The CPK may have had a long history
that went back to the 1930s, but its leadership in the 1970s was young
and inexperienced. Its original party leadership left for the maquis only
in the 1960s, had no expectation of early victory, and then faded away
in favor of a mixed group of much younger men and women who "took
control of the party by mid-1971."[52] However, these new party elite members—led by Pol Pot and a few others who formed a circle of "clandestine
camaraderie," bonded by their urban background and educational years
in France—were only a minority group within the CPK. During the early
1970s, the CPK leadership also "did not even control . . . the subdistrict
committees, much less village committees."[53] Subsequently they "presided
over a disparate cadre" and "apparently keenly felt its lack of control over
the administrative structure."[54] The CPK "did not [even] have the sophisticated cadre needed to control the towns."[55]

Most Cambodians who lived throughout the Khmer Rouge period
knew little or nothing about the CPK, whose existence was not officially
made known until 1977, but they learned every day from early on that
Angka (which basically means "faceless organization" associated with the
CPK) was the ultimate source of authority, whose debt of freedom they
owed, which deserved their praise, and to which they must subject themselves in complete obedience. One thing that could be said about this type
of secrecy is that the Pol Pot group became extremely and increasingly
obsessed with state and regime security to the point where it saw enemies (both external and internal, Cambodian and foreign) everywhere
and thus tried to project their fragile power by declaring that Angka had
"as many eyes as the eyes of the pineapple."

After 1975, the CPK leadership itself grew divided; political divisions
may have become more serious after the unexpected victory, when it sub-

sequently sought to consolidate state power. Because it lacked administrative control, the party leadership relied on secrecy and violence as the way to defend or sustain its regime. This obsession with secrecy reveals internal tensions among regions "which were kept isolated from each other to the point that nationwide study meetings were a rare, noteworthy occurrence."[56] Even Khmer Rouge leaders deeply distrusted each other, and struggles for power among themselves led to incessant purges.[57] Coup attempts on Pol Pot's life took place in 1976 and 1978, which helps explain why he conducted numerous intraparty purges across the country, targeting those who were perceived to be traitors. As Timothy Carney puts it, "the only conclusion is that the regime gave itself over to counterespionage paranoia."[58] Karl Jackson also makes an insightful observation: "Pol Pot's regime purged and repurged itself in a fratricidal search for ideological purity and internal security. In the end, striving for security at any price proved counter-productive."[59]

In short, the excessive state violence committed under the Khmer Rouge reign of terror was driven by radical egalitarianism, fears of perceived threats to personal and regime survival, and extreme institutional weaknesses. By destroying all existing nonsocialist institutions but being unable to build new ones on time, the illegitimate regime created an extreme imbalance between repressive and accommodative institutional capacity, and this exacerbated state violence. There was nothing—absolutely nothing—to stop the Pol Pot elite from being driven by extreme insecurity in their search for absolute power by using the violent means most readily available after their military conquest. State, regime, and subsequently personal insecurity drove the Khmer Rouge elites to struggle for hegemonic power without limits.

THE LIMITS AND POTENTIAL DANGERS OF RETRIBUTIVE JUSTICE

Scholars and policy makers have differed on how to deal with the legacies of Khmer Rouge atrocities. Those who are working for the United Nations and living in the West make arguments supporting retributive justice instead of punitive justice.[60] First, such justice would serve as a way to demonstrate that the Khmer Rouge regime committed crimes. Without such knowledge, the Cambodians would not learn that what the Khmer Rouge committed was a crime. These advocates generally assume that the Cambodians did not know what had happened and would now want to know. One of the tasks, then, would be to conduct research by collecting data revealing that genocide, war crimes, and crimes against humanity had been committed. Second, retributive justice would bring about peace based on a sense of closure and reconciliation and would deter Khmer Rouge leaders (and other potential criminals) from committing more crimes, especially after they had been put away in jail, where they belong. Third, without this type of justice there would be no democracy. Some even condemned the Paris Peace Agreements because they included the Khmer Rouge, advocating war as the best way to break their back and assuming that democracy would have been better promoted had the Khmer Rouge been destroyed. Fourth, the pursuit of retributive justice would further promote respect for human rights by ending the Cambodian culture of impunity and promoting accountability.

The pursuit of retributive justice has made some progress. In June 1997, the Cambodian government requested the United Nations to proceed in a joint effort to hold Khmer Rouge leaders accountable for their past crimes. The Cambodia–UN negotiations on how to conduct Khmer Rouge trials proceeded in fits and starts. Differences between the two sides remained. One issue was centered on the question of whether a justice institution would be able to enjoy independence. Another issue was the scope of the trials: whether or not to try all Khmer Rouge officials or just a small number of those most responsible for the crimes committed during their reign of terror. It was not until 2003 that both sides finally agreed on the need to establish the Extraordinary Chambers in the Court of Cambodia (ECCC)—a hybrid judicial body made up of Cambodian and international judges and prosecutors, with Cambodians in the majority: without their support, no effective action can be taken. The court has the mandate to prosecute only Khmer Rouge leaders "most responsible" for the crimes.

Further progress was made after the ECCC was inaugurated in July 2006. In June 2007, the court began its formal proceedings. Kaing Guek Eav (better known as Duch), the chief executioner at the infamous Tuol Sleng extermination center, was the first to face justice: charged with war crimes, crimes against humanity, torture, and premeditated murder, he was put on trial and accepted his personal responsibility for the torture and death of approximately fifteen thousand people. The trial was concluded late in 2009, when the prosecutors demanded that he be put in jail for forty years. On July 26, 2010, the ECCC finally sentenced him to nineteen years in prison. In March 2010, the international prosecutor finally announced that the ECCC would soon move toward bringing to trial four senior Khmer Rouge leaders who had been held in custody—Khieu Samphan (eighty years old, the Khmer Rouge's former head of state), Nuon Chea (seventy-nine years old, known as Brother Number Two, second only to Pol Pot), Ieng Sary (eighty-seven years old, former Khmer Rouge minister of foreign affairs), and Khieu Thirith (Ieng Sary's wife and former Khmer Rouge minister for social affairs). They were first charged with war crimes and crimes against humanity. Then in December 2009, the ECCC finally issued for the first time additional genocide charges against Khieu Samphan, Nuon Chea, and Ieng Sary. Their trials began on June 27, 2011, and it was expected that they would last more than a year.

The argument that retributive justice serves as an effective way to demonstrate that the Khmer Rouge regime committed crimes has a lot of merit. The new generation of Cambodians who were either too young to remember the country's tragic past or who were born after 1978 may benefit from the criminal trials in terms of having the opportunity to learn more about the mass atrocities committed under the old Khmer Rouge reign of terror. Such historical knowledge may help them do their part to deter or prevent the events of such a tragic past from recurring.

However, it is highly questionable whether the ongoing pursuit of retributive justice has met other major expectations that advocates of human rights had hoped for. The Cambodian administrative staff within the ECCC has also been marred by serious corruption scandals. The limits of retributive justice are quite evident. Having spent up to $135.4 million (by the end of 2010), the ECCC had sentenced only one ex–Khmer Rouge official to jail. The court was reported to have a budget shortfall of at least $40 million. Witnesses are said to have been blocked from testifying. In mid-2011, four other Khmer Rouuge leaders were on trial. Efforts to bring more cases against Khmer Rouge leaders have also been thwarted, however. Prime Minister Hun Sen has rejected any idea of bringing more former Khmer Rouge officials to justice, because he saw this move as having the potential to give rise to instability or civil war. He preferred to see the ECCC fail rather than succeed, especially when the court considered pursuing more suspects, and reminded ECCC officials that they would need to provide him with reasons for further investigation. In fact, several high-ranking government officials refused to testify in court when international judge Marcel Lemonde (from France) tried to summon them. Late in October 2010, Hun Sen told the UN secretary general Ban Ki-moon that he would not allow the ECCC to try other former Khmer Rouge officials not in custody, reiterating his concern that such an effort would plunge the country back into civil war. Foreign Minister Hor Namhong also told US Secretary of State Hillary Clinton (during her first two-day visit to Cambodia, from October 30 to November 1, 2010) that a move to bring more Khmer Rouge members to justice would jeopardize the peace and stability of his country.

Early in June 2011, ECCC judges also rejected calls for investigation into additional cases (Cases 3 and 4), associated with five further ex–Khmer Rouge leaders, who had served the Khmer Rouge regime as navy commander (Meas Mut), air force commander (Sou Met), district chief (Im Chaem), and zone deputy secretaries (Ta Tith and Ta An)—apparently due to the lack of support from Cambodian co-prosecutor Chea Leang (accused of toeing the government's line). Cambodian co-investigating judge You Bunleng was regarded in the same negative light: he had first authorized an additional investigation into alleged crimes committed by these ex–Khmer Rouge officials but then crossed out his signature after his authorization became public. He may not have acted on government instructions, as defense lawyers charged, but he was well aware of the government's resistance to additional investigations.

It is still far from clear that putting Khmer Rouge leaders behind bars would have promoted the cause of peace and democracy. As David Maguire, a professor of law and theory of law at Bard College and Columbia University, puts it, "The biggest problem facing the ECCC is living up to its own hype. Claims that such trials lead to healing, closure, truth and reconciliation are speculative at best. How does one measure 'healing, closure and reconciliation'?"[61] Few of the expectations, if any, that retributive justice would promote peace, democracy, and security have empirical support. Peace in negative terms did not result from retributive justice. The signing of the Paris Peace Agreements on October 23, 1991, among former armed enemies (including the three allies of the Coalition Government of Democratic Kampuchea, or CGDK—the Khmer Rouge; the Royalists, known as FUNCINPEC; and the Khmer People's National Liberation Front, or KPNLF—and the State of Cambodia, or SOC, whose party was named the Cambodian People's Party, or CPP) made it possible for the peace and democratic processes to get started. The peace process proceeded with UN intervention—in the form of the UN Transitional Authority in Cambodia, or UNTAC—from 1992 to late 1993. Although the Khmer Rouge party pulled out of the electoral process (just weeks before the election in May 1993), the other Cambodian signatories competed for public office and ended up forming a coalition government presided over by two co–prime ministers: First Prime Minister Norodom Ranariddh (FUNCINPEC) and Second Prime Minister Hun Sen (CPP). The Khmer Rouge leadership continued its armed rebellion afterward, but the new democratic process served as a powerful weapon to discredit and delegitimize the armed rebels. The rebels now could no longer count on the support of their former allies—the Buddhist Liberal Democratic Party (BLDP) and FUNCINPEC—as they had throughout the 1980s. Nor did the rebels any longer enjoy international support from the United States, the Association of Southeast Asian Nations (ASEAN), or China, all of which had lent them a helping hand throughout the 1980s. The introduction of democracy into Cambodia helped weaken the Khmer Rouge power base and put the rebels in disarray.

The recent peace also resulted from the disintegration of the Khmer Rouge's armed rebellion, especially after Pol Pot's death in April 1998. One reason for these developments was that the government had used an effective strategy to divide the Khmer Rouge leadership by granting an amnesty to one top Khmer Rouge official, former minister of foreign affairs Ieng Sary. The Khmer Rouge leadership's infighting then intensified and led to the arrest of Pol Pot by his "defense minister," Ta Mok (who subsequently put him on show "trial"), and his death. The Khmer Rouge disintegration from within was a blessing to Cambodia and the government, which subsequently agreed to grant informal amnesty to other Khmer Rouge officials.

Other factors have also contributed to the peace-building process—a form of deterrence against future crimes. As noted earlier, the Khmer Rouge leaders now on trial are quite advanced in age; they no longer command any armed rebels and would be unable to commit similar crimes again. None of the political parties, not even the CPP, has embraced the type of radical egalitarianism and autarky that the Pol Pot regime did; all of them have advocated globalization. Cambodia was the world's first "least developed" country to receive permission, in September 2003, to join the World Trade Organization. Since the early 1990s Cambodia has been a member of the United Nations; it joined ASEAN in 1999 and has maintained good relations with all of its neighbors. Only Cambodian-Thai ties remain far from ideal (because of minor armed border clashes that resulted from disputes over areas near the Preah Vihear temple).

Moreover, the new global security environment has helped stabilize Cambodian politics. Unlike during the Cold War period, when great powers dragged Cambodia into their proxy wars, the great powers have since the early 1990s shown strong support for the country. The international community has been quite supportive of the Hun Sen regime. Between 1998 and 2008, the total amount of international aid Cambodia received amounted to US$5.5 billion. The donor community continued to pledge more assistance. In 2009, it pledged US$950 million. In June 2010, it pledged another US$1.1 billion—one of the largest aid packages ever (particularly since the early 1990s). Other major powers in the region, especially China, Japan, and the United States, have shown growing interest in maintaining positive relations with Cambodia.

The argument that the pursuit of retributive justice has made Cambodia more democratic also still has little empirical support. Early in July 1997, soon after the Cambodian government had asked the UN for advice on how to go ahead with legal proceedings against Khmer Rouge leaders who still rebelled against it, Hun Sen staged a violent coup against his co-premier and has since consolidated power at the expense of democracy. After that, the CPP wanted to see criminal procedures restricted only to Khmer Rouge leaders who rebelled against the government. It was more about weakening their former enemy than about justice. Cambodia has since drifted toward a hegemonic-party system. The CPP has maintained a monopoly of power over the communes across the country. The election results between 1998 and 2008 allowed the CPP to win more and more seats in the National Assembly. Members of the CPP, especially powerful allies of Hun Sen, have also dominated the Senate. CPP leaders could not afford, and are unlikely, to give up power without relying on coercive means. Hun Sen has said that he intends to stay in power until he is ninety years old. Winning at all costs appears to be the only option now available to the CPP elites—the only guarantee of their security.

The CPP has also turned the judicial system into its own political instrument. The annual budgetary allocation to the judiciary remains far from sufficient (usually less than 1 percent of the national budget) and is much, much less than that for the armed forces. Opposition lawmakers who dare to challenge the prime minister often end up having their parliamentary immunity lifted, being charged with defamation, and brought to court, always losing and paying heavy fines. When he visited Cambodia late in October 2010, UN Secretary-General Ban Ki-moon urged the government to provide full cooperation and fully respect the independence of the ECCC, but Hun Sen said he would not allow additional cases against other ex–Khmer Rouge officials. His foreign minister, Hor Namhong, also told US Secretary of State Hillary Clinton (on her first visit to Cambodia) that his government wanted either the UN human rights office in Cambodia closed or the UN "special representative" and later its "special rapporteur" removed, accusing the latter of being a spokesman of the already weakened political opposition.

In addition to his efforts to consolidate political power by taking action to dominate the executive, legislative, and judicial branches of government, as well as the armed forces, Hun Sen has sought to protect his regime by moving closer and closer to other authoritarian states, most notably China. China has become the biggest investor in (with a cumulative amount of investment worth about $8 billion) and the largest aid donor to Cambodia, as well as the strongest defender of the Hun Sen regime. Chinese influence over Cambodia has grown so deep that US politicians can no longer afford to ignore it. During her 2010 visit to Cambodia, for instance, US Secretary of State Hillary Clinton urged the Cambodians to "look for partnerships that cut across geographic lines." She also urged them not "to get too dependent on any one country" (making reference to China) and reminded them of the need to raise important issues with China, such as the Chinese dams on the upper Mekong River, which could put Cambodia at risk.[62]

The perception of political insecurity thus seems to have driven the Hun Sen regime toward authoritarianism and helps explain why CPP leaders have sought to keep justice institutions weak or to prevent the judiciary and the legal system from becoming politically independent. The CPP elite is well aware of the fact that once power is lost, as for Khmer Republican and Khmer Rouge government officials, one simply lives at the mercy of the victor. The fear of prosecution among government officials remains widespread. A UN group of experts wrote: "The current Prime Minister [Hun Sen] and many of his colleagues in the . . . CPP . . . were once members of the Khmer Rouge before defecting to Vietnam."

Moreover, "FUNCINPEC and other parties were closely allied with the Khmer Rouge in the struggle against Vietnam and the PRK/SOC."[63] Foreign Minister Hor Namhong sued three journalists over allegations that he had been put in charge of prisoners in a camp where innocent people were tortured and executed; the journalists were found guilty and ordered to pay the minister $6,500 in compensation and $1,280 in fines to the state.[64] In June 2008, Dam Sith, a candidate for the Sam Rainsy Party and editor of the newspaper *Moneaksekar Khmer* (Khmer conscience), was arrested because he questioned the alleged role that the foreign minister had played during the Khmer Rouge period. Although there is no evidence against Hun Sen, files compiled by the Documentation Center of Cambodia provide "enough evidence to indict CPP President and Senate President Chea Sim and CPP Honorary President and National Assembly President Heng Samrin for crimes against humanity and/or war crimes." Chea was a district chief under the Khmer Rouge regime and "could be accused of mass killings." At the twenty-ninth anniversary marking the Khmer Rouge's January 1979 downfall, for instance, Chea Sim warned against politicizing the Khmer Rouge trials, calling those with the intent to do so "absent-minded elements" and "ill-willed political circles" who were opposed to the process of reconciliation after years of civil strife. In his words, "We condemn any acts to use the courts with the aim of creating instability or disrupting society."[65] International co-investigating judge Marcel Lemonde also asked top CPP officials (Hor Namhong; Keat Chhon [finance minister]; Chea Sim; Heng Samrin; and two CPP senators, Ouk Bunchhoeun and Sim Ka) to provide testimony, because of their alleged affiliations with the Khmer Rouge regime. Summoning the testimony of Hun Sen was ruled out by ECCC judges, but this does not mean that the judicial process no longer worries him.[66]

Whether a truth-and-reconciliation commission would have produced better outcomes for Cambodia (such as a stronger peace, more respect for human rights, and more progress on the democratic front) than the ECCC has is a matter of debate, but evidence suggests that it might. South Africa chose to go down this road and has since witnessed peace and stability through democratization. Indonesia has rejected retributive justice in favor of a truth commission yet has become far more democratic than Cambodia. In Timor-Leste, political leaders also adopted pragmatism, having realized that their country would need to coexist alongside Indonesia and thus choosing to go down the road of reconciliation.[67] As also noted by both Sung Chull Kim and N. Ganesan in this volume, there is much evidence to show that more than half of the relevant cases around the world, especially in Latin America and Eastern Europe, have rejected retributive justice in favor of restorative justice, particularly reconciliation.

The real issue here is not whether the Khmer Rouge regime committed mass atrocities, but rather what caused it to commit them. This is an important point because any prescriptions for peace, stability, and security must be in line with the causes of war, instability, and insecurity. Ideological commitment should not blind analysts to the point where they advocate strategies that perpetuate violence and insecurity. The thesis that racialism was the cause is far too simplistic and ideologically biased: it ignores well-documented socialist crimes. All socialist regimes were violently repressive, but some were far worse than others, and the Khmer Rouge regime stood among the worst of the worst. Culturalist perspectives help shed better light on the atrocities but still do not tell us why the Khmer Rouge committed violence that was far worse than under any other regime in Cambodian history. State-building, regime-changing, and regime-defending violence was committed not simply because the Khmer Rouge leaders were more evil in pure ideological terms than anyone else (their ideology was after all based on egalitarian justice and moral purity), but because they embraced a violent type of radical egalitarianism, using force to fight their way to power and preempt existing and potential threats to state- and regime-building efforts without any effective institutional support. Violent repression took place, escalated, and became uncontrollable when they perceived their vulnerability to be increasingly high and because they had access to more repressive than accommodative means.

The pursuit of retributive justice is likely to have minimal, if not harmful, effects on postwar societies, where state, political, and civil society institutions are extremely weak. This does not mean that retributive justice should not be pursued and that justice institutions should not be built (the International Criminal Court, for instance, may someday begin to play a useful role in promoting peace and security), but that such normative commitment should be informed of the empirical realities of security politics in conflict-prone societies. Retributive justice is not always the best or only way to deter mass atrocities but may, in fact, do more harm than good. The Cambodian experience shows that this type of justice may have contributed to the rise of political authoritarianism, entrenching the ruling elite's power base and hindering democracy and the promotion of human rights. Retributive calls for justice may also make it difficult for future peace negotiations or democracy and human rights promotion (in Cambodia and elsewhere) to succeed, especially when no warring party wants to lose or give up power due to fears of prosecution. The security-based institutionalist perspective suggests that effective truth-and-reconciliation commissions may serve the interest of peace, stability, and security better than a cry for retributive justice. Seek thus first the political kingdom, and the lofty tower of justice shall then be successfully constructed.

NOTES

1. The academic literature on the Khmer Rouge genocide is a growth industry. See, e.g., Howard Ball, *Prosecuting War Crimes and Genocide: The Twentieth-Century Experience* (Lawrence: University Press of Kansas, 1999); Donald W. Beachler, "Arguing about Cambodia: Genocide and Political Interest," *Holocaust and Genocide Studies* 23, no. 2 (2009): 214–38; Maureen S. Hiebert, "The Three 'Switches' of Identity Construction in Genocide: The Nazi Final Solution and the Cambodian Killing Fields," *Genocide Studies and Prevention* 3, no. 1 (2008): 5–29; James A. Tyner, "Imagining Genocide: Anti-geographies and the Erasure of Space in Democratic Kampuchea," *Space and Polity* 13, no. 1 (2009): 9–20; Sarah Williams, "Genocide: The Cambodian Experience," *International Criminal Law Review* 5, no. 3 (2005): 447–62; Edward Kissi, "Rwanda, Ethiopia and Cambodia: Links, Faultlines and Complexities in a Comparative Study of Genocide," *Journal of Genocide Research* 6, no. 1 (2004): 115–33; Scott Straus, "Contested Meanings and Conflicting Imperatives: A Conceptual Analysis of Genocide," *Journal of Genocide Research* 3, no. 3 (2001): 349–75; Patrick Raszelenberg, "The Khmer Rouges and the Final Solution," *History and Memory* 11, no. 2 (1999): 62–93; Alexander Laban Hinton, "Why Did You Kill? The Cambodian Genocide and the Dark Side of Face and Honor," *Journal of Asian Studies* 57, no. 1 (1998): 93–122; Khathaya Um, "Specificities: The Broken Chain; Genocide in the Reconstruction and Destruction of Cambodian Society," *Social Identities* 4, no. 1 (1998): 131–54.

2. Sorpong Peou, *Intervention and Change in Cambodia: Toward Democracy?* (New York and Singapore: St. Martin's Press and Institute of Southeast Asian Studies, 2000).

3. Stéphane Courtois, "Introduction: The Crimes of Communism," in *The Black Book of Communism,* ed. Stéphane Courtois et al. (Cambridge: Harvard University Press, 1999), 4.

4. Karl Jackson, "Introduction: The Khmer Rouge in Context," in *Cambodia, 1975–1978: Rendezvous with Death,* ed. Karl Jackson (Princeton: Princeton University Press, 1989), 4.

5. Ball, *Prosecuting War Crimes and Genocide,* 113.

6. See my book review in *Holocaust and Genocide Studies* 11, no. 3 (1997): 413–25.

7. Ball, *Prosecuting War Crimes and Genocide,* 112.

8. Julia Wallace, "Four Senior KR Leaders Indicted, Will Be Tried," *Cambodia Daily,* Sept. 17, 2010.

9. See, e.g., Gareth Porter and George C. Hildebrand, *Cambodia: Starvation and Revolution* (New York: Monthly Review Press, 1976). For a good review of this literature, see Beachler, "Arguing about Cambodia," 215–23.

10. Yale historian Ben Kiernan, e.g., falsely accuses me of being an apologist for the Pol Pot regime. I am not alone in feeling this way: Stephen Heder also writes: "Kiernan . . . pursues [a] crusade . . . against those who disagree with him. His ill manners in this regard are reminiscent of the Pol Potism which at other levels he despises. He suggests that those with contrasting views are subjectively or objectively in league with . . . the forces responsible for Pol Pot's genocide." Cited in Beachler, "Arguing about Cambodia," 231.

11. See also Beachler, "Arguing about Cambodia."

12. Courtois, "Introduction," 17.

13. *News Wires,* Dec. 16, 2009.

14. Timothy Carney, "The Unexpected Victory," in Jackson, *Cambodia,* 33–34; Karl D. Jackson, "The Ideology of Total Revolution," in Jackson, *Cambodia,* 51–52, 69–70, 75–76; Kenneth M. Quinn, "Pattern and Scope of Violence," in Jackson, *Cambodia,* 191; Francois Ponchaud, "Social Change in the Vortex of Revolution," in Jackson, *Cambodia,* 170–77; David Hawk, "The Photographic Record," in Jackson, *Cambodia,* 212.

15. Cambodian Genocide Group, May 3, 2005, cited in *WW4Report,* Dec. 18, 2009, http://www.ww4report.com/node/8086.

16. Bit Seanglim, *The Warrior Heritage* (El Cerrito, CA: Seanglim Bit, 1991). Some political theorists have developed arguments in which violence is seen as being deeply rooted in the political culture. Johan Galtung, e.g., sees "cultural violence" as an aspect of a culture that can be used to legitimize violence in its direct or structural form. Symbolic violence built into a culture does not kill or maim like direct violence or structural violence; however, it is used to legitimize either or both. See Johan Galtung, "Cultural Violence," *Journal of Peace Research* 27, no. 3 (1990): 291–305.

17. Elizabeth Becker, *When the War Was Over* (New York: Simon and Schuster, 1986), 85.

18. I have discussed culturalist perspectives in Sorpong Peou, *Conflict Neutralization in the Cambodia War* (Kuala Lumpur, Singapore, and New York: Oxford University Press, 1997); Peou, *Intervention and Change in Cambodia;* and

Sorpong Peou, *International Democracy Assistance for Peacebuilding: Cambodia and Beyond* (New York: Palgrave Macmillan, 2007). See also Alexander Laban Hinton, "A Head for an Eye: Revenge in the Cambodian Genocide," in *Violence: A Reader*, ed. Catherine Besteman (New York: New York University Press, 2002).

19. Hinton, "Head for an Eye," 147.

20. Zhou Daguan, *A Record of Cambodia: The Land and Its People,* trans. Peter Harris (Chiang Mai, Thailand: Silkworm Books, 2007), 64, 65.

21. Thomas Hammarberg, "Memorandum to the Royal Government of Cambodia: Evidence of Summary Executions, Torture, and Missing Persons since 2-7 July 1997" (unpublished report, UN Special Representative of the United Nations Secretary-General for Human Rights in Cambodia, Phnom Penh, Cambodia, 1997), 26.

22. See, e.g., Courtois et al., *Black Book of Communism;* Raphael Cohen-Almagor, "Foundations of Violence, Terror and War in the Writings of Marx, Engels and Lenin," *Terrorism and Political Violence* 3, no. 2 (1991): 1–24.

23. Jean-Louis Margolin, "China: A Long March into Night," in Courtois et al., *Black Book of Communism,* 521–22, 487.

24. Ibid., 527.

25. For more details, see Sorpong Peou, *Peace and Security in the Asia-Pacific: Theory and Practice* (Santa Barbara, CA: Praeger, 2010); Margolin, "China: A Long March into Night."

26. Many studies have indicated that the perception of threat and hostility does not necessarily correspond with the level of capability. According to Dina A. Zinnes, Robert C. North, and Howard E. Koch, "If a state's perception of injury (or frustration, dissatisfaction, hostility, or threat) to itself is 'sufficiently' great, this perception will offset perception of insufficient capability making the perception of capability much less important a factor in a decision to go to war. Under such circumstances, a state may go to war even though it perceives its power as relatively weak." See Dina A. Zinnes, Robert C. North, and Howard E. Koch, "Capability, Threat, and the Outbreak of War," in *International Politics and Foreign Policy,* ed. James N. Rosenau (New York: Free Press of Glencoe, 1961), 470. Even though he argues against the thesis that these are cases of pathological decision making, stating that war initiation can become a rational strategy, T. V. Paul accepts that weaker powers can initiate war with stronger ones; see T. V. Paul, *Asymmetric Conflicts: War Initiation by Weaker Powers* (Cambridge: Cambridge University Press, 1994).

27. Joel Migdal, *Strong Societies and Weak States: State-Society Relations and State Capabilities in the Third World* (Princeton: Princeton University Press, 1988), 207.

28. As Tilly puts it: "We discover a world in which small groups of power hungry men fought off numerous rivals and great popular resistance in pursuit of their own ends, and inadvertently promoted the formation of national states and wide-spread popular involvement in them." See Charles Tilly, *The Transforma-*

tion of National States in Western Europe (Princeton: Princeton University Press, 1975), 635. Tilly's analysis is based on states' reaction to challenges from groups seeking to improve their position; see Charles Tilly, *From Mobilization to Revolution* (Reading, MA: Addison Wesley, 1978), chap. 4.

29. David Mason and Dale T. Krane, "The Political Economy of Death Squads: Toward a Theory of the Impact of State-Sanctioned Terror," *International Studies Quarterly* 33, no. 2 (1989): 176–77.

30. Ibid., 177.

31. On the Khmer Rouge rise to power, see Matthew Edwards, "The Rise of the Khmer Rouge in Cambodia: Internal or External Origins?" *Asian Affairs* 35, no. 1 (2004), 56–67.

32. Jackson, "Introduction," 9–10; Timothy Carney, "The Unexpected Victory," in Jackson, *Cambodia,* 33–34; Karl D. Jackson, "The Ideology of Total Revolution," in Jackson, *Cambodia,* 46–47; Quinn, "Pattern and Scope of Violence," 181–83; Tyner, "Imagining Genocide," 14.

33. See Jackson, "Ideology of Total Revolution," 67.

34. Ibid., 46.

35. Jean-Louis Margolin, "Cambodia: The Country of Disconcerting Crimes," in Courtois et al., *Black Book of Communism.*

36. Tyner, "Imagining Genocide," 15–16.

37. David Chandler, *Brother Number One: A Political Biography of Pol Pot* (Boulder: Westview Press, 1999), 105; see also Timothy Carney, "The Organization of Power," in Jackson, *Cambodia,* 82–83.

38. A similar view is expressed in Tyner, "Imagining Genocide," 19.

39. On the Khmer Rouge's policy on industry, see Charles Twining, "The Economy," in Jackson, *Cambodia,* 132–37.

40. Edwards, "Rise of the Khmer Rouge in Cambodia," 59.

41. Ponchaud, "Social Change in the Vortex," 153; Ball, *Prosecuting War Crimes and Genocide,* 110.

42. Quinn, "Pattern and Scope of Violence," 181.

43. This author, for instance, was forced to witness a public execution in the village where he lived. A man and a woman were accused of adultery and brutally executed in front of villagers. Stealing a potato was also considered a crime punishable by death.

44. Hiebert, "Three 'Switches' of Identity Construction." The literature on Khmer Rouge violence includes perspectives on security. See, e.g., Peou, *Conflict Neutralization in the Cambodia War;* Jackson, "Introduction."

45. Jackson, "Ideology of Total Revolution," 69.

46. Kissi, "Rwanda, Ethiopia and Cambodia," 126.

47. Hiebert, "Three 'Switches' of Identity Construction," 17–20.

48. Although their defense of the Khmer Rouge policy is deeply flawed, Gareth Porter and George C. Hildebrand have a point when they argue that emptying the cities was justified on the grounds that they were swollen with refugees

from the countryside and that the Khmer Rouge regime could not cope with the food and health crises in 1975. See their *Cambodia: Starvation and Revolution*.

49. Wilfred P. Deac, *Road to the Killing Fields: The Cambodian War of 1970–1975* (College Station: Texas A&M University Press, 1997), 147, 166.

50. Arnold R. Isaacs, *Without Honor: Defeat in Vietnam and Cambodia* (Baltimore: Johns Hopkins University Press, 1999), 284.

51. Carney, "Unexpected Victory," 13, 35; Philip Short, *Pol Pot: The Anatomy of a Nightmare* (New York: Henry Holt and Company, 2004), 220.

52. Carney, "Unexpected Victory," 35.

53. Carney, "Organization of Power," 85.

54. Ibid., 95.

55. Carney, "Unexpected Victory," 33.

56. Carney, "Organization of Power," 95.

57. On purges within the CPK, see Quinn, "Pattern and Scope of Violence," 194–207.

58. Carney, "Organization of Power," 97; Raszelenberg, "Khmer Rouges and the Final Solution," 67.

59. Jackson, "Introduction," 3.

60. On the various reasons for transitional justice, see Sorpong Peou, "The East-Asian Challenge for Collaborative Action on International Criminal Justice," in *Human Security in East Asia: Challenges for Collaborative Action*, ed. Sorpong Peou (New York and London: Routledge, 2008); Sorpong Peou, "Reassessing the Role of Senior Leaders and Local Officials in Democratic Kampuchea Crimes," in *Bringing the Khmer Rouge to Justice: Prosecuting Mass Violence before the Cambodian Courts*, ed. Jaya Ramji and Beth Van Schaack (Lewiston, NY: Edwin Mellen Press, 2005).

61. Peter Maguire, "Cambodia's Tribunal, Already Troubled, Has Hard Times Ahead," *Cambodia Daily*, July 29, 2010.

62. John Pomfret, "Clinton Urges Cambodia to Strike Balance with China," *Washington Post*, Nov. 2, 2010.

63. United Nations, "Report of the Group of Experts for Cambodia Pursuant to General Assembly Resolution 52/135" (New York: United Nations, 1999).

64. *Cambodia Daily*, Sept. 15–16, 2001.

65. *Agence France-Presse*, Jan. 7, 2008.

66. Douglas Gillison, "Tribunal Judges Ruled Out Summoning Testimony of Hun Sen," *Cambodia Daily*, Feb. 11, 2010.

67. Peou, "East-Asian Challenge for Collaborative Action."

6

Counterrevolutionary Violence in Indonesia

Douglas Kammen

In October 1965, the Indonesian Army and an alliance of anti-communist civilian forces initiated a systematic attack on the Indonesian Communist Party (Partai Komunis Indonesia, PKI). Over the course of the next three years pogroms against the PKI left at least five hundred thousand people dead, hundreds of thousands more under detention, and unknown numbers dislocated within their communities. So horrific was the attack on the PKI that it is often counted as one of the worst cases of mass violence in the twentieth century.[1] That much is clear. But what sort of attack was it? Among scholars of Indonesia, debate emerged primarily over the question of perpetrators, with those on the political left typically arguing that the army organized and directed the violence, those on the political right tending to highlight the primacy of societal actors (running "amok" or even civil war). Within the broader field of mass and political violence, by contrast, there is general agreement that this was a case of state-led violence, but there are sharp differences over the question of intent and victims, best characterized by the contested usage of the terms "genocide," "politicide," and "ethnocide."[2]

Often missing in these debates is sensitivity to the *process* by which the violence took place and the position of the violence with respect to regime change. For the attack in Indonesia was not limited to members of the PKI or those suspected of being sympathetic to the party. The mass detentions, torture, and murder of communists and those accused of being "fellow travelers" were in fact only the first stage in a much broader attack on President Sukarno; the system of Guided Democracy he had proclaimed in 1959; the creative amalgam of nationalism, religion, and communism that formed the basis of Sukarno's thinking; and the social forces (including non-communist nationalists) most closely associated with Sukarno's regime. This chapter will argue that the mass violence between 1965 and 1968 was a counterrevolution against the ideals and popular mobilization unleashed by the Indonesian Revolution (1945–1949) and, a decade later, precariously institutionalized under Guided Democracy (1959–1965). Furthermore, the chapter seeks to demonstrate how and why the constellations of both perpetrators and victims shifted over the course of the attack. While the initial violence was perpetrated by an army-led coalition that included the active participation of civilians, as the army consolidated control over the state apparatus, it systematically marginalized its erstwhile allies. As such, what began as a seizure of the state and attack on the regime became a state-led attack. Conversely, the initial pogrom against the PKI was, over time, broadened to include repression of all groups associated with Sukarno and Guided Democracy, the construction of a new regime, and the establishment of new modes of political behavior.

The chapter is organized into three parts. The first section provides a brief historical account of political polarization under Guided Democracy and the September 30th Movement that provided the "pretext" for the army-led counterrevolution.[3] The second section examines the course of the violence, paying particular attention to regional variation, the forms of violence employed against the political left, the gradual consolidation of central state power and regime construction, and the eventual exclusion of civilian actors from the new regime. A final section turns to the legacies of mass violence, considering both the institutional violence during three decades of Suharto's rule and the ambitious but flawed efforts to address the legacy of counterrevolutionary violence during Indonesia's post-1998 transition to democracy.

BACKGROUND

The violence against the political left in 1965–1968 cannot be understood in isolation from Indonesia's political development over the previous two decades. The Japanese invasion in 1942 shattered the colonial myth of white supremacy and breathed new life into the nationalist movement. The Japanese occupation was brutal, though for many young Indonesians it also introduced exhilarating new experiences of military training and mass political mobilization. Immediately after the Japanese surrender in 1945, the nationalist figures Sukarno and Muhammad Hatta declared the independence of the Republic of Indonesia. The Dutch were intent to reclaim their colony, however, and four years of diplomatic maneuvering, further mass mobilization, and guerilla struggle ensued. The broad nature of the revolutionary movement inevitably led to sharp differences over strategy (negotiation vs. armed struggle) and ideology (among secular nationalists, devout Muslims, and more radical communists).[4] The mass mobilization of the revolution ensured that when independence was achieved in 1949 the new political system would be highly inclusive: all major ethnic groups had contributed leaders, and secular-nationalist, Islamic, and socialist parties coexisted.

During the early 1950s, Indonesia's fledgling system of parliamentary democracy experienced acute growing pains. In the absence of national elections, elite squabbling led to a succession of short-lived cabinets. The transformation of the revolutionary guerilla army into a standing military resulted in an attempted coup in 1952 and growing tensions between homegrown regional military commanders and Jakarta.[5] When the first national election was finally held in 1955, the vote was split among four big parties: the secular Indonesian National Party (PNI), the largely Java-based "traditionalist" Islamic party Nahdlatul Ulama (NU), the modernist Islamic party Masyumi, and a revived and astonishingly dynamic Indonesian Communist Party (PKI). Two years later, when regional elections were held in Java, the PKI polled even better, and it became clear that the PKI, though largely based in Java, was the fastest-growing party in the country. At the same time, Dutch intransigence over the return of Papua, which had not been included in the 1949 independence settlement, prompted Sukarno to retaliate by nationalizing all Dutch industries, which were then placed under army management.

The combination of elite friction in Jakarta, army hostility to the upstart new PKI, and the outbreak of the 1958 PRRI (Pemerintahan Revolusioner Republik Indonesia) rebellion in Sumatra and the Permesta rebellion in Sulawesi sounded the death knell of parliamentary democracy.[6] In 1959, declaring that the national revolution was not yet over,

President Sukarno proclaimed a new system of "Guided Democracy" and a return to the 1945 constitution, which gave the president far more authority. Paradoxically, the absence of elections drove the political parties into increasingly intense competition to recruit members into their mass-based organizations.[7] A combination of organizational expertise, a clean image, and programs targeting the poorest sectors of society made the PKI particularly successful at this extra-parliamentary party competition. The party's labor, peasant, youth, and women's organizations grew dramatically. During the early 1960s, as the Indonesian economy spiraled downward and hyper-inflation gripped the country, the PKI placed new emphasis on agrarian issues, made a concerted effort to expand its membership in the outer islands, and became a staunch supporter of Sukarno's international campaigns for the return of Dutch-held Papua and Confrontation against the formation of Malaysia.

These initiatives, however, resulted in increasingly direct conflict between the PKI and the army and conservative social forces. The focus on agrarian issues and support for unilateral actions (1964–1965) against landlords who refused to abide by the 1960 Agrarian Law created serious tensions with rural Islamic elites, particularly Nahdlatul Ulama in Java. Party expansion outside Java brought the PKI into conflict with the surviving aristocracy, regional military commanders, and supporters of the Darul Islam and PRRI/Permesta rebellions. The party's support for Confrontation and calls for the arming of a "fifth force" of peasants and workers was viewed by the army as a bid to arm itself in preparation for a seizure of power. As the PKI demanded greater restrictions on non-communist Islamic organizations and the media, religious groups and the army struck back. In East Java, Nahdlatul Ulama's youth wing (Ansor) and Multipurpose Brigade (Banser) launched widely reported attacks against the PKI. In early 1965, a combination of accurate news reports and wild rumors of PKI violence against Muslims in East Java prompted Islamic groups in Aceh to carry out attacks on newly established PKI offices in coastal towns. And in North Sumatra, where there were also a growing number of violent incidents, the all-Sumatra military commander ordered that army-affiliated labor and peasant unions be armed.[8] By August 1965 a number of political observers noted that opposition to the PKI within the army, in the Islamic community, and even within the right wing of the PNI was coalescing into an anti-communist alliance.

In the early morning hours of October 1, a small group of conspirators within the army carried out an action intended to arrest most of the army high command, though they wound up killing their targets. That morning Colonel Untung, the self-proclaimed leader of the September 30th Movement, issued a radio announcement explaining that the movement was acting to protect President Sukarno from a CIA-backed Council of Generals that was alleged to be planning to carry out a coup.[9] Major General Soeharto, the commander of the Army Strategic Reserve (Kostrad), initiated counteroperations, and by late afternoon he had secured the surrender of some of the September 30th Movement troops and flushed the remainder out of central Jakarta. The following day Kostrad and Army Para Commando Regiment (Resimen Para Komando Angkatan Darat, RPKAD) units surrounded the Halim Air Force Base, on the eastern outskirts of the city, and ultimatums resulted in the surrender of most of the remaining rebel forces. Air force commander Omar Dhani, PKI chairman D. N. Aidit, and a number of their associates managed to board two Hercules transport planes and escape to Central Java, where fellow conspirators had seized control in Semarang, Solo, Salatiga, and Yogyakarta.[10] By October 3, however, the movement in Central Java had dissolved. With no foreknowledge of the September 30th Movement and little information about what had actually transpired, PKI leaders told party members and supporters to keep a low profile.

With the exhumation of the bodies of the six murdered generals on October 4, Soeharto and the army set in motion a public relations campaign to downplay the involvement of army and air force personnel in the September 30th Movement and lay full blame on the PKI. The army also encouraged the "nationalist" (PNI, Partindo) and "religious" (NU, Masyumi, Katolik) parties to stage massive demonstrations calling for the PKI to be dissolved, often resulting in violent attacks on party offices and homes. On October 10, Soeharto announced the establishment of an Operations Command to Restore Order and Security (Kopkamtib).[11] Much like the Grand Committee of Public Safety established in Paris in 1793, Suharto's Kopkamtib was the precursor not to order but to a reign of terror aimed at fundamentally reordering social forces and their relations to state power. This was the beginning of a counterrevolution against the participatory and populist energies unleashed during the revolution and awkwardly institutionalized under Sukarno's left-leaning Guided Democracy.

COUNTERREVOLUTION, 1965–1968

The physical attack on the left involved a wide range of violence (arrests, torture, short-term detention, mass killings, forced relocation, and long-term imprisonment) over a period of more than three years. During this time there was a marked shift in the perpetrators and their relationship to the state, as well as in the aims of the violence. Building on Boudreau's discussion in chapter 1 of this volume, the point can be made that struggle against political rivals and for control over the state was characterized by highly instrumental violence, whereas subsequent regime construction was marked by a shift toward the monopolization of violence by the state and the use of exemplary violence to establish society-wide behavioral norms. For purposes of analysis, it is useful to break the counter-revolutionary violence into distinct phases: (1) October–December 1965, during which time the army seized control over provincial state apparatuses and oversaw the detention and massacre of several hundred thousand people; (2) January–July 1966, during which time the army wrested full control over the central state organs, continued the systematic purge of the civil service and armed forces, and initiated new witch hunts and further mass killings in provinces that had previously not been affected; and (3) the consolidation of Soeharto's New Order regime, the processing of detainees, and clean-up operations, most notably in West Kalimantan, beginning in 1967, and back on Java in 1968.

October–December 1965

During the last quarter of 1965 the most intensive violence against the PKI, its sympathizers, and those loyal to Sukarno was concentrated in six provinces—Aceh, North Sumatra, West Java, Central Java, East Java, and Bali. The aim of the attack was overwhelmingly instrumental: the destruction of the PKI as an organization, the establishment of military control over provincial-level state organs, and the gradual erosion of President Sukarno's authority. Although the army and most of its civilian allies shared these aims, there was significant variation in the timing, the constellation of perpetrators, and the patterns of violence.

    The first mass killings began in Aceh, at the northern tip of Sumatra. Although the PKI was a minor party in the province, during the first week of October the regional military commander, Brigadier General

Yusuf Ishak, encouraged anti-communist Muslims to stage rallies in the provincial capital and subdistrict towns to demand that the PKI be dissolved.[12] Members of the PKI and its affiliates were detained at various military facilities, then, beginning on October 7, released back into the hands of civilians and massacred. The violence also spread to target Javanese migrants, who were prominent smallholders in the coffee sector, and the property of ethnic Chinese, who dominated trade and retail. According to reports, victims were decapitated, and their heads were mounted on spikes along roadsides. The mass killings in Aceh took place with spectacular speed: by the second week of November newspapers cryptically reported that "Atjeh is calm" and a month later noted that the province had been "cleansed" of communists.[13] Reporting to the US embassy in Jakarta, the American consul in Medan wrote: "General Mokoginta [the All-Sumatra military commander] on December 25 told me there are only 120 PKI left in Atjeh, and a [word deleted] source on Mokoginta's staff reported 6,000 have been killed there."[14]

In Jakarta and across Java, by contrast, the first three weeks of October were characterized by uncertainty and fear, but not mass killings. Following the exhumation of the murdered generals, the army encouraged the formation of an Action Front to Crush the September 30th Movement (KAP-Gestapu), which staged frenzied demonstrations opposing the PKI and attacked PKI property. These actions in Jakarta were quickly replicated in the provinces, where provincial branches of NU, PNI, and other anti-communist parties mobilized mass demonstrations and demanded that the PKI be banned. In East Java, for example, NU held simultaneous rallies in a number of district cities on October 13, and the action in the town of Kediri culminated in an attack on PKI headquarters and the slaughter of eleven PKI members.[15] But mass killings in Java did not commence until *after* Suharto's appointment as army commander-in-chief on October 16. This alone is powerful evidence that the violence was the product of military leadership and not, as some have claimed, civilians "run amok."

Central Java, which was the only province in which the September 30th Movement had temporarily seized power, was the army's top priority. The Diponegoro Regional Military Command was severely depleted because of deployments to Sumatra, and five of the remaining seven battalions had initially sided with the September 30th Movement. For this reason, Soeharto chose to send units from the small but well-trained

RPKAD to spearhead the army's response. It was their arrival—first in the provincial capital, Semarang, on October 18, then by road through Magelang, Boyolali, and into Surakarta—that set in motion the mass arrests and killings of PKI members and other alleged leftists. Despite scholarly claims to the contrary, there is evidence that PKI members in the greater Surakarta area responded to the arrival of the feared RPKAD by attempting limited defensive actions (felling trees to blockade roads, cutting telephone lines, and a strike by railway workers in Solo) and are reported to have killed an estimated two hundred to three hundred political enemies.[16] Claiming that the PKI was preparing to launch a reign of terror, Diponegoro commander Brigadier General Surjosumpeno declared martial law, and RPKAD commander Sarwo Edhie set about mobilizing and arming tens of thousands of civilians to assist in the anticommunist killings.[17] The NU and PNI youth organizations contributed the largest component of these paramilitary killing squads, but Catholic Party and Muhammadiyah youth appear to have been particularly active in Yogyakarta and other urban centers. By late December tens of thousands had been killed. Although the massacres were to continue in Central Java through early 1966, on Christmas day the RPKAD units began a one-week "victory tour" of the province before returning overland to Jakarta.[18]

The political situation in East Java differed in important respects from that in Central Java. Here, the PKI and NU were the two largest parties, with PNI a distant third. The unilateral actions carried out by the Indonesian Peasants' Front (Barisan Tani Indonesia, BTI) in 1964 had led to extreme tension in lowland areas, and by early 1965 NU was responding with its own campaign of violence against the PKI. On October 1, members of the September 30th Movement in Surabaya issued a single radio announcement, but the movement never attempted to seize power in East Java. The regional military commander, Brigadier General Basuki Rachmat, who was known to be a Sukarnoist, was slow to respond, and hence much depended on local conditions and the political inclinations of subregional military officers. Mass killings in East Java erupted almost simultaneously with those in Central Java, beginning in areas in which the NU and PKI were evenly balanced (e.g., the Jombang-Kediri-Tulungagung and the Banjuwangi-Jember corridors) and where the local military commanders were staunchly anti-communist. By contrast, in areas of relative PNI strength, such as Madiun, or where there was a strong navy and marine presence, such as Surabaya and Pasuruan, there was far less immediate violence.[19] The influx of people into the relative safety of Surabaya led to violent clashes and killings between Ansor/Banser and the navy. In mid-December the caretaker mayor of Surabaya, Lieutenant Colonel Sukotjo, was sufficiently concerned about PKI members and sympathizers taking refuge in the city (as well as the emergence of violence between the marines/navy and Ansor) that he declared Surabaya a "closed city" and posted roadblocks to control movement in and out.[20] By late December, the US consulate in Surabaya reported: "Killing of PKI suspects continues but evidently on lesser scale and in more discreet manner. Generally victims are taken out of populous areas before being killed and bodies are buried rather than thrown into river. According [to an] NU source . . . NU campaign to exterminate PKI now being carried out throughout whole East Java."[21]

The army's response in West Java was shaped by at least four key factors. First, with the exception of the theft of a small number of weapons from a military warehouse in Cimahi on October 1, the September 30th Movement had not taken action in West Java.[22] Second, the West Java branch of the PKI was far smaller than those in Central and East Java. Third, the legacy of the Darul Islam rebellion, particularly in the mountains around Tasikmalaya and Garut, may have deterred the army from arming and encouraging Muslim youth to take direct action against their political opponents.[23] Fourth, and perhaps of most importance, Siliwangi commander Major General Ibrahim Adjie was anti-communist but also loyal to President Sukarno and hence was less likely to condone wholesale killings. In early October military commanders encouraged PKI branches to voluntarily disband, and there were reports that villagers were handing PKI members/sympathizers over to the army.[24] By mid-November, however, massacres were well under way. The US embassy noted "receiving reports [that] Ansor [is] slaughtering PKI a la Kediri in many areas [of] West Java."[25] The killings were particularly severe in the Cirebon-Indramayu-Subang region and, to a lesser extent, in the southern Priangan highlands.[26]

The situation in North Sumatra developed more slowly than in neighboring Aceh, Central Java, and East Java and in some respects most closely resembled West Java. This was in part because of the relative strength of the PKI and the left wing within PNI, in part too because of sharp differences between the All-Sumatra Military Command (Koanda

I), headed by the anti-communist Major General Mokoginta, and the left-leaning North Sumatra Regional Military Command, Brigadier General Darjatmo. Anti-communist forces allied with Mokoginta staged anti-PKI rallies and attacked property belonging to the PKI, its affiliates, and the ethnic Chinese and left-leaning Consultative Body for Indonesian Citizenship (Badan Permusyawaratan Kewarganegaraan, Baperki), at times resulting in the murder of party officials. But throughout October there were no mass killings in North Sumatra. The turning point came in the last week of October, when Kodam commander Darjatmo was finally replaced, and mass purges were carried out within the civilian administration.[27] A huge anti-communist rally in Medan on November 2 provided the cue for the start of the pogroms. Three weeks later, the US embassy described the "systematic drive to destroy PKI in northern Sumatra" and "wholesale killings."[28] The limited evidence suggests that members of the PKI plantation workers union were the primary target of the killings. In late November, however, at least some elements in the army sought to end what they called "unauthorized killings," and a struggle emerged between the army and the more radical anti-communist forces, intent on continuing "silent killings" beyond the east coast.[29] By late December, a US telegram sought to downplay the severity of the massacres: "North Sumatra still bloody but situation never really out of control there except perhaps in certain districts."[30]

Bali presented an entirely different dynamic. With the island's predominantly Hindu population, political allegiances were evenly divided between the PNI and the PKI. Throughout October and the first half of November the situation was tense, but there were no killings, leading the NU newspaper *Duta Masjarakat* to allege that Javanese communists were seeking refuge across the narrow strait.[31] By late November, however, the US embassy received reports that "house burnings have become nightly entertainment and stabbings frequent" in the Denpasar area but noted that West Bali, where the PKI was particularly strong, "remained quiet."[32] The Fact-Finding Commission appointment by President Sukarno in December 1965 concluded that a violent incident in Jembrana on November 30 between a local army unit and Ansor Youth, on one side, and Pemuda Rakyat, on the other, had provided the spark for mass violence. During the first week of December several thousand alleged communists were killed in West Bali.[33] With the arrival of RPKAD in the provincial capital, Denpasar, killings spread rapidly across the island. At the end of December the Udayana military commander told the Fact-Finding Commission that fifteen thousand people had been killed, but off the record he reportedly told Commissioner Oei Tjoe Tat that the army's real estimate was forty-five thousand.[34]

By the end of 1965, several hundred thousand people had been murdered, and hundreds of thousands more were under detention. While there was considerable variation by time and place, the violence described above typically occurred in three distinct stages. The first attacks in a given locale—carried out by the army, civilians, or a combination of the two—often involved the slaughter of entire communities. A US embassy telegram describes one such attack in Kediri, East Java: "American Missionary from Baptist Hospital in Kediri told us that 3400 PKI activists were killed by Ansor with probably [sic] assistance from [PNI] Marhaenist youths over period Nov 5 to Nov 9. . . . After seizing victim concerned, they took him to river banks, where PKI allegedly had prepared mass graves prior to Oct. 1, and cut his throat." In the second stage, army units and civilian militias conducted patrols to arrest PKI suspects, who were then detained by the army at makeshift detention centers. In the third stage, individuals already under detention were "transferred" (typically at night) to a new location but while en route were then "handed over" to civilian killing squads. One of the most explicit descriptions available again comes from East Java: "Source described how a column of prisoners would be taken through villages and the commander would shout 'Do you want some?' and five or six prisoners would be pushed into the crowd where they would be killed on the spot."[35]

Throughout this initial period the army's attack was (with the exception of Aceh) focused on the provinces in which the PKI had the largest membership and enjoyed the greatest political clout. It is important to account for variation in the timing of the outbreak of violence in these provinces. This was in part a function of the speed with which anti-communist army officers could consolidate full control over their own ranks and effective dominance over the provincial-level state apparatus. But it also depended on how quickly the army could form an alliance of anti-communist civilian forces to participate in the attack. When these conditions were met, the violence was directed against entire categories of people and organizations identified as subversive, without regard for an individual's involvement in or even knowledge of the September 30th Movement, aimed at not only eliminating communism but destroying the social bases of the regime.

By mid-December the army leadership was confident that the PKI had been destroyed as an organization, allowing Soeharto and his allies to recalibrate the attack. With the start of the Muslim fasting month, military officials and their civilian allies made repeated statements in the press and to foreign diplomats about plans to order a halt to the killings. In East Java, the US consulate reported being told that an order would be issued to end the killings on December 15, though NU sources had made it clear that they would not obey such a directive.[36] In Bali, similarly, in mid-December RPKAD commander Colonel Sarwo Edhie is reported to have stated that it was necessary to "bring the killings under control."[37] At precisely the same time, the army forced Sukarno to acquiesce to the appointment of a new triumvirate within the Supreme Operations Command (KOTI)—General Nasution for military affairs, the sultan of Yogyakarta for economic affairs, and Ruslan Abdulgani for political affairs—a move US sources described as "an elliptical procedure for assuming control of government."[38] In the words of a US embassy telegram, the "real stage was the Army versus Sukarno." Phase two was about to begin.

January–October 1966

In January 1966, Soeharto and the army trained their sights on President Sukarno, though they clearly wished to avoid a direct confrontation and prevent angering the PNI and other nationalist forces. Outraged by the army's lies and horrified by the violence unleashed against the PKI, Sukarno fought back as best he could. Loyal ministers announced the formation of a Sukarno Front (Barisan Sukarno) to counter the anticommunist Action Front to Crush the September 30th Movement (KAP-Gestapu). The plan collapsed in the face of army intransigence, however, and the army set about arresting Sukarno's top aides and further curtailing the president's movements. Of greater importance, the army began to mobilize urban youth into new action fronts to denounce the president. This was the beginning of a convoluted struggle in Jakarta and other major cities between Soeharto and President Sukarno. The standoff culminated in the Letter of 11 March (Surat Perintah 11 Maret, abbreviated Supersemar), transferring administrative authority to Soeharto, which Harold Crouch has called a "disguised coup."[39] In June, intent on consolidating full control over the central state organs, the army oversaw a closely orchestrated special session of the People's Consultative Assembly

(Majelis Permusyawaratan Rakyat Sementara, MPRS). Under the watchful eye of the military, the assembly delegates dutifully confirmed the powers contained in Supersemar. With full control over state institutions, regime construction could begin. In October 1966 Soeharto and the army signaled that they would no longer tolerate independent violence perpetrated by civilians and indicated that Sukarno, who was still president in name, would be dealt with through constitutional mechanisms.

While these political struggles played out in Jakarta, violence continued elsewhere in the country. Three dynamics are of particular importance. The first concerns the ongoing attack against the political left in the worst-affected areas. In Central Java, mass killings continued, though at a much reduced level, until a devastating flood in March brought the Surakarta region to a standstill and marked the end of the violence.[40] In East Java, too, killings continued throughout the first half of the year. In Bali, where mass violence had only commenced in early December 1965, the killings raged on. This period also saw the emergence of significant new lines of friction. As the army sought to exert greater control over the activities of its anti-communist civilian allies, tensions arose within the anti-communist alliance.[41] This was exacerbated in those provinces where the left wing of the PNI was ascendant (Jakarta, East Java, North Sumatra) and by accusations, often well founded, that the PNI was providing refuge for communists. Further conflict was fueled by NU opposition to the emergence of another Islamic political party.[42] In East Java, the primary tension was between NU, which sought to remain relevant in the hopes of winning representation within the post-Sukarno political regime, and the PNI. This split was paralleled by tensions within the security forces, with the staunchly Sukarnoist Marines (and at times the police) siding with PNI and local army troops siding with NU. This resulted in serious clashes, including loss of life.[43] A similar split emerged in North Sumatra, where the League of Upholders of Indonesian Independence (IPKI) and PNI youth squared off in violent clashes.

Friction within the anti-communist alliance was compounded by the thorny issue of detainees. This issue had already surfaced in December 1965, albeit fleetingly. In North Sumatra, for example, the army had announced plans to build major new detention centers, but limited funds made this impractical; instead, there were reports that many of the ten thousand detainees in the province would simply be trucked to Aceh for execution.[44] The question of detainees took on new urgency in early 1966.

In his struggle to regain authority, Sukarno issued an order in February for communist detainees (officially estimated to number 120,000, though the actual number was certainly far higher) to be handed over from the army to the attorney general for legal processing. In early March, Soeharto reluctantly agreed to comply with this order, but the most bloodthirsty of the anti-communist groups sought to kill detainees before they could be transferred.[45] In some instances the military or civilians in charge of makeshift detention centers simply increased the nightly quota of executions; in other cases NU and IPKI forces carried out brazen attacks on detention centers and their terrified inhabitants. It is impossible to estimate the number of detainees who were executed as a result, though it appears that this was far higher in East Java than in Central Java.

The third development during this period was the initiation of anti-communist violence in regions previously unaffected. While information is often limited, three provinces illustrate this new dynamic. In Lampung, which had remained relatively quiet in late 1965 because of the very limited army presence, naval operations commenced in early January and netted more than five thousand PKI suspects in the first week alone.[46] In West Sumatra, where there had been relatively minor clashes in late 1965, military operations and direct violence by anti-communist civilians increased during the first months of 1966.[47] In Nusatenggara Timor, attacks on the PKI and mass killings only commenced in mid-January 1966, eventually leaving several thousand dead.[48] In these provinces and elsewhere, the pattern was much as it had been in Java and Bali a few months earlier: army sponsorship of civilian paramilitaries, brutal attacks on known PKI figures, and then witch hunts resulting in mass detentions and the execution of prisoners. The scale of the killings in these locales, however, was far lower than on Java or in the northern part of Sumatra.

In addition to these broad developments, it is crucial to note that there was a spike in violence—detentions as well as killings—before and during the June Special Session of the People's Consultative Assembly. One reason for this may have been explicit orders for regional military commanders (now effectively in control of provincial government) to ensure "stability" during this crucial political exercise. Of greater importance, however, was the desire of anti-communist groups to press for particular outcomes (e.g., the removal of Sukarno from the presidency, a reversal of the plan to process detainees through the legal system, etc.), as well as a last-ditch effort to remain politically relevant in the hope of securing institutional representation within the new regime. NU, IPKI, and other such groups were to be sorely disappointed on both counts: these groups having outlived their usefulness, the army was determined to reassert its monopoly over the use of violence. In the following months some of these groups made further efforts to remain relevant, but by October 1966 Soeharto had signaled that the state and law, not mass mobilization, was to be the cornerstone of the New Order. This marked the decisive shift from crudely instrumental violence to exemplary violence intended to proscribe behavior and acceptable means of identification for the entire population.

The Final Stage, 1967–1968

The full consolidation of the new regime was accompanied by a very real effort to enforce social order, right the economy, and complete the realignment of Indonesia's foreign policy. But the violence against the left was far from over. The third and final period—from 1967 to 1968—was marked by the processing and internment of hundreds of thousands of prisoners, as well as "clean-up" operations against leftist remnants.

The first of these operations was necessitated by an attack carried out against a small air force facility in West Kalimantan, not far from the Malaysian border. Although the military believed that the attack had been perpetrated by members of the ethnic Chinese and communist Sarawak People's Guerrilla Force (Pasukan Gerilya Rakyat Sarawak) and the allied North Kalimantan People's Force (Paraku), it was in fact the work of the largely ethnic-Chinese West Kalimantan branch of the PKI, together with its Sarawakian fellow travelers. After several months of preparatory operations, again spearheaded by RPKAD, in November 1967 the army once again turned to the use of civilian paramilitaries: ethnic Dayaks were mobilized to attack the large ethnic Chinese population in the rural interior, resulting in an estimated three thousand deaths in November–December alone. This was followed, over the next few years, by the forced relocation of over one hundred thousand ethnic Chinese, many into concentration camps on the coast.[49]

The final spasm of killings occurred in 1968, when the Indonesian military uncovered evidence of underground PKI activity and even small-scale rural bases in Java. The locations ranged from Indramayu, in West Java; to the Merapi-Merbabu mountain complex and the greater

Purwodadi area, in Central Java; to Blitar and Mount Lawu, in East Java. The army wasted no time in launching new operations, first in the Blitar-Tulungagung region of East Java and then in Purwodadi and other areas of Central Java.[50] Thousands of people were reportedly killed, and many more were taken into custody and subjected to torture and long-term imprisonment. These final operations brought the direct pogroms against the PKI, its sympathizers, and staunch Sukarnoists to a close.

Up to this point, the discussion has emphasized the forms and intensity of violence and the shifting alignment of perpetrators within a primarily chronological framework. Moving up the ladder of abstraction, it is now necessary to situate these findings within the analytical framework of larger political processes and the aims of violence outlined by Boudreau earlier in this volume. What is most immediately apparent is that the analysis of the mass violence against the Indonesian left presented here is not limited to the geographic expansion and deepening of state authority (state building), the establishment and regularization of new rules for the exercise of state power (regime construction), and politics under "settled political arrangements" (regime maintenance). It requires the addition of a prior category: violence against and the dismantling of an existing regime with the explicit intention of producing regime change. As the Indonesian case illustrates, regime change is far more likely than either state building or regime construction to involve the widespread use of the most extreme forms of violence (e.g., killings rather than detention) to proscribe identities (as opposed to activities) and, because of the scale and problem of identifying opponents, is more likely to involve the deployment of civilian allies (as opposed to strictly state actors). In Indonesia, the attack on the "old" regime lasted from October 1965 until March 1966, when President Sukarno was forced to cede administrative authority to Lieutenant General Soeharto.

With the successful seizure of central state power, those who led the attack on the old regime were faced with the overlapping tasks of state building and regime construction. In Indonesia, the logic of state building is seen in the geographic spread of anti-communist violence to every province during the first half of 1966. Purges, detentions, and killings against alleged communists in provinces were conducted even where the PKI had a minor presence. This appears to have had little to do with an actual threat in the outer islands and more to do with involving (and by extension implicating) provincial authorities in the foundational act of the new regime and ensuring that it was not possible for the decimated PKI to regroup in peripheral areas. To this extent the violence was largely instrumental. This contributed, of course, to a simultaneous process of regime construction and ongoing consolidation: setting the parameters of accepted political identity and behavior, enforcing the state's monopoly over the legitimate use of violence, specifying a new economic model of natural resource–based growth, and offering side payments for compliance to the general population.

Legacies

If blunt coercion was the external hallmark of the counterrevolution, from the earliest days the army high command sought to shroud the use of force under a cloak of consent. The murder of six generals on the morning of October 1, 1965 (the details of which were falsified and embellished), was presented as necessitating action to "save" the nation; the mass mobilization of anti-communist forces, encouraged and in large part directed by the army, was portrayed as evidence of societal outrage; and the mass killings were only unleashed after Soeharto had been granted formal authority as head of Kopkamtib and commander of the army. More telling still, the army's propagandists made every effort to deny that the violence was even taking place. While the fancied crimes of the September 30th Movement and the alleged plans of the PKI to wage a reign of terror dominated the carefully controlled press, the mass media was silent on the actual pogroms under way. Occasional reports—such as the article in December declaring Aceh to be "calm"—might have hinted otherwise, but one searches the Indonesian press and later military publications in vain for information about the mass killings. Periodic articles about detentions and arrests lent a further air of legality to the assault. Only later, as John Roosa has convincingly shown, did antimonies between and within New Order accounts appear.[51]

With the consolidation of the new regime in 1967 and the final operations in Java in 1968, the fury of the counterrevolution gave way to the "icy institutional violence" of authoritarian rule.[52] Several hundred thousand Indonesians were shunted through a jerry-rigged judicial process and classified by their alleged degree of involvement in the September 30th Movement and their association with the PKI. Many were in fact released, though the stigma of the PKI and their status as detainees were indelibly marked on identity cards and in government dossiers. Less fortunate were the tens of thousands more incarcerated in the existing prison system and in newly established detention centers, where they languished for a decade or more.[53] The direct repression was accompanied by a ban on Marxism, prohibition on the use of Chinese characters, and strict censorship. The regime also placed tight restrictions on the freedom of association, making it impossible for victims to commemorate either the national tragedy or individual suffering and loss. Memory of the violence was harbored within families, though even there many tried to hide the past so as to protect their children and grandchildren.

State violence was one of the hallmarks of Soeharto's rule over the course of the next three decades. Counterinsurgency operations were waged against communist remnants in West Kalimantan until 1974 and against ethno-nationalist separatist movements in Papua (throughout the New Order) and Aceh (1976–1979 and from 1989 onward). The 1975 invasion of Portuguese Timor in 1975 and its formal annexation the following year added another protracted "internal" war of pacification. These groups were geographically contained and far from Jakarta, and it was thus relatively easy for the New Order to portray their members as "subversives" and to limit what the general populace knew about the regime's use of violence against them. What is perhaps most interesting about these counterinsurgency operations is that in each instance Soeharto's military drew on the foundational experience of 1965–1968, organizing and arming civilian groups to operate alongside the existing military and intelligence network. Indeed, the hallmark of Soeharto's rule was that the New Order repeatedly eschewed its rightful claim to a monopoly over the legitimate use of violence by employing paramilitaries, militarized youth groups, and informers to commit violence on behalf of the state against fellow citizens. In this sense, the violence was not just the product of a finely tuned security apparatus but was literally state led.

Three decades of violence and silence were finally shattered by the massive *reformasi* protests in early 1998 and Soeharto's eventual resignation in May of that year. Regime transitions, scholars argue, provide a key opening within which the past may be addressed and injustices redressed, though they disagree on questions of sequencing (transition as a precondition for retributive/restorative justice or some form of justice as a precondition for democratization). What these arguments generally lack, however, is a specific examination of the class character of regime collapse. Where middle classes were a principal victim of repression and came to spearhead opposition to the regime, one might plausibly argue that that some form of transitional justice is more likely to take root. Redress of past human rights violations may be less likely in cases where subordinate classes or religious/ethnic minorities were the primary target of regime violence but educated and urban sectors led the demand for democratization. In Indonesia, the mass killings in 1965–1968 took place overwhelmingly in rural areas and targeted lower classes; urban dwellers and those with higher education were more likely to be subjected to detention, though the numbers pale in comparison to the victims of murder. Three decades later, the foot soldiers of the reformasi movement in 1998, in contrast, were overwhelmingly urban—most obviously students and intellectuals. The economic crisis threatened all three groups, which came to agree that Soeharto had become a liability.

The catch-call of the movement, hence, became "try Soeharto." But the call for Soeharto to be put on trial was not centered on the mass violence in 1965–1968 or the institutionalized violations of rights thereafter; not on the illegal invasion and massive loss of life in East Timor, the fraudulent integration and genocidal policies in West Papua, or the brutal military operations in Aceh; nor on the repression of Islamic actors in Tanjung Priok in 1984 and in Lampung in 1989. Instead the demand that Soeharto be tried betrayed middle-class concerns: the vast sums Soeharto had accumulated while in power.

Meanwhile, other voices did demand that the legacy of human rights violations be addressed. Although these actors typically viewed themselves as part of a progressive front, there were two distinct approaches to the issue of transitional justice. On the one hand, academics, nongovernmental organizations (NGOs), and the student bodies established at the height of the 1998 reformasi protests focused on legal reform, free and fair elections, and the promotion of human rights.[54] While the past may have animated their campaigns, they were typically focused on the present and future. On the other hand, a smaller number of human rights NGOs and newly created "victims" associations (Paguyuban Korban Orde Baru [Association of Victims of the New Order], Yayasan Penelitian Korban Pembunuhan 1965/1966 [Foundation for Research on Victims of the 1965–1966 Killings], Sekber '65 [Joint Secretariat on '65], etc.) demanded redress for past human rights violations. The focus of these efforts varied along a spectrum that included explicit calls for retributive justice, truth-seeking, rehabilitation, and reconciliation. Both streams had to engage with powerful New Order elements—including the military and police, the judiciary, and Golkar and Soeharto cronies—that had outlived the dictatorship.

The political landscape initially appeared quite promising. Soeharto's chosen successor, B. J. Habibie, waged a campaign to recast himself as a true reformer, only to lose the 1999 election. With no party winning a majority, lines were drawn between the secular-nationalist PDI-P, led by Megawati Sukarnoputri, the daughter of former President Sukarno, and a hastily assembled alliance of Islamic parties and pretenders to state power. These were, of course, the inheritors of the "nationalist" and "religious" constituencies that had participated in the anti-communist violence of 1965–1968. Out of the electoral deadlock compromise was found in the selection of Abdurrahman Wahid, the long-time head of Nadhlatul Ulama (which, of course, had provided the shock troops for the killings in Java and elsewhere in 1965–1966). But Wahid was an eccentric: an on-again, off-again critic of Soeharto, a champion of democracy but an opponent of reformasi, and a renowned joker. In early 2000, President Wahid proposed lifting the 1966 ban on Marxism-Leninism and made a highly public apology for NU's involvement in the 1965–1966 killings.

It was under Wahid's presidency that a Jakarta-based NGO, the Institute of Policy Research and Advocacy (Elsam), and the National Commission on Human Rights (KomnasHAM) began to lobby for the formation of a truth and reconciliation commission. Although new laws on human rights protection had already been passed under the Habibie administration, it was during the early months of Wahid's presidency that the People's Consultative Assembly passed several key pieces of legislation. Of particular importance was MPR Decision V/2000 on National Unity, which called for the formation of an extra-judicial truth and reconciliation commission.[55]

The reform era appeared to be off to a promising start. NGO activists took the lead, writing the draft legislation for the truth commission, with solid backing from KomnasHAM. Beginning in 2001, however, the process slowed considerably, in part because of opposition from the administration of the new president, Megawati Sukarnoputri, who was concerned about alienating political Islam, in part too because opposition political parties were eager to use the threat of a resurgent left to their advantage. And they were not alone. Anti-communism had become a compelling issue for conservative groups, at times involving physical threats. Nevertheless, in 2004 the People's Consultative Assembly finally passed the Law on the Truth and Reconciliation Commission, and a list of candidate commissioners was compiled.[56] Concerned about both popular opposition to the TRC, as well as who and what the commission might investigate, newly elected president Susilo Bambang Yudhoyono put off the review and appointment of commissioners.[57] The stalling tactic worked: in December 2006, the Constitutional Court ruled that the TRC law was unconstitutional. Since then all but a handful of civil society organizations have abandoned the issue, and once-vibrant victims' organizations have fallen silent.

Why did various formal mechanisms for addressing past violence fail? It can be argued that the social and institutional forces that perpetrated the counterrevolution were still present throughout the political transition to and consolidation of democracy and forestalled calls for redress of past abuses. Such reasoning is clearly attractive: the Indonesian Armed Forces and Islamic organizations and lobbies did oppose President Wahid's apology; they resisted calls for the establishment of a truth commission and opposed the rehabilitation of former political prisoners. But this relatively crude "negotiated transitions" approach fails to account for two equally important dynamics. On the one hand, the 1965–1968 violence and the subsequent institutional stigmatization of the political left were not the only cases demanding redress in 1998. Indonesia was under intense international (and more modest domestic) pressure to address the much more recent atrocities committed in East Timor, to resolve the ongoing conflicts in Aceh and Papua, and to face demands for justice over past cases of state repression of Islam. The TRC mandate had come to encompass all of these cases, but this was never a realistic undertaking. The simplest solution was to jettison the TRC and instead treat the other human rights violations on a case-by-case basis. On the other hand, the lobby supporting the TRC and other transitional-justice mechanisms was from the outset small, and it floundered in the face of mainstream ignorance and apathy about the country's violent past.

The violence of 1965–1968, this chapter has argued, was not simply an attack on the left, but in fact a far broader attack on Sukarno, Sukarnoism, and the participatory values of the national revolution. It was, in other words, a counterrevolution spearheaded from within by the army against the very structures of the state, necessitating a gutting of the old institutions and civil service personnel before construction of a new regime could even begin. Viewed in this light, the Indonesian counterrevolution bears greater resemblance to the Cultural Revolution, which Mao hoped would prevent the stultifying bureaucratization characteristic of the USSR, than it does to Stalinist repression, which was carried out exclusively by the state's own highly developed internal security apparatus against the populace.[58] Paradoxically, the "mass" involvement of nationalists and religionists in the Indonesian violence made possible the construction of a far stronger central state that, for the first time since independence, could conclusively exclude not only the left but also the anti-communist forces that had been so eager to eliminate their rivals. This also sheds light on the failures of the many initiatives for transitional justice after 1998. Those seeking justice ran up against not only the now old "New Order" holdovers but, more important, the religious right, which was intent on using the specter of communism in its bid for a place in the new Indonesia.

NOTES

1. For claims in the general literature on mass violence, see Matthew Krain, "State-Sponsored Mass Murder," *Journal of Conflict Resolution* 41, no. 3 (1997): 339; for scholarship specific to Indonesia, see Robert Cribb, "Problems in the Historiography of the Killings in Indonesia," in *The Indonesian Killings, 1965–1966: Studies from Java and Bali*, ed. Robert Cribb (Clayton, Victoria: Centre of Southeast Asian Studies, Monash University, 1990).

2. Samuel Totten, William S. Parsons, and Israel Charny, arguing for a broader definition of genocide, include the 1965–1968 mass killings in Indonesia in their volume *Century of Genocide*, 2nd ed. (New York and London: Routledge, 2004). Barbara Harff and Ted Robert Gurr, by contrast, categorize the killing of large numbers of communists as "repressive politicide" and the killing of a far smaller number of ethnic Chinese (five hundred to one thousand) as "xenophobic genocide"; see their "Toward Empirical Theory of Genocides and Politicides: Identification and Measurement of Cases since 1945," *International Studies Quarterly* 32, no. 3 (1988): 359–71.

3. The term "pretext" is borrowed from John Roosa, *Pretext for Mass Murder: The September 30th Movement and Suharto's Coup d'État in Indonesia* (Madison: University of Wisconsin Press, 2006).

4. During an ill-fated putsch to gain control over the course of the revolutionary struggle in 1948, communist forces in Madiun were crushed by the secular-nationalist leadership of the Indonesian National Army.

5. Ruth McVey, "The Post-Revolutionary Transformation of the Indonesian

Army," parts 1 and 2, *Indonesia*, no. 11 (Apr. 1971): 157–76, and no. 13 (Apr. 1972): 147–82.

6. Dan Lev, *The Transition to Guided Democracy: Indonesian Politics, 1957–1959* (Ithaca: Southeast Asia Program, Cornell University, 1966).

7. Benedict Anderson, "Elections in Southeast Asia," in *The Spectre of Comparisons: Nationalism, Southeast Asia and the World*, ed. Benedict Anderson (London and New York: Verso, 1998), 281.

8. Reported in Airgram A40, US Consulate Medan to US Embassy Jakarta, Mar. 15, 1965, POL 2 INDON, US National Archives and Records Administration (hereafter NARA). Remarkably, PKI members were included in this scheme.

9. It is worth noting that Benedict Anderson, whose "preliminary analysis" in 1966 argued that G30S was largely an internal military affair, more recently has suggested that Suharto was privy to the conspirators' plans. John Roosa, however, has argued that, via the mysterious Sjam, PKI chairman Aidit and his secret "Special Bureau" were in fact involved in the plot. See Benedict Anderson, "Petrus Dadi Ratu," *New Left Review* 3 (May–June 2000): 7–15; and Roosa, *Pretext for Mass Murder*.

10. Benedict R. Anderson and Ruth T. McVey, *A Preliminary Analysis of the October 1, 1965, Coup in Indonesia* (Ithaca: Modern Indonesia Project, Cornell University, 1971), 32–41, 54–56.

11. Harold Crouch, *The Army and Politics in Indonesia* (Ithaca: Cornell University Press, 1978), 160.

12. Pusat Penerangan Angkatan Darat, *Fakta2 Persoalan Sekitar "Gerakan 30 September"* (Jakarta: P. N. Balai Pustaka, 1966), 180; Jessica Melvin, "A Silent Massacre: The Indonesian Communist Party and the Mass Killings in Aceh" (BA thesis, University of Melbourne, 2010).

13. "Atjeh tenang," *Berita Yudha*, and "Atjeh kembali tenang," *Angkatan Bersendjata*, both Nov. 11, 1965; "Atjeh bersih dari PKI," *Api Pantjasila*, Dec.11, 1965.

14. Telegram A-20, US Consulate Medan to US Embassy Jakarta, Jan. 6, 1966, POL 2 INDON, NARA; Telegram 924A, US Embassy Jakarta to US State Department, Dec. 27, 1965, POL 23-9 INDON, NARA. See also Kodam–1, "Laporan Tahunan Lengkap Kodam-1/Kohanda Atjeh, Tahun 1965" (n.p., n.d.), 6–7.

15. Crouch, *Army and Politics*, 147, 151; Hermawan Sulistyo, *Palu Arit di Ladang Tebu: Sejarah Pembantaian Massal Yang Terlupakan 1965–1966* (Jakarta: Gramedia, 2000).

16. *Fakta2*, 204–11, 276–77; Crouch, *Army and Politics*, 149–50. Military sources report that PKI forces killed "nationalist" and "religious" opponents in Boyolali (ninety-eight dead), Klaten (forty-four dead), Solo (fourteen dead), and Djatinom/Manisrenggo (eighty-two dead); see *Fakta2*, 287–88.

17. Twenty-four thousand youths were mobilized into paramilitary units in Surakarta alone. Scattered evidence suggests that the general plan was for a platoon of one hundred men in each village.

18. "Mengikuti Operasi RPKAD: Pulang kekandang," *Berita Yudha*, Dec. 29, 1965.

19. See Telegram 930A, US Embassy Jakarta to US State Department, Nov. 26, 1965, POL 23 INDON, NARA; incoming Telegram 1617, US Embassy Jakarta to US State Deparment, Dec. 2, 1965, POL 23-9 INDON, NARA; and Telegram 36, US Consulate Surabaya to US Embassy Jakarta, Nov. 18, 1965, POL 23-8 INDON, NARA.

20. Idea first reported in Telegram 52, US Consulate Surabaya to US Embassy Jakarta, Dec. 16, 1965, POL 23-8 INDON, NARA; actual closure reported in Telegram 724A, US Embassy Jakarta to US State Department, Dec. 20, 1965, POL 23-9, INDON, NARA.

21. Incoming Telegram 55, US Consulate Surabaya to US Embassy Jakarta, Dec. 28, 1965, POL 23-8 INDON, NARA.

22. This is all the more remarkable given the rumors in circulation since mid-1965 that the PRC had smuggled one hundred thousand small arms into Indonesia for the PKI and that these were stored in three caches in West Java.

23. Major General Adjie was well aware that Masjumi and socialist elements were joining the army-Muslim alliance against the PKI, but with aims of turning the situation to their own advantage.

24. Outgoing Telegram 1317A, US Embassy Jakarta to US State Department, Oct. 28, 1965, POL 23-9 [INDON], NARA: "In other parts West Java Miltag officer just returned from Bandung reports villages clearing out PKI members and affiliates and turning them over to Army."

25. Telegram 18R, US Consulate Surabaya to US Embassy Jakarta, Nov. 21, 1965, POL 23-8 INDON, NARA.

26. Sundhaussen reports that the worst killings occurred in Subang, with an estimated five thousand deaths, or half of the total for the entire province. See Ulf Sundhaussen, *The Road to Power: Indonesian Military Politics, 1945–1967* (Oxford: Oxford University Press, 1982), 216–17.

27. See Yen-ling Tsai and Douglas Kammen, "Anti-Communist Violence and the Ethnic Chinese in Medan, North Sumatra," in *The Contours of Mass Violence in Indonesia, 1965–1968,* ed. Douglas Kammen and Katharine McGregor (Singapore: NUS Press for the Asian Studies Association of Australia, 2012).

28. Telegram 798A, US Embassy Jakarta to US State Department, Nov. 22, 1965, POL 12 INDON, NARA. A few days earlier, however, the US consulate in Medan had commented that although the "attitude [of] Pemuda Pantjasila leaders can only be described as bloodthirsty, while reports of wholesale killings may be greatly exaggerated, number and frequency of such reports plus attitude of youth leaders suggests that something like real reign of terror against PKI is taking place." See Telegram 391, US Consulate Medan to US Embassy Jakarta, Nov. 16, 1965, POL 23-9 INDON, NARA.

29. Telegram 1037A, US Consulate Medan to US Embassy Jakarta, Nov. 30, 1965, POL 23-9 [INDON], NARA. A civilian anti-communist leader told the US consul that he "is not rpt [repeat] not under direction of Army which he regards as too slow and too uncertain in their attack on PKI. He stated Army

had detained him for a week recently because he [was] suspected of complicity in unauthorized killings. He said he denied everything to Army authorities but was in fact responsible."

30. Telegram 991A, US Embassy Jakarta to US State Department, Dec. 29, 1965, POL 23-9 INDON, NARA.

31. Telegram 1403A, US Embassy Jakarta to US State Department, Oct. 30, 1965, POL 23-9 INDON, NARA.

32. Telegram 885A, US Embassy Jakarta to US State Department, Nov. 24, 1965, POL 23-9 INDON, NARA.

33. US embassy telegrams noted reports that by Dec. 8 three thousand PKI members/suspects had already been killed in West Bali. See Telegrams 386A and 685A, US Embassy Jakarta to US State Department, both Dec. 10, 1965, POL 23-9 INDON, NARA.

34. Oei Tjoe Tat, *Memoar Oei Tjoe Tat: Pembantu Presiden Sukarno* (Jakarta: Hasta Mitra, 1995), 186–87. Given that the killings were then at their peak, this figure fits well with subsequent estimates that eighty thousand were killed in Bali in 1965–66.

35. Airgram A-391, US Embassy Jakarta to US State Department, Dec. 9, 1965, POL 2 INDON, NARA.

36. Telegram 562A, US Embassy Jakarta to US State Department, Dec. 15, 1965, and Telegram 05RA, US Consulate Surabaya to US Embassy Jakarta, Dec. 16, 1965, both POL 23-9 INDON, NARA. Despite a wealth of evidence to the contrary, in a telegram to the secretary of state, US ambassador Green noted that the "military is deeply concerned over extensive killings of PKI suspects in East Java." See Telegram 33A, US Embassy Jakarta to Secretary of State, Dec. 1, 1965, POL 23-9 INDON, NARA.

37. See discussion in Geoffrey Robinson, *The Dark Side of Paradise* (Ithaca: Cornell University Press, 1995), 295–97.

38. Telegram 562A, US Embassy Jakarta to US State Department, Dec. 15, 1965, POL 23-9 INDON, NARA.

39. Crouch, *Army and Politics,* 158–96.

40. See Incoming Telegram 2819, US Embassy Jakarta to US State Department, Apr. 1, 1966, POL 2-1 INDON, NARA.

41. Downplaying this, Edward Masters, the political affairs officer at the US embassy in Jakarta, noted that "the traditional bickering among right-wing groups—cemented by fear and hatred of the PKI into the Army-religious coalition —has resumed, surprising many observers who have been dazzled by the scintillating cooperation of the anti-PKI front into forgetting the jealousies and hostilities endemic within the right-wing." See Airgram A-440, US Embassy to US State Department, Jan. 7, 1966, POL 2 INDON, NARA.

42. NU was particularly suspicious of the banned Masjumi, which had provided many of the most militant shock troops. See Airgram A-145, US Embassy Jakarta to US State Department, Sept. 24, 1966, POL 2 INDON, NARA.

43. Such clashes first occurred in early Dec. 1965 but became far more severe

in early 1966. See, e.g., Incoming Telegram 15R, Jan. 19, 1966, and Incoming Telegram 03R, Feb. 2, 1966, both US Consulate Surabaya to US Embassy Jakarta, POL 23-8 INDON, NARA.

44. Airgram A-16, US Consulate Medan to US Embassy Jakarta, Dec. 6, 1965, POL 2 INDON, NARA; J. B. Wright to British Embassy, Feb, 8, 1966, Records of the Foreign Office, 810-25, 1966, United Kingdom National Archive.

45. Incoming Telegram 222A, US Embassy Jakarta to US State Department, Mar. 7, 1966, POL 23-9 INDON, NARA.

46. Airgram A-444, US Embassy Jakarta to US State Department, Jan. 11, 1966, POL 2-1 INDON, NARA.

47. Narny Yenny, "Violence in the Anti-Communist Tragedy in West Sumatra" (paper presented at the conference "1965–1966 Indonesian Killings Revisited," June 17–19, 2009, Singapore).

48. Steven Farram, "The PKI in West Timor and Nusa Tenggara Timur, 1965 and Beyond" (paper presented at the conference "1965–1966 Indonesian Killings Revisited," June 17–19, 2009, Singapore).

49. See Jamie Davidson and Douglas Kammen, "Indonesia's Unknown War and the Lineages of Violence in West Kalimantan," *Indonesia,* no. 7 (Apr. 2002): 53–87.

50. On Blitar, see Vannessa Hearman, "South Blitar and the 1968 Trisula Operation," in Kammen and McGregor, *Contours of Mass Violence.* On Purwodadi and other areas in Java, see Triyana, "Peristiwa Purwodadi: Kasus Pembunuhan Massal Anggota dan Simpatisan Partai Komunis Indonesia di Kabupaten Grobogan Tahun 1965–1969" (BA thesis, Universitas Diponegoro, 2003).

51. John Roosa, "The September 30th Movement: The Aporias of the Official Narratives," in Kammen and McGregor, *Contours of Mass Violence.*

52. Benedict Anderson, "Introduction," in *Violence and the State in Suharto's Indonesia* (Ithaca: Cornell Southeast Asia Program, 2001), 13.

53. On the release of political prisoners, see Greg Fealy, "The Release of Indonesia's Political Prisoners: Domestic Versus Foreign Policy, 1975–1979" (Working Paper 94, Centre of Southeast Asian Studies, Monash University, 1994).

54. Suzannah Linton, "Accounting for Atrocities in Indonesia," *Singapore Year Book of International Law* 10 (2006): 202.

55. "Ketetapan MPR No. V/2000 tentang Pemantapan Persatuan dan Kesatuan Nasional," Aug. 18, 2000, http://sosialisasi.mpr.go.id/mpr/arsip/ketetapan/putusan%20MPRRI%202000.pdf.

56. "Undang Undang Republik Indonesia Nomor 27 Tahun 2004 tentang Komisi Kebenaran dan Rekonsiliasi," *Tambahan Lembara Negara Republik Indonesia,* no. 4429 (2004).

57. Yudhoyono is married to a daughter of Sarwo Edhie Wibowo, the commander of the army Paracommando Regiment that oversaw the pogroms in Central Java and Bali in 1965–66 and subsequently regional military commander in North Sumatra and Irian Jaya.

58. See Perry Anderson, "Two Revolutions: Rough Notes," *New Left Review,* no. 61 (Jan.–Feb. 2010): 91–92.

7

Getting Away with Murder in Thailand

State Violence and Impunity in Phatthalung

Tyrell Haberkorn

> Every side, every circle, wants one thing only: to conceal the
> wickedness. This will make it possible to continue to kill, and
> then deny that it is real.
> — Yotthong Thabtiumai, *Thang Daeng, Na Sai, Ko. Oo. Ro.*
> *Mo. No., Phraratchabandit To Tan Kommunit*

In February 1975, student activists exposed a series of brutal murders of
citizens by the Communist Suppression Operations Command (CSOC)
and other state security forces that had taken place two and a half years
earlier in Phatthalung province in Thailand.[1] The *thang daeng*, or "red
drum," killings gained their name from the method of killing employed.
Accused of engaging in communist activities or tacit support for them,
citizens were arrested, or simply taken, in large sweeps across districts
throughout the province and brought to detention camps for interrogation. While some detainees were released after being interrogated, others
were tortured and then killed. At night, after being beaten until uncon-

scious or with irons around their necks, individual citizens were placed into empty two-hundred-liter oil drums at the edge of the detention camps, doused in oil, and then burned alive. While the bodies were burning, truck engines were revved to partially mask the screams of those who were being murdered. The engines only partially masked the evidence of what was occurring, because those who survived recalled both the screams and the sounds of the engines. Villagers and students estimated that several thousand people in Phatthalung, perhaps as many as three thousand, were killed as alleged communists in this manner.

Between February and March 1975, the killings became open knowledge as details of them, sometimes conflicting, were brought to light in newspapers and at public events. Nearly every day for two months, most major Thai newspapers carried extensive coverage of the exposure of the thang daeng killings, including the testimonies of survivors and of the families of those who were killed and the varied state responses to the exposure.[2] This information then became the foundation for debate as survivors, students, and state officials discussed and disagreed about what should be done in the aftermath of the killings. When the thang daeng killings were perpetrated in late 1972, the dictatorial and severely anti-communist regime of Field Marshal Thanom Kittikachorn, Field Marshal Praphat Jarusathien, and Colonel Narong Kittikachorn ensured that there was no public outcry or opposition. In sharp contrast, the public exposure of the killings occurred during the brief period of democratic politics and increased political participation from all sectors of society that began with the end of dictatorship, with the October 14, 1973, movement.[3]

While the open murder of citizens was possible under a dictatorship, within the context of open politics, survivors and student activists demanded that the state officially investigate the killings, and the state was forced to respond. In mid-February 1975, the minister of the interior, Atthasit Sitthisunthorn, created a committee to investigate the allegations; Atthasit claimed that if state officials had acted improperly, then they would be punished according to the law.[4] But a little over a month later, when the committee concluded that state officials had acted improperly, they were not punished. The summary of the investigation released to the press stated that yes, innocent citizens had been killed in thang daeng, but only seventy or eighty people were involved, rather than thousands. No one was punished, and the work of the Internal Security Operations Command (ISOC), which replaced the CSOC in 1973, continued as usual.[5] Over thirty years later, the ISOC remains active in protecting the nebulously defined "national security" of Thailand; questions continue to be raised about the precise role of ISOC within the Thai military and security apparatus and where the protection of human rights falls in their policies and actions.

While the exposure by students and villagers was marked, and made possible, by the events of October 14, 1973, the Ministry of the Interior investigation perhaps foreshadowed the return to dictatorship that came a year and a half later in the form of the October 6, 1976, massacre and coup.[6] Yet for a variety of reasons, and heralding the production of impunity that contributed to making it possible for unarmed students to be killed in broad daylight on October 6, 1976, the calls for state accountability for the thang daeng killings were silenced and then refuted by the 1975 Ministry of the Interior report.

In *Unsettling Accounts: Neither Truth nor Reconciliation in Confessions of State Violence*, Leigh Payne examines state confessions in four nations—Chile, South Africa, Brazil, and Argentina—undergoing both democratization and a range of judicial processes focused on past violence. Payne argues that "confessions do not settle accounts with the past; rather, they unsettle them."[7] Public discussion and telling of what happened does not create a single truth about the past but instead facilitates what she calls "contentious coexistence." This mode of being and relating socially and politically in the aftermath of violence "rejects infeasible official and healing truth in favor of multiple and contending truths that reflect different political viewpoints in society" and "is stimulated by dramatic stories, actors, or images that provoke widespread participation, contestation over prevailing political viewpoints, and competition over ideas. Contentious coexistence, in other words, is democracy in action."[8] Payne's analysis is provocative and hopeful, suggesting that it is precisely at the moment that past state violence becomes public, even when denied by perpetrators, that it becomes challengeable by citizens. It is this sense of possibility that makes contentious coexistence a part of democratization. Yet what happens when exposure of past violence and confessions of state involvement occur not during a period of democratization, but while a nation is precariously perched between democracy and dictatorship and hurtling toward dictatorship? Is it possible that then exposure, discussion, and ultimately a lack of accountability contribute to the production of increased impunity, manifested in the failure to stop the violent actions of state officials and hold them accountable?

This question is the point of departure for the remainder of this chapter. Forty years after the killings occurred, what is known about them remains plagued by inconsistencies, lacunae, and a persistent lack of resolution. The duration of the killings is unknown, although survivor and family accounts cite August 7, 1972, as the beginning of the arrests. The number of people who disappeared and were murdered varies widely, with some state officials estimating approximately eighty deaths and student activists instead estimating three thousand deaths. Most troubling, the precise nature of state involvement—including units, motivation, actions, and recordkeeping—remains obscured. The involvement of the Thai monarchy, even at the level of knowledge of the killings, remains obscured and unquestionable given the sanctions raised by the specter of Article 112 of the Thai Criminal Code (the lese majeste law). At a minimum, these questions will require the Thai state to make its documents about the killings available.[9] State documents related to the killings, including the 1975 report, remain unavailable in the National Archives of Thailand.

In Vince Boudreau's terms (see chapter 1, this volume), the thang daeng killings and the subsequent failure to secure accountability were examples of both instrumental and exemplary violence. The public production of impunity served as both an event silencing dissent and a pedagogical reminder to dissident (and nondissident) citizens of the lack of paths for redress and justice open to them. My contention in the case of the thang daeng killings in Phatthalung province is not only that the public exposure of the killings, and subsequent failure to hold state actors accountable, led to the further consolidation of impunity, but that an end to impunity can, and perhaps must, begin with understanding this process. This means tracing how the thang daeng killings were exposed, how state officials publicly responded, and how the decision not to take action to hold officials responsible emerged. In so doing, questions of how citizen fear of violence at the hands of state actors is consolidated, how state actors systematically evade responsibility, and ultimately how justice is foreclosed come to the surface.

Perhaps surprisingly, given that a blanket restriction on the release of documents pertinent to "national security" means that state documents related to the thang daeng killings in 1972 will not be publicly available in the foreseeable future, there *are* documents in the National Archives that can aid in this endeavor. In particular, there is a file of news clippings about the exposure in 1975, comprising three folders containing a total of 149 pages of news coverage about "the work of the Internal Security Operations Command and the case of thang daeng" (kan damnoen ngan khong amnuaeykan raksa khwam mankhong phai nai lae karani thang daeng).[10] The presence in the National Archives of the thang daeng file, which is a document of inaction and what was *not* done, provides a sliver of hope. The Thai state records and preserves the public accounting of its inaction, even as its own documents are unavailable for survivors, scholars, and others concerned about the thang daeng killings. Before turning to the exposure, I begin with the stories of Teacher Lim and Teacher Ploy, which I summarized from reports in *Thai Rat,* the largest-circulation daily Thai-language newspaper, contained in one of the folders.

TEACHER LIM

On August 7, 1972, Lim Phaosen, a teacher in Phatthalung province, was taken from his home and never returned. Teacher Lim left the house in the morning to go observe a school in another district as part of his work as the acting head teacher in his village. While he was out, an army soldier came looking for him. His mother-in-law, Kloy Ketsang, said he was not home and told the soldier to come back later. The soldier searched and found Teacher Lim in the other district and forced him to come with him. He took Teacher Lim home and asked him to change his clothes, as he was wearing a sarong, and then took him to a nearby army camp to meet his superiors. Chaweewan, Teacher Lim's eight-year-old daughter, was home from school while this series of events occurred and pleaded with the soldier not to take her father away. Chaweewan and her grandmother cried and asked the soldier to let them come to the camp too, but he refused. When Khruawan, Teacher Lim's wife, arrived home in the evening, she became immediately concerned. Teacher Lim suffered from chronic illness and had not taken his medication with him. But the soldier had not given Kloy or Chaweewan information on where precisely he was taking Teacher Lim.

Chom Kaewpong, another man from Teacher Lim's village, was taken on August 7, 1972, as well, but he was released a few days later. Chom told Khruawan that he had seen Teacher Lim at the camp where he was held. She quickly prepared a supply of medicine for Teacher Lim and rushed to the stated camp. When she arrived at the army camp where Chom had been held and released, the soldiers told her that they had not arrested Teacher Lim and that he was not there. Khruawan then went from camp to camp in Phatthalung but did not find Teacher Lim or anyone who had information about him. She went to neighboring Songkhla and Pattani provinces but was still unable to find her husband. Finally, she learned from a survivor of Thachiet camp that he had been burned in a thang daeng. The same person told her that Teacher Lim had been killed because he opposed the corrupt dealings of a locally influential person who wanted a contract to build a new school. Teacher Lim had been a civil servant for over ten years, but Khruawan was unable to obtain his death benefit or even his last month's salary. The reason: there was no body, no death certificate.[11]

TEACHER PLOY

Ploy Prap-in, age thirty-nine, was a teacher who narrowly escaped the thang daeng in Phatthalung. On August 10, 1972, he was taken and stuffed with others from his village into a GMC truck and transported to Thachiet army camp. In language reminiscent of earlier and later periods of extrajudicial detention, Teacher Ploy was told that he was not being arrested but was "invited" (*choen*) to the camp. Once one is arrested (*chap*), certain procedures and record-keeping mechanisms must be followed under Thai law. "Invitation" is a slippery linguistic trick of obfuscation. If Teacher Ploy was "invited," it was an invitation without the possibility of refusal.

Upon arrival at Thachiet, officials accused Teacher Ploy of working with his colleague Teacher Lim to foment unrest. They were allegedly going to make Xeroxes of tracts from the Peoples' Liberation Army of Phatthalung to distribute in the market. Then they were going to burn government buildings, including a health center, and kill army soldiers and Village Defense Volunteers. At the close of this interrogation, Teacher Ploy was told that if he did not confess to these crimes, then he would be killed in a thang daeng. A soldier took Teacher Ploy to a large tent at the edge of the camp. He saw blood staining the ground near the tent. When he entered the tent, he saw over sixty villagers, many of them with obvious marks of torture on their bodies. Teacher Ploy was interrogated every day while at Thachiet. His fellow villagers told him that if you were called for interrogation at night, then you were going to be killed. The villagers told Teacher Ploy that even though the soldiers guarding the tent told those who left at night that they were being released, this was not true. Instead, people were forced to sign a statement confirming that they were being released, and then they were killed. Every night those inside the tent saw the fires as the oil and bodies in the thang daeng burned.

On his fifth night in the tent, Teacher Ploy was taken to be interrogated. He was forced to sign a paper stating he had been released. Then, a high-ranking officer came into the room and said that he was innocent and to take him back to the tent. Teacher Ploy was held for seven more days. During those days, he underwent "training" (*kan fuek obrom*) in the camp. He was very surprised to see himself in documents distributed by trainers from the CSOC. Apparently he and Teacher Lim had turned themselves into the CSOC and confessed to planning to distribute communist documents and destroy government property. He had neither turned himself in nor confessed. After his release, Teacher Ploy remained afraid but felt lucky to be alive and returned to work.[12]

THE ARBITRARY BOUNDARY BETWEEN VILLAGERS AND COMMUNISTS

The thang daeng killings unfolded in a part of Thailand that is remote, marked by relatively difficult terrain, and with a persistently violent history. Phatthalung is located in southern Thailand, bordered by Trang, Nakhon Sri Thammarat, and Songkhla provinces. The province is contained within the Fourth Army Region, which has a long record of presiding over the violation of the rights of citizens in the service of alleged counterinsurgency during the 1970s and alleged counterterrorism since 2004.[13]

When thinking about the thang daeng killings, whether there was an actual communist insurgency in Phatthalung is not an issue. There *was* an insurgency, and Phatthalung later became a stronghold of the Communist Party of Thailand (CPT). Instead, what is of concern is understanding how violence emerged in response to both actual insurgency and a fear of unbridled possible insurgency. What is of concern is how people were killed as communists even when they were not and understanding how it became possible to blur the line between communist and ordinary

villager. What is of concern is how it became state policy, official or unofficial, to arbitrarily select people to be brutally killed and destroyed.

Although the thang daeng killings took place over a period of months
beginning in August 1972, both CPT activity and repression of villagers by state officials began many years earlier in Phatthalung. Many of
the inhabitants of Phatthalung are rubber tappers, and John Dennis
argues that the physical characteristics of Phatthalung, as well as the
rubber tappers' connections with the global market, may have helped
the CPT develop there.[14] The CPT became active in Phatthalung province and neighboring Trang province in southern Thailand in 1963.[15] In
1963, several hundred police and army officers conducted mass arrests
of over two hundred people, including lawyers and teachers. Within two
months, almost all of those arrested were released due to a lack of evidence sufficient to bring official charges of communism against them.[16]
Then, in 1964, in a conflict between a policeman and alleged communists, an alleged communist was killed and the policeman injured. Writing about the events in the years leading up to the thang daeng killings,
Thanet Aphornsuvan cites this event as the beginning of intensified violence against villagers—communist or not—in Phatthalung.[17] When one
reporter asked people in Phatthalung why they had joined the CPT, they
responded that "it all began when the people in the province decided they
were not receiving proper welfare and just treatment from government
servants." The same reporter estimated that by 1971, six hundred communists were active in Phatthalung.[18]

In 1971, Field Marshal Praphat Jarusathien, one of the three ruling
dictators in power until the October 14, 1973, movement, claimed that
within six months all traces of communists and communism would be
eradicated from Thailand.[19] One particularly proactive response to this
statement came from a teacher and Village Defense Volunteer from Khaochaison district in Phatthalung, Yongyut Dusithamo.[20] Teacher Yongyut
recruited a group of young men and instructed them to re-create the
appearance of having fought with communists. Thirteen young men were
given five guns and twenty bullets per night. After 9 P.M. every evening,
they shot the guns into the air and ran through the rice fields, trampling
the stalks and destroying the rice. Teacher Yongyut also provided chick-
ens for them to kill to create blood-laced messy evidence of their encounters with the communists. This nightly killing of a chicken was necessary
since the alleged communists were not real. With the chicken blood as

evidence of their presence, the young men could report that the communists always fled. After using their allotted bullets, the young men ran to tell the nearest village headman in a given area that they had fought the communists, but the communists had escaped.[21]

Teacher Yongyut and his fellow Village Defense Volunteers used similar strategies to produce a logic in which there was both a formidable communist presence in Phatthalung as well as a need for their increased financial support. Through their nightly fights with a chicken, his volunteers produced an idea of communists so fierce that they always escaped, unstoppable even when wounded. If this many communists allegedly existed and needed to be eliminated, but did not really exist, then who would be killed in their place?

One answer is in how the thang daeng killings unfolded. While a range of experiences are described in the various thang daeng accounts, common to all is a high degree of arbitrariness. Villagers were asked to inform state officials about who among their neighbors and colleagues was a communist. In some cases, this was an informal process, and in others, villagers were actually placed on the payroll of the CSOC as spies. One could end up on the communist blacklist due to a dispute over an unrelated issue with a neighbor; the blacklist became a way of eliminating one's enemy.[22] *Actually* being a communist was not a requirement for being taken, and reports indicate that the first to be arrested were those who knew about the corrupt, abusive actions of state officials, such as Teacher Lim. Within this context, personal connections could function to lead to either one's death or one's survival, as in the respective cases of Teacher Lim and Teacher Ploy. Aside from the use of blacklists, in many villages there were mass arrests. A large number of people would be arrested in a sweeping operation, and then those deemed to be innocent would be released after being interrogated.[23] Those who witnessed the operations reported that a large number of security officials—fifty to sixty in the middle of the night or one hundred during the day—surrounded the house of the alleged communist.[24]

Upon arrival at the camp, detainees were accused, similar to Teacher Ploy, of plotting and/or committing crimes against the Thai state. In the days that followed their initial detentions, many detainees were interrogated multiple times and frequently tortured. Villagers who were taken and those close to people who were taken reported that forms of torture used during interrogation included electric shock, withholding food, and being beaten and kicked in the chest and head until one passed out.[25] Through-out the period of detention, any physical torture was accompanied by fear of the possibility of what would happen when the security forces ceased their interrogation. Would one be released, like Chom Kaewpong and Teacher Ploy? Or would one be killed in a thang daeng, like Teacher Lim?

Exposing the Thang Daeng Killings

After the October 14, 1973, movement ousted the ruling dictatorial tri-umvirate of Field Marshal Thanom Kittikachorn, Field Marshal Praphat Jarusathien, and Colonel Narong Kittikachorn, King Bhumipol Aduly-adej appointed Sanya Thammasak, rector of Thammasat University, as the interim prime minister. The first elections during the period of open politics were finally set for January 26, 1975. In the weeks and months preceding the election, many student activists traveled throughout the country spreading information on democracy and talking with people about how to participate in politics. While doing this work in south-ern Thailand, Phinij Jarusombat, the head of the political wing of the National Student Center of Thailand (NSCT), heard stories of the thang daeng killings from villagers he met. From Chachoengsao province in the central region, Phinij was a fourth-year law student at Ramkhamhaeng University, the open university in Bangkok. After hearing about sweeping arrests, detention, torture, and killings in the thang daeng, Phinij wanted to investigate to have a fuller picture of what had happened in 1972 in Phatthalung province. When he returned to Bangkok, he brought the issue to his colleagues in the NSCT.[26]

The NSCT and the United Front against Dictatorship (UF), a pro-gressive network of students and nonstudents alike, formed a committee in early February to study and then disseminate information about thang daeng to the public. Their logic was that this was not an isolated case and that the Thai people needed to know what had happened during the time of the previous dictatorship.[27] In the month that followed, the NSCT and the UF brought villagers from Phatthalung to Bangkok and then sent a delegation of students, doctors, and journalists from Bangkok to Phat-thalung. The intention of bringing villagers from Phatthalung to Bang-kok was to create the opportunity for survivors of thang daeng to directly share their experiences with the people and the media. Then, they were going to meet with the newly elected government of Seni Pramoj to decide how to create justice for the survivors and families of those who had been killed or had disappeared. Finally, while the villagers were in Bangkok, the NSCT and the UF intended for them to meet with General Kris Sivara, the commander of the army, to figure out how to ensure the safety of the villagers, because they remained afraid of state security forces.[28] Then the delegation from Bangkok would use its time in Phatthalung to compile as much specific information about the thang daeng case as possible to present to the government.

Public Testimonies and National Demands

The NSCT planned an event on Sanam Luang, a public grassy space and frequent site of protests across the street from Thammasat University in the heart of Bangkok, as the centerpiece of its exposure of the thang daeng killings. In preparation for the event, Phinij Jarusombat and a group of villagers, including Abdulmanee Abdullah, a former CSOC employee, and Samart Rakradej, a village headman who had helped the NSCT organize the collection of evidence and the names of people killed in thang daeng, met with the prime minister and other state officials to inform them of their plans.[29] Together with the Socialist Party of Thailand (Phak Sangkhomniyom Haeng Prathet Thai, or SPT), the NSCT called for the dissolution of the ISOC.[30] The SPT viewed the ISOC as "creating great suffering for the people and the most vile criminal."[31]

Even before the event on Sanam Luang, villagers in Phatthalung who intended to speak out became the targets of criticism and threats. On February 9, a group of NSCT activists went to Phatthalung because the villagers planning to come to Bangkok had been threatened by four unknown figures (*khon luek lap*) who followed and threatened them, telling them "to not bring the issue to the public in Bangkok."[32] On February 10, there were reports of a murky declaration (*talaengkan mued*) saying that the conduct of the students was "a violation of the law and a dishonoring of Thai people" that would create chaos.[33] Yet what law was being violated by the exposure of state violence, and *who* stood to be dishonored by its exposure? While it is tempting to discard this statement solely as an inaccurate attempt by those against the exposure to discredit the individuals involved, taking it seriously reveals the existence of multiple layers of impunity. The *law* that was being violated was not one contained within the criminal or civil code, but rather the unchecked, unquestioned power of the state. By bringing to light what happened during the thang daeng killings, students made this latent law visible. If anything was being dishonored, it was the image of the ISOC and other state actors as protectors of the citizens.

Despite these threats, the NSCT, the UF, and the SPT continued with plans for the event on Sanam Luang. On February 14, at 4 p.m., there was a (Hyde Park–style) public hearing, entitled "Report of killing the people by throwing them into a red barrel and burning them," which was attended by over twenty thousand people.[34] Approximately thirty villagers from Phatthalung traveled with Samart Rakradej back to Bangkok to attend the event, and nineteen spoke about their own and their families' experiences of thang daeng.[35] One villager who came to Bangkok said that they had called on officials in Phatthalung before, but no action had been taken. This had "caused many people to feel afraid up until today."[36] Although those participating in the event on Sanam Luang were full of fear, this villager, joining with others, suggested that participation was also transformative.

In what might be read as a response to the allegation that students were violating the law, Sutham Saengprathum, a student leader, explained during the event that "the majority of Thai people believe in religion. [We have] laws that people who act wrongly are judged via a judicial process. But when the administrative class makes themselves those who decide (justice), the life of the people has no meaning."[37] Sutham's idea of law was one with no space for the unchecked power of the state. *Everyone* was subject to the same judicial process. On Sanam Luang, two demands were articulated: to dissolve the ISOC and to compensate those whose family members had been killed. The ISOC was identified as the common thread across the various accounts of terror in Phatthalung. While most of those who came to Sanam Luang supported the exposure of the thang daeng killings, a small number of members of Krathing Daeng, one of the right-wing parastate groups active in Thailand between 1973 and 1976, also attended the event.[38]

A day later, the two demands were lengthened into six:

1. For the government to protect the people of Phatthalung who have brought the issue out into the open, including both those who have spoken out about the issue and those who have called on the government to accept responsibility.
2. For the government to compensate people whose relatives were killed and people who were tortured by state officials.

3. For the government to remove soldiers and Village Defense Volunteers.
4. For the government to punish officials who acted in excess of the law.
5. For the ISOC to be dissolved.
6. For the Anti-Communist Activities Act to be repealed.[39]

The new set of demands went beyond identifying the ISOC as the perpetrator of the killings and asking for compensation to addressing the broader context of fear and the dangers of counterinsurgency. With the extended set of demands, the issue of holding the many different actors involved accountable also came to the fore. On February 15, the Phatthalung villagers met Minister of the Interior Atthasit Sitthisunthorn at his home in Bangkok. When presented with the demands, he said that "this is the first time he had received an official complaint about the case" and "that although no official protest had been lodged it is the duty of the provincial authorities to take the 'serious matter' up as soon as possible."[40] Since almost three years had passed since the killings took place, Atthasit believed that a period of study and research was needed before a response to the six demands could be made.[41] By the end of the month Atthasit had commissioned an official report on thang daeng to be carried out by the Ministry of the Interior, but his response to the demands led to the proliferation of other responses and rumors. One of these rumors cited an unnamed source within the army who said that an internal report commissioned by General Kris claimed that "government troops were 'used' by village headman to kill 16 personal enemies in a rival group," the parties engaged in rivalry over "mining and sexual relations issues." Ten additional people had allegedly been arrested in that sweep but then released.[42] While it is impossible to confirm whether this particular account is true, many within the state itself did confirm that arrests were arbitrary and based on personal conflicts in a given village or district. As students, doctors, and journalists prepared to travel to Phatthalung, rumors proliferated, and tensions in Bangkok and the south increased.

THE DANGERS OF SPEAKING ABOUT VIOLENCE

While a range of state officials reacted negatively to the events exposing the thang daeng killings in both Bangkok and Phatthalung, the lengths to which they went to attempt to stem the exposure in Phatthalung was dramatic. Abdulmanee Abdullah, a villager from Phatthalung who had worked with the ISOC prior to thang daeng but then resigned and later joined the efforts to expose the killings, commented that those who dared speak about the events lived in a "kingdom of fear" (anachak haeng khwamklua).[43] Abdulmanee and others who joined the exposure were threatened and followed by assassins.[44] Members of the security forces who were perpetrators during the thang daeng killings clearly did not expect that their actions would become the object of public scrutiny and stood to potentially suffer if they did. If the reaction to the exposure and those who spoke out can be read as diagnostic of the dangers of speaking out, the risks increased as the exposure moved from Bangkok back to Phatthalung itself. In other words, it may have been more dangerous to break silence locally, where the killings occurred, than in the national center of Bangkok. As the exposure, and the reaction to it, began in Bangkok and moved south a few weeks later, the right wing inside and outside the Thai state was gathering force. The increasingly violent reaction to the exposure of the thang daeng killings was both caused by and indicative of the disappearing space for dissent in Thailand in mid-1975.

These risks did not stop people from speaking, however, and shortly after the NSCT began its exposure, a group of Phatthalung villagers told the newspaper *Daily Time* of their willingness to be witnesses if the state decided to investigate. They shared their addresses and names with the newspaper, which then published the information. Mr. Somnuksang, a lawyer, told *Daily Time* about his brother, Mr. Chamsangkaew, who had been accused of allegedly supporting the CPT in 1972. He was interrogated and harangued by the village headman in front of his fellow villagers while Chamrat Mahapol, the provincial head of the CSOC, watched from the sidelines. One month later, CSOC officials came to find Mr. Chamsangkaew, but he had already fled to Bangkok. Mr. Banjong Khaekpheng, a teacher, had been taken and investigated by the CSOC for allegedly fomenting bad feelings against officials among villagers and being a communist during the time of thang daeng. Like Teacher Ploy, he was recognized by one of the CSOC officials and released from the tent before he was killed in a thang daeng. Mr. Kawisak Oonruang, a lawyer, had heard a loud noise outside his door while he was sleeping. He thought the noise was a villager with a problem. When he opened the door, he was surprised to see a group of sixty CSOC officials and Village Defense

Volunteers. Mr. Kawisak started to close the door, but one of the CSOC officials accused him of trying to flee as a dirty communist. Mr. Kawisak was not taken to an army camp but interrogated in the field of the local headman. Many people whom he had helped, or sat and chatted with while drinking, were there as Village Defense Volunteers, so one of them told the CSOC to release him. When they came forward with their stories in February 1975, all three were ready to be witnesses.[45]

Immediately after the event on Sanam Luang, the NSCT and the UF formed a committee to organize their trip to Phatthalung to interview people like Mr. Kawisak, Mr. Banjong, and Mr. Somnuksang. They went to speak with General Kris about their planned trip and to ask for cooperation from the army and the ISOC, as one of the other rumors circulating in mid-February was that soldiers were going to shoot at students if they came to the south. General Kris assured the NSCT committee that they would be safe in Phatthalung.[46] The trip was set for February 17–22; journalists from *Athipat, Prachathipatai, Prachachaat, Daily Time, Thai Rat, Bangkok Post,* and an international news wire service were also planning to join the expedition.[47] A total of sixty students, with representatives from Chulalongkorn University, Thammasat University, Mahidol University, and Ramkhamhaeng University, were going to split into six groups to visit different regions of the province. Two members of each group were medical students from Mahidol University, who would provide services for villagers lacking access to public health centers.[48] The primary purposes of the trip were to support villages who were courageously speaking out, to gather evidence and the names of people who had been killed or disappeared during the thang daeng killings, and to build networks to continue working for justice on the issue.[49] In a broader sense, the NSCT planned to use the trip as an opportunity to learn about additional problems faced by villagers in Phatthalung and southern Thailand.[50]

Yet from the moment of their arrival in Phatthalung, members of the delegation met with resistance from local officials despite the alleged cooperation that they were to receive.[51] Asa Monkholsiri, a district officer, was one of the loudest voices interfering with the NSCT delegation. Soon Khamnurak, whose three nephews had died in thang daeng, said that Asa Monkholsiri had called a district meeting on February 20 and told everyone present not to believe the newspapers. Instead, they should only believe village headmen and other state officials. Soon noted that Asa had "said that the students were going to incite us to go to the jungle. They did not come to spread democracy. If we didn't believe him, we would suffer more."[52] Another report alleged that Asa had given villagers food, clothing, and other items and told them to keep quiet about thang daeng.[53] Asa told *Prachathipatai* newspaper that he had not told people not to talk to the students. During his time as district officer, only two young children had come to see him about relatives who allegedly disappeared during the thang daeng killings. At the same time, however, he said that the news about thang daeng was a strategy of the CPT to convince people to go to the jungle.[54]

When the students arrived in Ban Phut subdistrict, Asa turned his warnings into action. He used a megaphone to attack the students, his verbal intimidation matched by the presence of fifty armed soldiers. Asa and the soldiers finally left at 5 P.M., and students then organized a debate and discussion. Many villagers spoke; the conclusion was that at least two hundred people had been killed in Ban Phut. Saphak Panui, who had worked as a patroller for the army in 1972, said that typically seven or eight people were killed each evening. He said that the soldiers drank while they killed people and as the bodies burned.[55]

Asa Mongkholsiri was not the only person who acted against the NSCT investigation. One deputy district officer, Surinthorn (last name unknown), told villagers that the students had come to agitate and advised against talking to them. In particular, he claimed that if they talked to students, "it will cause [our] homeland to become chaotic and return to dictatorship again."[56] Posters were put up saying that students should leave and go back to studying and reading books.[57] When students went to one village in Khaochaison district, they saw a poster that stated: "Dear children, commit yourselves to studying. Don't create divisions. Now they live together peacefully already."[58] In another part of Phatthalung, students faced accusations that they had come to burn down the market and incite the people to riot.[59]

Given the intimidation and harassment the NSCT delegation faced, Phinij Jarusombat estimated that it only covered one-tenth of the affected communities. Despite the difficulties, the delegation's members collected the names of 809 people who had been killed or who had disappeared during the thang daeng killings.[60] Perhaps unintentionally, the efforts of Asa Mongkholsiri and others to silence villagers and intimidate the NSCT delegation signaled the need for exposure. These efforts can be seen as a form of denial of wrongdoing, in which "perpetrators acknowledge the stories of victims and survivors and challenge the regime's jus-tifications."[61] If the stories of thang daeng did not matter, why would Asa give villagers free goods in an attempt to silence them? Why would sol-diers be willing to spend the day watching as Asa yelled at students? Why would posters be made and put up in communities telling students to go back to reading books, rather than seeking knowledge of recent vio-lence? And what forms of violence and intimidation against those who spoke out did not make it into the newspaper and other reports about the exposure?

What was at stake, it seems, was not only the issue of the facts of the thang daeng killings itself, but the capacity of the security forces to control life in a broader sense in Phatthalung. The importance of this was particularly clear in how state officials invested in keeping the kill-ings hidden reacted to state officials who joined the exposure efforts. For example, Chamlong Porndetch, appointed as the governor of Phatthalung province in early 1975, came into constant conflict with the head of ISOC for the province as well as certain district-level officials in Phatthalung. As soon as news of the NSCT/UF's exposure of the thang daeng killings emerged in early February 1975, Chamlong expressed his desire to learn more about the events, which had occurred before he became governor. Upon arrival in Phatthalung, he was made very aware that the people were afraid.[62] Chamlong told Phinij Jarusombat and the NSCT that "I have heard news about this kind of assassination of the people. But I don't have witnesses or evidence, because the people are terrified. They are afraid to talk openly with civil servants about it."[63] While Chamlong supported the exposure, his colleagues fought, openly and secretly, to put a halt both to the exposure and to his involvement in it. In mid-1975, after facing death threats and constant harassment, Chamlong asked the Ministry of the Interior to transfer him from Phatthalung to another province. Rather than being uniform, state responses to the exposure of the thang daeng killings were widely divergent. Some actors, such as Asa Mongkholsiri, were vehemently against the exposure, while others, Chamlong included, risked their position and even personal safety to push for further inves-tigation. In a different political moment, perhaps when Thailand was not hurtling toward a return to dictatorship, Chamlong Porndetch and his allies might have been able to force the emergence of accountability within the Ministry of the Interior or the state security apparatus that it attempted to monitor. Yet in mid-1975, his position within the bureaucracy was not even secure enough to keep him safe from threats. If state officials who dissent can be threatened or forced to resign or flee for their lives, what can happen to ordinary citizens?

THE PRODUCTION OF IMPUNITY

From the very beginning of the exposure of the thang daeng killings, citizens and state officials offered a range of often contradictory statements, what Payne calls "unsettling accounts," that created "political competition over how to interpret dramatic political events, how to use them, and what they mean for contemporary political life."[64] In a time of democracy, competition over interpretation of a violent past may "not end by killing off democracy or saving it. Instead, it puts into practice the art of competition over ideas and the possibility of building consensus around democratic values."[65] But extrajudicial violence was on the rise in Thailand in mid-1975, and public airing of the debate became an opportunity to demonstrate the sheer vulnerability of those who spoke out.

When he met with villagers who came to Bangkok, Interior Minister Atthasit said that a committee would be formed to investigate the allegations and that if state officials had acted improperly, then they would be held accountable.[66] The Ministry of the Interior could call any former and current employees to Bangkok for questioning, but it had to ask the Ministry of Defense for permission to investigate members of the army.[67] Viang Sakornsin, inspector general for the southern area, was appointed to head up a two-person committee to investigate all sides of the killings.[68] Viang and the second committee member, Montri Trangan, were given seven days to carry out their investigation.[69] In late March, the summary of the investigation released to the press stated that although innocent citizens had been killed in thang daeng, the number was much smaller than that offered by students and villagers. Rather than thousands, only seventy or eighty people had been killed. The report concluded that there should be no punishment of state actors because it would cause them to feel discouraged in their important work of fighting insurgency.[70] The ISOC could not be dissolved because it was needed to continue fighting insurgency. While the Anti-Communist Activities Act gave state officials license to arbitrarily arrest and detain suspected communists with a minimum of evidence, arbitrary murder was not legal. Shortly after a summary of the report (the report itself remained inside the Ministry of the Interior) was released, the NSCT criticized the hidden nature of the report and the apparent protection of wrongdoing by state actors.[71]

The assertion that state actors should not be punished for murdering citizens because punishment might make them feel discouraged recalls another contradictory acknowledgment of violence and refusal of accountability by a state actor. Police Major Anan Senakhan, a maverick and often inconsistent figure vis-à-vis progressive politics in the mid-1970s, publicly acknowledged in early February 1975 that the thang daeng killings had occurred. In 1972, he had been responsible for collecting and distributing the police news from the southern region, so he was aware of the sweeping arrests and killings. Anan disputed the number of people killed, arguing that it was not three thousand but approximately three hundred. He personally knew two people who had been killed. Yet despite this knowledge, Anan urged people not to think of soldiers as monsters lacking humanity. Instead, he urged people to see that they were "people who love the homeland too, we should give our sympathy to them too."[72] The difficulty with this is that if perpetrators are not held responsible, then they are the *only* ones who receive compassion. Without accountability for perpetrators, compassion for survivors of torture and for those who died in the thang daeng killings lacks meaning. Shortly before the release of the summary of the Ministry of the Interior report, a new government headed by Kukrit Pramoj, Seni's brother, came into power. Kukrit decided not to give compensation to the villagers, likely in order to not displease the counterinsurgency and the broader military apparatus.[73] As 1975 wore on, overt intimidation and violence against progressive activists increased; while the NSCT inquired as to how the Kukrit government was going to address the thang daeng killings, it was unable to force Kukrit to take action.

Benedict Anderson argues that what makes the October 6, 1976, massacre, which occurred a year and a half after the thang daeng killings were exposed, different from earlier state violence in Thailand is that it was "the culmination of a two-year-long right-wing campaign of public intimidation, assault and assassination best symbolized by the orchestrated mob violence of October 6 itself."[74] For example, rather than being hidden from public view, the assassinations of farmers, workers, and students often took place in broad daylight, as neighbors watched.[75] The exposure of the thang daeng killings, the calls for state accountability, and ultimately the foreclosure of the possibility of accountability were part of a resonant and complementary process. Through the exposure of the thang daeng killings, citizens across Thailand learned about the precise extent of what could be done to them by security forces if they became real or perceived enemies of the state. They also learned that even after broad public exposure, including a large demonstration in the center of Bangkok and high-profile meetings among survivors, activists, the commander of the army, and the prime minister, it was possible that no one would be held accountable for the violence. They learned that the committee appointed by the state could acknowledge that there had been wrongdoing by security forces and then decide against punishing those security forces.

What is most troubling about the thang daeng killings is not that they occurred and were never brought to light, but rather that they occurred, were exposed, and were investigated and confirmed by the state—which then chose to do nothing. I noted earlier that at the beginning of exposure of the killings, Sutham Saengprathum stated, "[We have] laws that people who act wrongly are judged via a judicial process. But when the administrative class makes themselves those who decide (justice), the lives of the people have no meaning."[76] When the administrative class acknowledges that they have committed crimes but then allows those crimes to go unpunished, the lives of the people who died become *filled* with meaning. Their lives, and their deaths, become a permanent reminder of the ability of the state to kill with impunity citizens seen as dissidents. They become a reminder of how state actors can get away with murder. The stories of Teacher Lim and Teacher Ploy—and the arbitrary way the security forces decided who would survive and who would die in the thang daeng—acquire an additional layer of meaning as part of the file about the ISOC and thang daeng in the National Archives. The file of news clippings documents the *lack* of state action, and the inclusion of the stories of these two teachers critiques this lack of action.

Yet in another, Benjaminian sense, these two stories are marked by "courage, humor, cunning, and fortitude. They have retroactive force and will constantly call into question every victory, past and present, of the rulers. As flowers turn toward the sun, by dint of a secret heliotropism the past strives to turn toward that sun which is rising in the sky of history."[77] The archival file documents the fact that no one was held accountable for Teacher Lim's death or for Teacher Ploy's suffering. Yet the very presence of the two stories in *Thai Rat* newspaper means that the file also documents the willingness of Teacher Ploy and Khruawan, Teacher Lim's widow, to speak out during a time of fear and certain violence. *This* remains a challenge to state impunity. The challenge, then, for concerned scholars is to detect these challenges to impunity. One of the additional pieces of information that came out during the exposure of the thang daeng killings in Phatthalung in February 1975 was that this was not an isolated incident.[78] Multiple reports cited similar mass arrests, disappearances, and killings in Surat Thani and Nakhon Sri Thammarat. In addition to being killed in thang daeng, villagers were reported to have been thrown out of helicopters.[79] Yet in the aftermath of official state impunity with respect to the thang daeng killings in Phatthalung, and with the filing of a slander and libel case against Phinij Jarusombat, these allegations went uninvestigated. They remain uninvestigated today. Even/especially in the absence of official documents, it is time to restart the investigations into these and many other reports of state violence from the 1950s, the 1960s, the 1970s and beyond.

Notes

I would like to thank N. Ganesan and Sung Chull Kim of the Hiroshima Peace Institute for their clarion advice during the workshops in which this chapter was developed and the other participants for their astute comparative comments. In addition, Kevin Hewison, Doreen Lee, Samson Lim, and Gayatri Menon provided useful comments for revisions. I would like to thank Thanet Aphornsuvan for sharing his unpublished paper and Prajak Kongkirati and Chaiyan Rajchagool for introducing me to Jularat Damrongviteetham. Although I do not discuss it here because my focus is elsewhere, Jularat Damrongviteetham wrote a brilliant master's thesis on thang daeng and memory in present-day Phatthalung. See Jularat Damrongviteetham, "Kansomsang Prawatisat Lae Khwamsongcham-lon: Kansuksa Kitchakam Chan Khwamsongcham Karanee 'Thang Daeng' Nai Chumchon Lamsun Amphur Srinagarinda Changwat Phatthalung" [Historical reconstruction and haunted memories: A study of activities based on memories of the "Red Barrel" incident in Lamsin Community, Srinagarinda District, Phatthalung Province] (MA thesis, Chiang Mai University, 2552 [2009]).

1. Yotthong Thabtiumai, *Thang Daeng, Na Sai, Ko. Oo. Ro. Mo. No., Phrarathabandit Totan Kommunist: Wannakam Kanmuang Samrap Phu Chai Panya Chut Prawat Chua Khong Chat Thai* [Thang Daeng, Na Sai, ISOC, Anti-Communist Activities Act: Political literature for wise people, terrible history of the Thai nation] (Bangkok, 2518 [1975]). 3. All translations in this chapter are my own. When citing Thai-language sources, I first specify the Buddhist Era publication date and then include the Common Era date in brackets immediately following.

When transliterating Thai into the Roman alphabet in the main text and in the bibliography, I do so following the system of the Royal Institute of Thailand, with three exceptions. I do not change the romanization of the names of individuals who have already transliterated their own names, nor do I alter established spellings of place names or romanization in quoted material.

2. In order to mark the inclusion of the articles in the file at the National Archives (NA), when citing newspaper articles contained in the file, I both note the standard bibliographic information and include the abbreviation "NA."

3. See National Student Center of Thailand, *Khabuankan Prachachon Tulakhom 2516* [Movement of the people, October 2516] (Bangkok: National Student Center of Thailand, 2517 [1974]), for detailed descriptions of the events of Oct. 1973, when thousands of students and citizens took to the streets to demand an end to dictatorship and a new constitution.

4. *Prachachaat,* Feb. 16, 2518 [1975].

5. *Chao Thai,* Mar. 28, 2518 [1975] (NA).

6. See *Bulletin of Concerned Asian Scholars* 9, no. 3 (1977), for a collection of articles about Oct. 6, 1976, when a massacre of unarmed students at Thammasat University in Bangkok by armed right-wing state and parastate actors ended this brief period of open politics.

7. Leigh Payne, *Unsettling Accounts: Neither Truth nor Reconciliation in Confessions of State Violence* (Durham: Duke University Press, 2007), 2.

8. Ibid., 281.

9. My point here is not to deny that knowing the number of people who were killed is important, but rather to note that in the absence of a reliable method of doing so, my focus in this chapter is necessarily elsewhere. Please see Robert Cribb, "How Many Deaths? Problems in the Statistics of Massacre in Indonesia (1965–1966) and East Timor (1975–1980)," in *Violence in Indonesia,* ed. Ingrid Wessel and Georgia Wimhöfer (Hamburg: Abera, 2001), 82–98.

10. Articles from the following newspapers are included in the folders: *Thai Rat, Sayam Rat, Prachathipatai, Prachachaat, Chaw Thai, Daily Time,* and *Daily Niu.* I draw on these articles as well as others from the same group of newspapers, additional newspapers, and other accounts in the remainder of this chapter.

11. *Thai Rat,* Feb. 7, 2518 [1975] (NA).

12. *Thai Rat,* Feb. 8, 2518 [1975] (NA).

13. The Fourth Army Region is headquartered in Nakhon Si Thammarat and covers the entire region of southern Thailand. In addition to Phatthalung, this area also includes Yala, Pattani, and Narathiwat provinces, which have been under martial law since Jan. 2004 and emergency rule since 2005, due to ongoing conflict among the central state, insurgents, and criminal elements inside and outside the state.

14. John Value Dennis, "The Role of the Thai Student Movement in Rural Conflict, 1973–1976" (MS thesis, Cornell University, 1982), 151.

15. Thanet Aphornsuvan, "Chak Thang Daeng Thung Tak Bai: Prasopkan

Nai Kan Kae Panha Khong Rat" [From Thang Daeng to Tak Bai: Experiences of solving the state's problems] (paper presented at Thammasat University, Jan. 23, 2005), 2.

16. Aroon Larnlue, "Phatthalung Terrorists: Constant Gnawing Sharpens the Teeth," *Nation*, June 20, 1971.

17. Thanet, "Chak Thang Daeng Thung Tak Bai," 2.

18. Aroon, "Phatthalung Terrorists."

19. Thanet, "Chak Thang Daeng Thung Tak Bai," 4.

20. The Village Defense Volunteers, which remains an organized force, is a village-based defense volunteer unit. Its members are often poorly trained in the use of their issued weapons, poorly and disparately supervised, and unprofessional. During the thang daeng killings in Phatthalung, accounts indicate that they reported directly to the CSOC.

21. Yotthong, *Thang Daeng*, 62–69.

22. *Prachathipatai*, Feb. 16, 2518 [1975].

23. Dennis, "Role of the Thai Student Movement," 142.

24. Yotthong, *Thang Daeng*, 76–77.

25. Ibid., 72-78; *Siang Puangchon*, Feb. 8, 2518 [1975].

26. *Prachathipatai*, Feb. 9, 2518 [1975] (NA).

27. Ibid.

28. Ibid.

29. *Sieng Puangchon*, Feb. 6, 2518 [1975].

30. *Sieng Puangchon*, Feb. 8, 2518 [1975].

31. Ibid.

32. *Sieng Puangchon*, Feb. 9, 2518 [1975].

33. *Sieng Puangchon*, Feb. 10, 2518 [1975].

34. *Sieng Puangchon*, Feb. 15, 2518 [1975].

35. Ibid.; *Prachachaat*, Feb, 15, 2518 [1975].

36. *Prachachaat*, Feb. 16, 2518 [1975].

37. *Sieng Puangchon*, Feb. 15, 2518 [1975].

38. *Prachachaat*, Feb. 15, 2518 [1975]. Among the right-wing groups active during the 1973–1976 period, Krathing Daeng's membership was drawn largely from the secondary and tertiary vocational student population.

39. *Sieng Mai*, Feb. 16, 2518 [1975]. Some of the temporary camps used during the thang daeng period remain in use.

40. *Voice of the Nation*, Feb. 16, 1975.

41. *Prachathipatai*, Feb. 16, 2518 [1975].

42. *Voice of the Nation*, Feb. 17, 1975.

43. *Prachathipatai*, Feb. 9, 2518 [1975].

44. Ibid.

45. *Daily Time*, Feb. 9, 2518 [1975] (NA).

46. *Prachathipatai*, Feb. 16, 2518 [1975].

47. *Prachathipatai*, Feb. 17, 2518 [1975].

48. *Prachathipatai,* Feb. 21, 2518 [1975].

49. *Sieng Puangchon,* Feb. 17, 2518 [1975].

50. *Sieng Mai,* Feb. 17, 2518 [1975].

51. *Voice of the Nation,* Feb. 24, 1975.

52. *Prachachaat,* Feb. 15, 2518 [1975].

53. *Sieng Puangchon,* Feb. 24, 2518 [1975].

54. *Prachathipatai,* Feb. 17, 2518 [1975].

55. *Prachathipatai,* Feb. 20, 2518 [1975].

56. *Sieng Mai,* Feb. 22, 2518 [1975].

57. Ibid.

58. *Prachathipatai,* Feb. 20, 2518 [1975]. The "they" may have been a mistake of either the person who made the poster or the newspaper that reported it. If villagers created the poster themselves, would they not use the pronoun "we"?

59. *Sieng Puangchon,* Feb. 24, 2518 [1975].

60. *Daily Time,* Feb. 24, 2518 [1975] (NA).

61. Payne, *Unsettling Accounts,* 170.

62. *Prachathipatai,* Feb. 4, 2518 [1975].

63. *Prachachaat,* Feb. 4, 2518 [1975].

64. Payne, *Unsettling Accounts,* 285.

65. Ibid.

66. *Prachachaat,* Feb. 16, 2518 [1975].

67. *Sieng Mai,* Feb. 25, 2518 [1975].

68. *Voice of the Nation,* February 25, 2518 [1975].

69. *Thai Rat,* Feb. 25, 2518 [1975] (NA).

70. *Chao Thai,* Mar. 28, 2518 [1975] (NA).

71. *Thai Rat,* Mar. 27, 2518 [1975] (NA).

72. *Prachachaat,* Feb. 11, 2518 [1975].

73. Dennis, "Role of the Thai Student Movement," 133.

74. Benedict Anderson, "Withdrawal Symptoms: Social and Cultural Aspects of the October 6 Coup," *Bulletin of Concerned Asian Scholars* 9, no. 3 (1977): 13.

75. For an analysis of the series of assassinations of leaders of the Farmers' Federation of Thailand in mid-1975, please see Tyrell Haberkorn, "An Unfinished Past: The 1974 Land Rent Control Act and Assassination in Northern Thailand," *Critical Asian Studies* 41, no. 1 (2009): 1–43.

76. *Sieng Puangchon,* Feb. 15, 2518 [1975].

77. Walter Benjamin, "Theses on the Philosophy of History," in *Illuminations: Essays and Reflections,* ed. Hannah Arendt, trans. Harry Zohn (New York: Schocken Books, 1968), 254–55.

78. This is why I have not capitalized *thang daeng* in this chapter.

79. *Sieng Puangchon,* Feb. 8, 2518 [1975]; *Sieng Mai,* Feb. 4, 2518 [1975]; *Prachathipatai,* Feb. 6, 2518 [1975]; *Prachathipatai,* Feb. 12, 2518 [1975]; *Daily Time,* Feb. 7, 2518 [1975] (NA).

8

The End of an Illusion

The Mendiola Massacre and Political Transition in Post-Marcos Philippines

Rommel A. Curaming

The Epifanio de los Santos Avenue (EDSA) People Power uprising in February 1986 was a pivotal event in the recent political history of the Philippines. The demise of the Marcos authoritarian regime—unthinkable to many until it actually happened—unleashed high hopes for what democracy can and ought to do to a nation ravaged by dictatorship, underdevelopment, and corruption. While certainly not everyone was optimistic, the restoration of the wider democratic space enticed various interest groups to aspire for something much better and to position themselves more favorably within the emerging sociopolitical order. There were groups or institutions, as expected, that found the onrush of the potential and actual changes disturbing. Struggles to define the future ensued, and these struggles manifested in various forms, including state violence.

As ground for exploring the complex role of state violence in democratic transition, the Philippines in the post-Marcos years may offer valuable insights. On the one hand, its being prone to violence coincided with a common pattern among new and struggling democracies. State violence during this period varied from clandestine, extra-judicial killings, involving a small number of targets, to massacres in both isolated and open public spaces. On the other hand, the Philippine state or the regime during this time had a rather peculiar character: it may not be easily cast as weak, owing to the enormous popularity of the president; at the same time it cannot be classified as strong, for failing to control its arms, particularly the military. An analytically salient question arose of who best embodied the state: the popular president or other state actors or institutions such as the military? This ambiguity poses a challenge, but it also offers an opportunity for complicating and deepening our understanding of the interplay between state violence and political transition.

What this chapter seeks to do is document and analyze the trajectory of events leading up to and following from the Mendiola massacre of January 22, 1987, which caused over a dozen fatalities. The choice of this event was informed by a number of considerations. First, as this event helped define the trajectory of political development during the Aquino years, it offers a good platform for exploring the main theme of this book—the link between state violence, on the one hand, and political transition, consolidation, and reconciliation on the other. Second, the complexity of this event offers a good illustrative example of what Boudreau (in chapter 1 of this volume) has noted to be the overlapping features of instrumental and exemplary violence, as well as of state building and regime definition or construction. Third, relatively small in scale yet with visible and immediate political impact, this case offers an opportunity to examine the interplay between the scale of violence and its political consequences.

This chapter assesses the role of this tragic event in political transition: from the initial, "honeymoon" period, characterized primarily by Aquino's commanding popularity, to the succeeding years of Aquino's struggle to keep the democracy agenda alive and to survive threats from various fronts. The main argument is that this incident spelled the end of the suppositions, illusions, expectations, and pretensions held for a range of reasons by stakeholders about the new government and about how Philippine politics would unfold in the immediate post-Marcos years. What came with this tragic incident was "the passing away of innocence," as one journalist evocatively put it.[1] This was a moment of truth, the realization of which helped shape the transition process, specifically the terms, the direction, and possibly the outcome of the engagement among key political stakeholders.

THE MENDIOLA MASSACRE

The organized peasantry was one of the sectors that saw, and acted on, a window of opportunity within the newly expanded democratic space. Banking on Aquino's earlier promises and testing the limits of the reformist spirit of the time, they repeatedly pressed the new government for agrarian reform. Seeing the Aquino government's apparent indecisiveness on the issue, they grew suspicious of the government's design. Their suspicion was matched by growing impatience and militancy in acts and pronouncements.

Following a number of previous demonstrations, the farmers under Kilusang Magbubukid ng Pilipinas (KMP, Farmers Movement of the Philippines) camped for a week, starting January 15, 1987, outside the Ministry of Agrarian Reform building in Quezon City to press for their demands. Detesting what they viewed as lack of attention from officials and the media, they went to the extent of blockading the compound to prevent employees from entering it. Provocatively, they raised their own flag side by side with the Philippine flag. It was a potent symbolic act of protest.[2] When Minister Heherson Alvarez talked to their representatives, the farmers were told to wait for the ratification of the Philippine Constitution and the convening of Congress. This was precisely what the farmers wished to avoid because they were afraid that Congress, dominated by landlords, would not enact a "genuine" agrarian reform law. On the following day, January 22, the group led by KMP president Jaime Tadeo marched over a dozen kilometers to Malacañang Palace, purportedly to present its demands to the president.[3] Along the way, they gathered throngs of sympathizers from the organized labor unions, farmers, students, the urban poor, and intellectuals.

Meanwhile, informed that the demonstrators would proceed to Mendiola and Malacanang, the police and the marines deployed civil-disturbance and crowd-control units on Mendiola Bridge and around the palace. Later investigations revealed that military intelligence indicated "heavy infiltration" of the crowd of protesters by members of the Communist Party of the Philippines and its armed wing, the New Peoples' Army (NPA). Also disclosed was the presence of civilian-clothed and armed military operatives in the crowd.[4]

At around 4:30 P.M. the protesters arrived and inched closer to the first section of the three-tier blockade on Mendiola. As marchers pushed their way forward, clashes ensued. The commission's report described the situation thus:

There was an explosion followed by throwing of pillboxes, stones and bottles. Steel bars, wooden clubs and lead pipes were used against the police. The police fought back with their shields and truncheons. The police line was breached. Suddenly shots were heard. The demonstrators disengaged from the government forces and retreated towards C. M. Recto Avenue. But sporadic firing continued from the government forces.[5]

Soon, the nation was stunned by the news that a huge crowd of largely peasant protestors, estimated at ten to fifteen thousand, had clashed with, and been fired upon by, the police and marine crowd-control units at the historic Mendiola Street/Bridge in Manila. Other than being a major access point to Malacañang Palace, Mendiola was highly symbolic of the people's struggle against Marcos. The choice of this place sought to dramatize a crucial test for Aquino's strong avowal that hers was the exact opposite of the previous regime.

Twelve or thirteen were immediately confirmed dead, and over a hundred were wounded.[6] Six more reportedly died later from injuries sustained during the clash, but this was not verified. Popularly known as the Mendiola Massacre, this was a tragic end to the weeklong protest. It served as a catalyst for the Aquino government's response to the clamor for agrarian reform. Within the broader political developments of the time, it seemed to have hastened as well the process of drawing up the lines along which the left, the right, and the center would navigate the difficult period of political transition and/or consolidation.

The killing shocked many. It "severely put to test" Aquino's ties with a broad coalition of progressive organizations.[7] Enraged, a number of highly respected government figures such as Jose Diokno resigned in protest. Barely a year after the euphoric EDSA "revolution," this tragic event curtly brought back the painful memories of Marcos's violent years, which everyone had thought were gone for good. Aquino's painstaking effort to present her administration as opposite to that of Marcos was badly tarnished: the incident made Marcos appear gentle by comparison.[8] Visibly distraught and concerned, Aquino acted quickly to commiserate with the families and friends of the victims. She condoled with the families of the dead and visited some of them in the hospital.[9] She also talked to the leader of KMP and renewed the promise to act on agrarian issues. As if to underscore her decisiveness, she issued Administrative Order 11, forming a fact-finding body, the Citizens' Mendiola Commission (CMC), and assigned respected retired Supreme Court justices to investigate "the disorder, deaths and casualties that took place in the vicinity of Mendiola Bridge and Mendiola Street and Claro M. Recto Avenue, Manila, in the afternoon of January 22, 1987." She ordered that the report be submitted within two weeks.

THE ROAD TO MENDIOLA

The agrarian problems in the Philippines are deeply rooted in the country's long colonial history. The feudal arrangements perpetuated by the *encomienda* and *hacienda* systems during the Spanish period had been largely carried over during the American period with the failure of the colonial government, eager as it was to win elite support, to seize the opportunity for land redistribution.[10] All Philippine governments since Aguinaldo's Malolos Republic (1899–1901) and Quezon's Commonwealth (1935–1941) had at least paid lip service to the need for social justice, in which the issue of more equitable land ownership occupied a prominent place. As part of efforts to neutralize the brewing Huk Rebellion that threatened the republic in the late 1940s and early 1950s, Magsaysay (1953–1957) pushed a land reform program rather forcefully. The landlord-dominated Congress, however, effectively watered down the outcome of the initiative. The struggle between Magsaysay and Congress set a pattern that continued in later periods under the administrations of Macapagal (1962–1965), Marcos (1966–1972), and beyond.[11]

When Cory Aquino was swept into power by the EDSA "revolution," hopes soared among peasants that agrarian problems would be addressed more seriously. Notwithstanding the skepticism shared by not a few, owing primarily to Aquino's elite and landed background, the prevailing atmosphere was one of anticipation.[12] It was further encouraged by the overall reformist tenor of the early years after EDSA. Soon enough, however, observers began to notice that Aquino's attitude toward land reform had become increasingly complacent, evasive, or ambiguous. During the campaign against Marcos, she had bitterly critiqued Marcos's agrarian reform program for being a "mockery" of the peasants' aspirations and promised a "genuine" agrarian reform.[13] Possibly as a portent of what was to come, such declarations were tempered into calls for "viable" agrarian reform a few weeks before the February 1986 elections.[14] In her first eleven months upon ascension to power, Aquino said and did little about agrarian reform, despite concrete proposals and protest marches undertaken by farmers' groups.[15] Observers have bitterly regretted that rather than using her unlimited power under the Freedom Constitution—which was promulgated on March 26, 1986—to mandate by decree a genuine agrarian reform program, she issued instead a few days before Congress convened in July 1987 a considerably emasculated version of Executive Order (EO) 229. This decree left the most crucial questions—scope, retention limits, and compensation—for Congress to decide.[16] Doing this, critics contended, she let go of the rare opportunity to put in place a legal mechanism to address the country's centuries-long agrarian problems. By appointing as minister of agrarian reform someone like Heherson Alvarez, who had little background in agriculture and no track record of championing agrarian reform issues, Aquino gave the impression that she was less than serious in pursuing a genuine agrarian reform agenda.[17]

Several factors help explain Aquino's apparently lukewarm or ambivalent attitude toward reform. Often cited is her class background: she is herself a member of a family that owns one of the country's largest haciendas.[18] While Aquino may have personally harbored sympathy toward pro–peasant reform efforts, this sympathy could not have been enough given the strong family-affair character of Philippine politics and the opposition of other landed elites to reform.[19] In his analysis of agrarian reform legislation process during the Aquino years, Simeon Gilding argues that it was the landlord-dominated Congress rather than the executive that spelled doom for the genuine agrarian reform effort.[20] But even from within her own cabinet support for agrarian reform was at best half-hearted, with some strongly supportive while others were indifferent or openly opposed. Likewise, stung by criticism for earlier dictatorial tendencies in the use of her unlimited decree-making power, Aquino opted to go slowly, which could account at least partly for her ambivalence regarding the use of this power to enact decisively pro-farmers agrarian reform.[21]

Given the enormity and wide range of problems left behind by Marcos, some have argued that Aquino's priorities understandably lay in other areas: political consolidation, restoration or reinvigoration of pre–martial law democratic institutions, economic revitalization, the recovery of Marcos's ill-gotten wealth, and reconciliation with communists and Muslim rebels.[22] Starting in mid-1986, the need for Aquino to survive destabilizing plots by Marcos loyalists, politicized groups within the armed forces, and other disgruntled civilian and military elements became an urgent concern.[23] These concerns predominated, crowding out land reform.

Among the first things that Aquino did upon assuming the presidency was to release political prisoners, including top-ranking officers of the Communist Party of the Philippines. Notwithstanding stiff opposition from the military and others on the right, including the United States, Aquino did this to demonstrate her resolve to achieve national reconciliation. She actively pursued peace talks with Muslims and communist rebels and created the Human Rights Commission to look into human rights violations by the military.

Aquino's conciliatory policy toward communists and Muslims posed a big headache for the military. In tandem with efforts to look into human rights abuses by the military, this move, they believed, was a threat to national security. This perception significantly contributed to the brewing dissent and dissatisfaction with the Aquino government that was demonstrated in six or seven coup attempts from 1986 to 1990, two of which came close to toppling the Aquino government.[24]

Certain factions on the left viewed Aquino's early moves as an indication of her liberal inclinations and apparent sincerity. This emboldened them to argue for a critical collaboration with the government. Having blundered in their decision to boycott the 1986 snap presidential election and not to participate in the climax of the effort to oust Marcos—the EDSA "revolution"—the leaders of the movement now faced a barrage of criticisms that opened up opportunities for them to seriously question even the movement's overall strategy. The ensuing debates helped spell the end of unity within the movement, leading to the "split" in 1993.[25] Indeed, the movement struggled to define its bearings and maintain unity in the sharply altered post-EDSA situation.

Aquino's peace overtures toward the left and the military's opposition to them increasingly became the fulcrum around which civilian-military tensions revolved.[26] At stake, some scholars observed, was the question of which side would have the upper hand in defining the direction of the government. For a while the sixty-day ceasefire that the government and NDF negotiators had agreed would take effect on December 10, 1986, seemed to vindicate Aquino's approach and strengthened the civilian position, at the expense of hawkish elements in the military. On the other hand, so Gareth Porter warned, if Aquino were to be persuaded or pressured to abandon negotiations with the left, "it could mark the transition to a military-dominated regime."[27]

Those on the left could not ignore Aquino's peace initiatives because they figured it would be politically costly to seem belligerent in the face of Aquino's overriding popularity and apparent sincerity.[28] They also thought that the negotiations offered them opportunities to gain legitimacy and the media exposure necessary for them to better explain themselves to the public. Moreover, here was an opportunity to penetrate areas for political education that hitherto had been difficult to reach.[29]

On the other hand, they were afraid this would cause a loss of momentum toward the military goal of reaching the "strategic counter offensive" (SCO) stage against the armed forces (AFP), which were growing ineffective and vulnerable. A ceasefire, from this point of view, would give the AFP a chance to regroup. In addition, it might create an impression among the cadres that political rather than armed struggle ought to be given greater emphasis.[30]

From the vantage point of the Aquino government, peace initiatives served to fulfill promises made during the anti-Marcos campaign. In addition to the initiatives' image-enhancing purpose, they were necessary if the government were to be able to devote its limited resources and energy to the task of economic recovery.[31] Eager to show her regime as the opposite of Marcos's, and believing, rather naively, that the rapid growth of communist insurgency had mainly arisen from Marcos's abuses, Aquino thought it was worthwhile to pursue a conciliatory policy to win over communists beyond the circle of the hard-core groups.[32] She might also have hoped to establish a justificatory mechanism for a more forceful later approach in case the initiatives failed. Later events lent credence to this view.

The public in general felt supportive and hopeful about Aquino's initiatives. After long years of turmoil, the mood was upbeat regarding the peaceful resolution of conflicts. Many believed that the excesses of the Marcos regime had brought forth rebellions. With Marcos gone, they hoped that peace was on the horizon and believed that Aquino's peace initiatives deserved to be seriously pursued. Thus, despite their knowledge of the deep and complex roots of the conflicts and the extreme difficulty of resolving them, political stakeholders from the right, the left, the center, and beyond could not but take part at least grudgingly in what Robert Reid and Eileen Guerrero have called the "peace charade," which in their words "proved little more than a public relations exercise."[33]

In a sense, what the Mendiola Massacre did was put an end to this "charade" and put on course a trajectory that could have started earlier. This is not to say that that such a trajectory was inevitable: objective conditions and the configuration of power within the left, the right, and the center made this trajectory a very strong possibility, but its realization was by no means assured. If the Mendiola Massacre had not happened as it did, it might have been more difficult for the NDF to justify withdrawal from peace talks, putting pressure on them to extend the "charade" for some time. While a major breakthrough in the peace negotiations was unlikely, a protracted "honeymoon" could probably have resulted in a different configuration of events and relationships among various stakeholders.

Aftermath

The first thing the NDF did in response to the Mendiola Massacre was to withdraw from the ceasefire, never returning to the negotiating table under the Aquino administration. For weeks, the NDF was growing exasperated at the conduct of the negotiations with the government panel, and the Mendiola Massacre opened the door for a graceful exit.[34] Rumors abound that even before the massacre, the NDF already intended to withdraw for a number of possible reasons. Speculation had it that the NDF was afraid that many rebels who had come down from the hills during the ceasefire and tasted what it was like to be with their families again, during the Christmas season at that, might find it difficult to willingly go back if the ceasefire continued for long.[35] The benefits for the left of the aboveground propaganda afforded by the ceasefire appeared to be canceled out by the cadres' exposure to intelligence monitoring by the military. Apparently more important was the fact that hardliners had gained the upper hand within the NDF at the expense of proponents of critical engagement with the Aquino government. While the provocative rearrest of NDF chair Rodolfo Salas and the slaying of labor leader Rolando Olalia did not lead to the withdrawal of the NDF, the government's insistence on negotiating within the parameters set by the constitution provided a pretext for the hardliners to claim that the negotiation was at a dead end.

If Aquino's iconic stature posed a serious problem for the left, the carnage in Mendiola seriously damaged her status and offered the left an opportunity to claim that Aquino was no different from Marcos: her administration could be as brutal, perhaps even more so.[36] The blood spilled in Mendiola effectively demystified Aquino's moral authority. At the same time, it denied the moderates in the NDF an excuse for further engaging the government. Soon the fighting between the NPA and AFP was renewed.

More important, this tragic event put an end to the Aquino government's indecision toward agrarian reform. Aware of the massacre's potentially devastating impact on the popularity and legitimacy of the Aquino regime, it acted swiftly by inviting the leaders of farmers' organizations to a dialogue and by agreeing practically to all demands for "minimum" agrarian reform, tabled but rejected earlier, during talks with the minister of agrarian reform. The day after Mendiola, the Inter-Agency Task Force on Agrarian Reform (IATFAR), formed a month earlier to look into the financing aspect of the program, immediately proposed expanding the scope of land reform to include private lands, not just public ones. It also proposed fast-tracking the implementation to six years.[37] Aquino also hurriedly formed the Cabinet Action Committee (CAC) for land reform a few days later, tasked to work with IATFAR to draft the text of the executive order.

The outburst of government effort to address the agrarian reform agenda in the wake of the Mendiola massacre had the effect of alarming anti–agrarian reform groups, including landlords and the agribusiness sector. Their opposition proved vigorous and sustained, putting the Aquino government in a dilemma: "Either she decree agrarian reform and face the immediate threat of destabilization by those opposed to land reform, or she leave the task to Congress and perhaps forfeit legitimacy among the rural poor."[38] The content of EO 229 showed that Aquino opted for the latter. After six months of debates and hard work to draft a progressive, pro-redistribution executive order, the version produced by CAC was superseded by that produced by the combined conservative interests of landlord, bankers, and businesses.[39] It was, in Gilding's words, "a rational response by a regime primarily concerned with preserving its own stability and promoting its own legitimacy."[40]

The strong initiatives taken by Aquino in the wake of the Mendiola massacre, and her later backtracking in the face of strong pressure from the landed interests, may be interpreted differently. One possibility is that her efforts were plain theatrics, just a show to save her image.[41] Right from the very start, that is, she did not seriously mean to fulfill her promise of genuine agrarian reform. Another possibility is that political imperatives forced her to defer to the "strongest groups and most pressing crisis."[42] The latter interpretation, in my view, seems to be the case.

The opening of the Congress in July 1987 shifted the struggle for genuine agrarian reform from the executive branch to the legislature. Debates raged for months in the halls of the Congress. The law that was eventually passed—called the Comprehensive Agrarian Reform Law—was hardly an improvement from EO 229. It left much to be desired by the farmers, its provisions saddled with loopholes that effectively exempted 80 percent of private lands, in addition to those that rendered implementation difficult. For their part, many landlords were also unhappy about the passage of the law. It appears that if they could have their way, a totally toothless agrarian reform law would have been passed, if any at all. With the memory of the Mendiola massacre constantly invoked by the law's greatly outnumbered proponents in the Congress and a sympathetic media, advocates for reform put up a good fight, making it less easy for the landlord bloc to get what it wanted. It is not farfetched to say that without the Mendiola massacre, the struggle would have proven much tougher.

With its ability for violence blatantly exposed, the Aquino government shed the "burden" of pursuing peace. True to Aquino's promise, the "sword of war (was) . . . unsheathed" once peace efforts failed. Soon anti-insurgency operations were renewed in earnest. By the following year credible results had been achieved, with the capture of important leaders of the opposition, the significant loss of its base, and growing demoralization and division within its ranks.

The massacre also had an impact on the image of the military. In the early months after EDSA, the armed forces enjoyed tremendous popularity on account of their role in the ouster of Marcos. Bearing a shameful reputation for doing the bidding of Marcos during the martial law years, many now believed that they had redeemed themselves through their central role in the EDSA "revolution." However, with the first military coup attempt in July 1986, and the killing of progressive elements of civil society, this newfound positive image had begun to be sullied. With the Mendiola massacre, the wrecking was complete, as it rivaled, or perhaps even exceeded, the brutality inflicted by Marcos operatives in other famous state-inflicted violence, such as Lapiang Malaya massacre in Pasay (1967), the Jabidah massacre in Corregidor (1968), and the Escalante Massacre in Negros (1985). The shooting was justified by claims that intelligence reports indicated heavy infiltration by communists within the ranks of the protesters, who planned to occupy the schools nearby in preparation for the eventual takeover of Malacanang.[43]

Rumors circulated that the military might have deliberately killed precisely to discredit Aquino and put an end to the government's peace efforts. For a long time, the military had bewailed Aquino's peace initiatives, which in its view sidelined, sidetracked, or hampered any serious anti-insurgency effort.[44] It became clear to many that regardless of the president—Marcos or Aquino—the military could not be controlled and trusted. What Mendiola did was reveal the armed forces' true "odor," temporarily masked by the euphoric post-EDSA atmosphere.

On the left, rumors also abounded that the military's provocation was a deliberate attempt to scuttle peace efforts, which by January 1987 had already proved burdensome.[45] Certain hardcore elements on the left were also said to wish for this tragic event so they would be vindicated for their widely unpopular decision to desist from participation in the snap election and the subsequent EDSA "revolution."[46] They might also have been afraid that the ceasefire could enhance commitment to political struggle at the expense of military struggle.[47] Whether or not the Mendiola massacre was a conspiracy or a tragedy willed to happen by the rightists and/or the leftists may never be proven. One thing is sure: the massacre ended a chapter in the government's engagement with nonstate political actors. Very soon, another chapter began.

The potentially much more damaging political fallout from the Mendiola massacre was averted when a few days later, on January 25–27, 1987, public attention was diverted to the rightist threat stemming from the military: a badly planned coup d'état launched by a military faction allegedly loyal to Marcos. This event allowed the government a more centrist position, thus helping to channel blame for the Mendiola incident to the military.[48] The attempted coup followed from the "Manila Hotel incident" in July 1986, which appeared to be tied to an effort to bring Marcos back to power. This coup did not succeed, but another attempt ten months later, in November 1987, came close. With rightist threats seriously jeopardizing the survival not only of the Aquino government but also of the democratic space that the EDSA revolution spawned, the memories of the Mendiola massacre and Aquino's early engagement with the left gradually receded in the public imagination.

(Ir)resolution

The fact-finding panel called the Citizens' Mendiola Commission (CMC) that Aquino quickly formed to investigate the incident released its report on February 27, 1987. The commission noted the following: the rallyers did not secure a permit; the members of crowd-disturbance units were armed with .38- and .45-caliber pistols and armalites; armed soldiers in civilian clothes were in the crowd; some of the demonstrators carried weapons; and Jaime Tadeo, KMP's leader, uttered words that incited sedition. Likewise noted were four uniformed men who could be seen firing on the marchers in photos and video footage. Unfortunately, the commission failed to identify these men and recommended further investigation by the National Bureau of Investigation (NBI). Overall, the findings were not conclusive as to who should be held responsible for the killings.[49]

The commission recommended that Jaime Tadeo be charged for inciting sedition and that administrative sanctions be meted out to the highest-ranking officers for "failing to make effective use of skill and experience in directing the dispersal." Compensation to the families of the victims was also recommended.[50]

The outcome of the investigation left many infuriated. The failure of the government to punish those responsible made it clear that in yet another aspect, the Aquino government was no different from Marcos's. Several months later, in late July 1987, when the government, saddled by serious coup d'état threats, failed to act on the commission's recommendations, the families of the victims formally demanded compensation. When nothing came of this, a 6.5-million-pesos damage suit was filed in the Manila Regional Trial Court on January 20, 1988, by the families of the victims and the survivors against the State. It was dismissed on May 31, 1988, by the court on the basis that the State cannot be sued without its consent. A petition for reconsideration was filed, arguing that the Citizens' Mendiola Commission's earlier recommendation that the victims be compensated implied the State's waiver of immunity from lawsuit. The petition was dismissed by the Supreme Court on August 8, 1988, for lack of merit, with the claim that such a recommendation did not necessarily mean a waiver.[51]

The victims' quest for justice dragged on. Ten years later, in 1998, a group called Kilusang Enero Beinte Dos (January 22 Movement) was formed, consisting of the families of victims and survivors of the Mendiola massacre.[52] They filed a class-action suit against Aquino and some officials of her administration, including Fidel Ramos. This case was also dismissed by the court for lack of merit.[53]

Succeeding governments did not consider land reform a high priority. For instance, the Ramos administration—with Ramos a general and the secretary of defense at the time of the Mendiola massacre—could hardly be expected to pursue the case seriously. Ramos knew too well its adverse impact on the morale of the military. Notwithstanding his pro-poor posturing, Estrada was too close to big players in agribusiness. Farmers' groups berated him for his plan for a "corporative agrarian reform" that could effectively exclude over two hundred thousand hectares of commercial farms.[54]

In response, organized militant groups continued in pressuring succeeding governments for a "genuine" reform program. Every year in various parts of the country, militant groups remember the anniversary of the Mendiola massacre with a protest march, among other commemorative activities.[55] The anniversary serves as an occasion to reiterate demands for genuine agrarian reform and to remind the public of the injustices committed against not just the victims of the massacre but also the entire peasantry.[56] When agrarian-related violence such as the 2004 massacre in Hacienda Luisita happened, the memories of the Mendiola massacre resonated. This prompted the filing of a bill in Congress urging that January 22 be declared National Farmers' Day, although it failed to pass into law.[57] Also in 2004 representatives for farmers in Congress considered passing a bill to compensate the massacre's victims, but again, nothing came to fruition.[58] In 2007, a granite marker with the names of the massacre's fatalities was installed at the Bantayog ng mga Bayani (Monument of Heroes). This in effect formalized the long-standing status of the victims as heroes or martyrs to the cause of social justice.

Under the presidency of Noynoy Aquino, who rode into power on the back of sympathy for the death of his mother, Cory Aquino, the son's tack seems to be a reprise of his mother's. Just as Cory Aquino's early promises to redistribute the land soon gave way to intricate legal maneuvers to avoid reform, a close look at Noynoy Aquino's pronouncements reveals that it is heading in the same direction.[59] The government continues to dodge the calls for justice for those who died in the Mendiola massacre and other state-sponsored violence. As the state ignores or erases the memories and the symbolism of these gruesome events, civil society groups install commemorative markers and work to keep their memories alive. They serve as a fulcrum around which continuing protests against the government's neglect of the plight of the poor revolve.

CONCLUSION

State-sponsored political violence is fairly common in the Philippines. Practically all regimes, whether authoritarian, such as Marcos's, or "democratic," such as Aquino's, have had a fair share of blood debt owed to the people. While this is not to say that a culture of violence thrives in or pervades the country, it may be said that enough cultural capital for dealing with political violence has long been in place. Spectacular as the Mendiola massacre was, the context in which it was carried out, its consequences for the country's political dynamics, and the manner in which its memories have been appropriated by activists lend it some distinction.

The case of the Mendiola massacre confirms the vulnerability of new or transitional democracies to political violence. It is well known that the Aquino government had a record of human rights violations that rivaled that of Marcos and was even worse in some aspects. That the Mendiola incident took place indicates Aquino's failure to rein in the military, which raises a question regarding the supposed singularity of regime or state as agent of violence. Beholden to the military for her regime's survival, Aquino grew more ineffective in imposing discipline, much less so in holding the military accountable for its crimes.

The overall Cold War atmosphere also set the broader context, which was conducive for the outbreak of political violence, including the case examined here. Aquino's early handling of insurgency, particularly the release of all political prisoners, made the United States nervous. While no clear evidence has linked the United States to the Mendiola massacre, the US Central Intelligence Agency was among the groups identified by observers as possible "conspirators" in the event and US strategic interest among its beneficiaries. Insofar as the US attitude toward land reform was concerned, the Mendiola massacre prompted a turnaround in US policy, from neglect of the country to active support, with an initial offer of aid amounting to $50 million.[60] It must also be noted that the military was quick to justify the use of violence by referring to intelligence reports that the protesters had been heavily infiltrated by the communists and that they planned to attack and occupy Malacanang. Time and again, it proved convenient to invoke anti-communism as a pretext for committing violence. In short, state- or regime-building efforts that trigger or justify state violence often have deeper structural roots beyond the boundaries of the nation-state and to which more attention must be paid.

As a "technology of modern politics," the Mendiola massacre, like other episodes of political violence, was consequential and strategic.[61] It was consequential in that it helped shape the course of succeeding events. Notwithstanding the eventual triumph of anti–agrarian reform conservatives, the Mendiola massacre made such a victory more difficult to attain as the memories of this tragic event enabled pro-reform groups to put up a good fight.

Beyond agrarian reform, this event also helped forge the sharp boundaries within the broader political platform that framed the engagement among key stakeholders. If enormous popularity lent Aquino enough power to disrupt the unfolding of history, leading it to a detour of sorts, the Mendiola massacre robbed Aquino of some of her powers, thus allowing the logic of realpolitik to run its course. This violent incident, in other words, was "constitutive" of ensuing political dynamics.[62]

It was strategic in at least one of three possible senses. First, while it is difficult to prove the rumor of conspiracy—that the shooting was a deliberate, premeditated act by the military—circumstantial evidence suggests that such a conspiracy is a strong possibility that cannot be dismissed. Shooting, without first using the water cannon and tear gas on standby, and doing so just when the first part of the three-tier line of defense was breached (each line ten meters apart), can hardly be considered a defensive, accidental act. It seems a tragedy willed to happen. Second, both the military and the left needed such an incident to happen for their own political purposes, so one side's provocation made the other more easily provoked. And third, even if we grant that neither the military nor the left deliberately willed the massacre in pursuit of a predetermined political purpose, it cannot be denied that all key stakeholders—the government, the right, and the left—capitalized on the political fallout from this incident to advance their own agenda. In short, the structure of power relations and the configuration of competing interests at the time made such a violent incident likely to occur.

The case of the Mendiola massacre seems to complicate analysis of the nature of state violence. While it was clear that government operatives fired the fatal shots, there was no doubt that no other branch of the government—executive, legislative, or judiciary—could have sanctioned or defended these actions. Aside from the massacre being a case of a possible breakdown of command responsibility, it also raises a number of queries that may have a bearing on the unity or efficacy of the concept of state violence. For example, should the state or regime always be taken as singular? What is the implication of notions of the contested state or contested regime on the nature of state violence?

It also flags possible issues of intentionality and audience. While I highlighted above the strategic character of state violence, other questions also ought to be asked: From whose standpoint was the massacre strategic, and with what audience in mind? Can there be only one state viewpoint, and is the intended target or audience necessarily the same as the actual one? Questions also arise as to whether nonstate actors are always the targets or victims of state violence. Can the state or regime be the target or victim of state violence, as one possible interpretation of the Mendiola massacre suggests? Is state violence always a self-serving measure? Or could it also be inflicted to weaken at least parts of itself? And if, indeed, leftist elements deliberately provoked the killings to serve their own purpose, then the picture becomes all the more complicated. With the situation viewed against these questions, we may have to rethink overly rational assumptions about the nature of state violence: particularly the typologies of exemplary and instrumental violence, spelled out by Vincent Boudreau earlier in this volume (see chapter 1), and assumptions about the determinate character of its target and purpose, in addition to the purported singularity of the state or regime as agent.

The case of the Mendiola massacre also sheds light on the relationship between the scale of violence and the manner it is staged, on the one hand, and the political repercussions of violence, on the other. The number of fatalities may have been small relative to other cases discussed in this volume, but the political fallout of this event was not insignificant. It was the manner in which the violence in this case was carried out, in great contrast to what the regime stood for, that determined the magnitude and character of its political consequences.

Like many other episodes of state violence in the Philippines, the Mendiola massacre was never resolved. Cory Aquino quickly expressed regret for the tragic incident, apologizing as she offered apparently heartfelt condolences to the victims, but resolution or closure have yet to come more than two decades later. Despite truth-finding exercises that point to possible culprits, no further investigation has been fruitfully carried out to hold them legally accountable. The least the state could have done was provide compensation, as the fact-finding commission recommended. Up to now, however, under the presidency of Cory Aquino's son, nothing has happened. The government has expressed its willingness to compensate the victims, but legal technicalities have gotten in the way. Another possible reason for the lack of closure is that Cory Aquino's government's stability depended on the goodwill of the military. Serious efforts to investigate and hold the military accountable easily raised displeasure within the ranks, resulting in the instability of the regime.

Perhaps inherent in the concept of "political violence" is the absence of full resolution or reconciliation. Probably in addition to the strategic intent of violence, the broad and deep structure of conflicts, and violence's targeted consequences, violence is political in character because of its openness to contestation and its ability to generate capital for one or the other among competing stakeholders. This seems clear in the ways civil society groups in the Philippines continue to commemorate and appropriate the memories of various episodes of state-sponsored violence, including the Mendiola massacre.

NOTES

1. Jo-Ann Q. Maglipon, ed., *A Smouldering Land* (Manila: National Council of Churches in the Philippines and the Forum for Rural Concerns, 1987), xiiv.

2. Supreme Court, *Republic of the Philippines et al. vs. Sandoval, Caylao et al.* (G.R. No. 84607); "The LawPhil Project: Philippine Laws and Jurisprudence Databank," Mar. 19, 1993, http://lawphil.net/judjuris/juri1993/mar1993/gr_84607_1993.html.

3. For a perceptive and detailed account of what happened during the negotiations, see Maglipon, *Smouldering Land,* xxviii–xxxi. See also Supreme Court, *Republic of the Philippines et al. vs. Sandoval, Caylao et al.* (G.R. No. 84607).

4. Supreme Court, *Republic of the Philippines et al. vs. Sandoval, Caylao et al.* (G.R. No. 84607).

5. Ibid.

6. Ibid.

7. Francisco Lara and Horacio Morales, "The Peasant Movement and the Challenge of Rural Democratisation in the Philippines," *Journal of Development Studies* 26, no. 4 (1990): 143.

8. Even rabid anti-Marcos activists and sympathizers with Aquino conceded that this was worse than what Marcos had done to them when they held rallies on the same spot. See Maglipon, *Smouldering Land,* xxxvii.

9. Eduardo Tadem, "The Agrarian Question Confronts the Aquino Government," *Kasarinlan: Philippine Journal of Third World Studies* 2, no. 4 (1987): 37.

10. The *encomienda* system refers to a trusteeship or land grant given by the Crown to people who have done exemplary service in exchange for a number of responsibilities, including collecting tributes, teaching the Spanish language, and converting natives to Christianity. The *hacienda* system refers to the large land-holdings of certain individuals or families.

11. See Jeffrey M. Riedinger, *Agrarian Reform in the Philippines: Democratic Transitions and Redistributive Reform* (Stanford: Stanford University Press, 1995), 86–104, for an overview of the history of land reform in the Philippines. See also Yujiro Hayami, Ma. Agnes R. Quisumbing, and Lourdes S. Adriano, *Toward an Alternative Land Reform Paradigm: A Philippine Perspective* (Quezon City: Ateneo de Manila University Press, 1990), chap. 3; James Putzel, *A Captive Land: The Politics of Agrarian Reform in the Philippines* (London: Catholic Institute for International Relations, 1992), chap. 2.

12. Her family owns Hacienda Luisita, one of the largest haciendas in the country at 6,400 hectares.

13. As cited in Riedinger, *Agrarian Reform in the Philippines,* 105.

14. Ibid., 122.

15. In early Apr. and late May 1986, Aquino reiterated her pro–agrarian reform position but not much else; see ibid., 125. Before the Mendiola massacre, land reform was never discussed in the cabinet. In fact, before July 1987, when EO 229 was signed, land reform was tabled for discussion only once, and the overall tenor was opposed to it; see Putzel, *Captive Land,* 247.

16. For a bitter critique, see Joel Rodriguez, *Genuine Agrarian Reform* (Manila: Urban Rural Mission, National Council of Churches in the Philippines, 1987).

17. Ibid.

18. See, e.g., Joel Rocamora, *Breaking Through: The Struggle within the Communist Party of the Philippines* (Manila: Anvil Publishing, 1994), 63–68.

19. Alfred W. McCoy, ed., *An Anarchy of Families: State and Family in the Philippines* (Madison: University of Wisconsin, Center for Southeast Asian Studies, 1993).

20. Simeon Gilding, *Agrarian Reform and Counter-Reform under the Aquino Administration: A Case Study in Post-Marcos Politics* (Canberra: Department of Political and Social Change, Division of Politics and International Relations, Research School of Pacific Studies, Australian National University, 1993).

21. Tadem, "Agrarian Question," 35.

22. Riedinger, *Agrarian Reform in the Philippines,* 127–28.

23. See chap. 6 of David G. Timberman, *A Changeless Land: Continuity and Change in Philippine Politics* (Singapore: Institute of Southeast Asian Studies, 1991).

24. Coup attempts were carried out in July 1986, Nov. 1986, Jan. 1987, Aug. 1987 (which came close to succeeding), Dec. 1989 (which came even closer to succeeding), and Oct. 1990. See Criselda Yabes, *The Boys from the Barracks: The Philippine Military after EDSA,* 1st ed. (Manila: Anvil Publishing Inc., 1991), for a detailed account of these coups d'état.

25. For a perceptive analysis of this crisis, see Rocamora, *Breaking Through*.

26. Timberman, *Changeless Land,* 252.

27. Gareth Porter, *The Politics of Counterinsurgency in the Philippines: Military and Political Options,* Philippine Studies Occasional Paper, No. 9 (Honolulu: Center for Philippine Studies, Centers for Asian and Pacific Studies, 1987), quoted in Timberman, *Changeless Land,* 253.

28. Robert H. Reid and Eileen Guerrero, *Corazon Aquino and the Brushfire Revolution* (Baton Rouge: Louisiana State University Press, 1995), 77–78.

29. Timberman, *Changeless Land,* 294–95.

30. Ibid., 294.

31. Francisco Nemenzo, "From Autocracy to Elite Democracy," in *Dictatorship and Revolution: Roots of People's Power,* ed. Aurora Javate de Dios, Petronilo Bn Daroy, and Lorna Kalaw-Tirol (Manila: Conspectus, 1988), 257.

32. Seth Mydans, "Aquino's Widow Says She Will Run against Marcos," *New York Times,* Dec. 3, 1985.

33. Reid and Guerrero, *Corazon Aquino and the Brushfire Revolution,* chap. 5, esp. 89.

34. Ibid., 88.

35. "Reds Cite Massacre for Breaking off Talks," *New Sunday Times,* Feb. 2, 1987.

36. Bobby M. Tuazon, "The Challenge of Militants," *Manila Standard,* May 15, 1987.

37. Jose J. Magadia, *State-Society Dynamics: Policy Making in a Restored Democracy* (Quezon City: Ateneo De Manila University Press, 2003), 64.

38. Gilding, *Agrarian Reform and Counter-Reform,* 11.

39. Putzel, *Captive Land,* 223–36.

40. Gilding, *Agrarian Reform and Counter-Reform,* 13.

41. Reid and Guerrero, *Corazon Aquino and the Brushfire Revolution;* Rocamora, *Breaking Through*.

42. Gilding, *Agrarian Reform and Counter-Reform,* 41.

43. *Republic of the Philippines et al. vs. Sandoval, Caylao et al.* (G.R. no. 84607).

44. See, e.g., Letty Magsanoc's article in *Inquirer,* cited in Maglipon, *Smouldering Land,* xv.

45. Belinda Cunanan, quoted in Maglipon, *Smouldering Land,* xxviii. See also David Wurfel, "Civil Society and Democratization in the Philippines," in *Growth and Governance in Asia,* ed. Sato Yoichiro (Honolulu: APCSS Publication, 2004).

46. As noted in Tadem, "Agrarian Question," 37.

47. Kathleen Weekley, *The Communist Party of the Philippines, 1968–1993: A Story of Its Theory and Practice* (Quezon City: University of the Philippines Press, 2001), 190.

48. Putzel, *Captive Land,* 224.

49. Supreme Court, *Republic of the Philippines et al. vs. Sandoval, Caylao et al.* (G.R. No. 84607).

50. Ibid.

51. Jeannette Andrade, "Mendiola Massacre Victims Seek Justice," *Manila Times*, Feb. 20, 2006.

52. The group's title refers to the day of the Mendiola massacre.

53. Gerry Corpuz, "Compensation Bill for Mendiola Massacre Victims Sought," *Bulatlat*, Jan. 25, 2004, http://www.bulatlat.com/news/3-50/3-50-mendiola.html.

54. Kilusang Magbubukid ng Pilipinas (Farmers Movement of the Philippines), "Mendiola Massacre Widows Hit Estrada's Bogus Land Reform," Jan. 22, 1999, http://www.hartford-hwp.com/archives/54a/105.html.

55. Thea Alberto, "KMP: Jan 22 Protest Is to Remember Mendiola Massacre," *INQUIRER.net, Philippine News for Filipinos*, Jan. 14, 2008, http://newsinfo .inquirer.net/breakingnews/nation/view/20080114-112251/KMP-Jan-22-protest-is-to-remember-Mendiola-massacre.

56. See, e.g., Jessica Mora, "Oldest Survivor of Mendiola Massacre Still Traumatized," *Manila Times*, Jan. 22, 2010, http://www.manilatimes.net/index.php/top-stories/10126-oldest-survivor-of-mendiola-massacre-still-traumatized.

57. Rorie Fajardo, "The Mendiola Massacre: Old Causes, New Paths," *GMA News.TV—Official Website of GMA News and Public Affairs*, Jan. 22, 2007, http://www .gmanews.tv/story/27740/the-mendiola-massacre-old-causes-new-paths.

58. Corpuz, "Compensation Bill for Mendiola Massacre Victims Sought."

59. Stephanie Dychiu, "Hacienda Luisita's Past Haunts Noynoy's Future—Special Reports," *GMANews.TV—Official Website of GMA News and Public Affairs*, Jan. 18 2010, http://www.gmanews.tv/story/181877/hacienda-luisitas-past-haunts-noynoys-future.

60. W. Scott Thompson, *The Philippines in Crisis; Development and Security in the Aquino Era, 1986–92* (New York: St. Martin's Press, 1992), 53. See Putzel, *Captive Land*, chap. 9, for analysis of the role of the United States in agrarian reform during the Aquino regime.

61. Meredith L Weiss, Edward Newman, and Itty Abraham, "Introduction—The Politics of Violence: Modalities, Frames and Functions," in *Political Violence in South and Southeast Asia*, ed. United Nations (New York: United Nations University Press, 2010), 2, 3.

62. Weiss, Newman, and Abraham, "Introduction."

9

The Four-Eights Democratic Movement and Political Repression in Myanmar

Kyaw Yin Hlaing

The Four-Eights democratic movement is one of the most crucial events in the history of state-society relations in Myanmar, for it opened up a long period of violent state repression against certain societal groups. Myanmar's ruling military, which was initially known as the State Law and Order Restoration Council (SLORC) in 1988 and later renamed the State Peace and Development Council (SPDC) in 1997, came to power by forcefully cracking down on the Four-Eights protests. In addition, the junta has continued to repress the members of opposition groups throughout the period of its rule to keep itself in power. That is why the SLORC/SPDC has been referred to as a fascist regime, a government that imposed a reign of terror or an Orwellian state on its own people.

In fact, it is hard to exaggerate the repressiveness of the Myanmar military government. It kept high-profile politicians like Tin Oo and Aung San Suu Kyi under house arrest and sentenced several leading pro-democracy activists to prison terms ranging from 10 to 103 years. Many political prisoners have also been physically tortured. Since the junta took control of the country, soldiers have also acted strictly in line with the warning of their former leader Ne Win: "When the army shoots, it shoots to hit."[1] Therefore, the bulk of the existing study of state-society relations in Myanmar has been on how the junta brutally repressed its own citizens, especially members of the political opposition.

This chapter posits that Myanmar's military regime could be ruthless in dealing with its challengers. However, it has to be noted that the reality is far more complex than what one would learn from most scholarly and journalistic accounts. Regardless of the stunning evidence of the ruling military government's ruthless repression of its opponents, one cannot argue, as done by most of the existing studies, that the actions of the military government against the opposition were consistently severe. At the same time, one cannot simply claim that the government will not tolerate any of its critics. Rather, a more nuanced reading of the situation is required.

It is true that the government was not tolerant of most of its critics and challengers in the early 1990s. Along with leading activists who called for the public to do whatever they could to bring down the government, many people were arrested simply for giving interviews to foreign journalists or for helping family members of opposition leaders. The government practiced a zero-tolerance policy during that time. In the second half of the 1990s, however, the government came to show some tolerance toward its critics. The ways the government dealt with societal groups became more complex in the 2000s. On the one hand, the government became more tolerant of its critics. The government has also come to tolerate local civil society organizations that were closely working with international nongovernmental associations (INGOs) and foreign funding agencies, although they were not formally registered. Both senior government officials and their agents also became friendly with former opposition leaders whom they had imprisoned in the 1990s. On the other hand, the government came to take more severe actions against the activists who posed credible challenge to its rule. Only beginning in 2000 were political activists in Myanmar given more than forty-year prison terms.

This chapter will examine the nuances in the ways the government dealt with the political opposition. In so doing, it argues that one has to understand the way the military government repressed its opponents in light of the state-building and regime-construction processes. Following Vince Boudreau and others, state building "involves more or less direct efforts to bring people living *outside* state authority under state control and includes the construction of institutions and capacities that enable those efforts"; regime construction "involves the regularization of rules for the exercise of power, including the principles according to which leaders are selected [and] how governments are structured."² The military government resorted to a zero-tolerance policy when it had to undertake both state-building and regime-construction activities simultaneously in most parts of the country. The government is more tolerant when it has to undertake only regular regime-construction or -maintenance activities. In that process, the government will severely punish those who are perceived as participating in activities that would later require the government to undertake all-out state-building activities. In other words, actions perceived as threatening the state, especially in terms of its territoriality and sovereignty, will be dealt with much more harshly. And this policy is well in keeping with the military government's portrayal of itself as the defender of the nation and its inhabitants from threats within and without.

The military junta in power and the elected members of parliament drawn from the military are generally not interested in sharing power with the political opposition. This is certainly the case with Aung San Suu Kyi and the National League for Democracy (NLD). The general strategy is to slowly acquire political legitimacy and erase memories of the military's defeat in the 1990 election. Additionally it has regarded political repression, including the violence associated with the 1988 incident, as a law-and-order issue. Consequently there is no need for any kind of truth-finding mission or political reconciliation. And even if such reconciliation were to occur, it would certainly be in accordance with the terms set by the military. The government has also sought to acquire greater internal and international legitimacy by introducing a new constitution that was "ratified" in 2008 and handsomely won the national election in November 2010 amid allegations of vote rigging and monopolistic practices. The newly elected government has an automatic 25-percent seat allocation in parliament and in states and regions through military representatives. Additionally it has complete control over the ministries of Home Affairs, Defense, and Border Areas. And apart from complete autonomy, the military also has six out of eleven members on the National Security and Defense Council. Finally, Prime Minister Thein Sein officially "retired" from the military to assume the civilian appointment, as did many of the other ministers. The conversion of the Union Solidarity and Development Association (USDA), a corporatist-type peak organization, into the Union Solidarity and Development Party (USDP) just before the election also allows the military to maintain a mass-based political party in order to metamorphose itself to suit procedural democratic requirements. Since the by-elections of April 2012, however, the government has recognized the NLD as a legitimate political party and its leader Aung San Suu Kyi as an elected member of parliament. As part of a process of political liberalization, the Thein Sein government has released political prisoners, negotiated ceasefires with many ethnic insurgent groups, and liberalized the political and economic situation in the country.

THE LEAD-UP TO THE FOUR-EIGHTS MOVEMENT

When Burma gained independence in 1948, its regime was a part of the phenomenon that Samuel Huntington has called second-wave democracies. Although Burma's parliamentary democracy was by no means perfect, opposition parties were allowed to exist, and elections were held regularly. The military coup staged by the Revolutionary Council on March 2, 1962, brought an end to this brief period of electoral democracy in Burma. A long period of military rule began. The Revolutionary Council instituted a one-party socialist system by forming the Burma Socialist Program Party (BSPP) and banning all opposition groups. This new government ruled the country with an iron fist.

The 1964 National Solidarity Act warned all potential challengers to the government that high treason was punishable by death. The BSPP government's actions did not, however, bring an end to autonomous political organizations. When they could not engage in autonomous political activities legally, students, teachers, lawyers, and writers created informal discussion groups and engaged in illegal political activities. As a result of political constraints, membership in such organizations was strictly confined to the social networks of their initial founders. Many ambitious informal organizations were loosely connected to illegal political groups, especially the Burma Communist Party (BCP).

Because the socialist government was prepared to do whatever was necessary to eliminate its foes, it was not easy for informal political organizations to organize overt protests. The government cracked down on all antigovernment demonstrations in a consistently forceful manner. Several members of the two major anti-socialist movements—commonly known as the U Than movement and the Hmaing Centenary movement—were shot dead on the streets by government security forces. Others received long prison terms. Those who wanted to engage in open antigovernment activities joined one of the insurgent groups operating in various border areas. In the latter half of the 1980s, however, sociopolitical and economic developments allowed these informal study groups to organize a nation-wide democratic movement.

The 1980s were, in fact, bad years both for the socialist government and for the people. The country's economic growth had stalled, and the cost of living was exorbitant. In 1985, some 40 percent of the population was living below the absolute poverty level.[3] Since the socialist government controlled the entire economy, it was responsible for the poor economic conditions. Then, in an attempt to control the illegal money circulating in the black market, the government carried out demonetization in 1956 and 1987. As a result, the country's two most valuable banknotes became worthless in the first demonetization initiative, and the next three banknotes followed suit in the second. During the first demonetization, people who had paid taxes on their income could convert all of their demonetized banknotes into legal-tender notes; those who could not prove their tax payment could convert only 75 percent of their banknotes; the government confiscated the rest as a fine for presumed tax evasion.[4] But in the second exercise, there was no systematic conversion of demonetized bills to legal-tender status.

Not only did the government's negligence have a negative impact on many people, but the Burmese banking system was so inefficient that most people chose to keep their money in cash rather than depositing it in a bank. Many lower-middle-class families in fact lost their life savings owing to the inefficient banking system, and all business transactions came to a halt in the second demonetization exercise. Taking advantage of this situation, BCP-affiliated student study groups in Yangon and Mandalay distributed a series of pamphlets urging college students in Rangoon to rise up against the government. At the outset, most students distanced themselves from such activities—the cost of participating in antigovernment protest would be too high—but an unexpected development brought changes in favor of opposition groups. In the middle of March 1988, a minor off-campus brawl between some engineering students and some outsiders broke out near the Rangoon Institute of Technology (RIT). Initially, the incident was nonpolitical, but it grew into a violent riot because of mismanagement by local authorities. In the course of its suppression, a student was fatally wounded, infuriating students at

Rangoon University and RIT. Taking advantage of the situation, leaders of informal study groups publicly urged students to express their unhappiness with the government's handling of the incident by participating in antigovernment rallies at the university. On March 17, when leaders of an independent group marched to RIT with five thousand Rangoon University students, they were stopped on the way by well-equipped riot police. When students refused to comply with their orders, the police crushed the demonstration by force. The cost of launching an antigovernment protest proved to be very high. A number of students were allegedly beaten or shot dead, hundreds of students were arrested, and forty-one students suffocated inside an overloaded police van.

As people's resentment of the government mounted, study groups tried to arrange mass rallies at Rangoon University and RIT, and more antigovernment pamphlets began circulating on campus. To control the situation, the government closed down every university in the country. When universities were reopened in May, students at Rangoon University and RIT found many of their friends missing. By this point it was not difficult for opposition groups to provoke students into joining antigovernment rallies. Moreover, various study groups turned themselves into full-fledged social movement organizations (SMOs). Small independent study groups began joining bigger BCP-affiliated or independent groups. When student-led SMOs from Rangoon University and RIT undertook antigovernment activities on their respective campuses, the government again suspended classes at all universities. While informal study groups–turned-SMOs were pondering their next step, the BCP instructed its agents to organize nationwide antigovernment rallies with the help of its affiliated and sympathizer groups. At this time, there were three major student-led groups at Rangoon University: the communist sympathizers, led by Min Ko Naing and Moe Thee Zun, and two independent groups, led by Min Zaya and Than Win. Although the political ideologies of these three groups were different, they did not have any ideological problems as they all placed emphasis on bringing down the BSPP government.

Because the BCP-affiliated SMOs appeared stronger and better organized than their independent counterparts at Rangoon University and RIT, they often managed to present their demands as the demands of all the students. In June 1988, for example, a BCP-affiliated SMO asked the government to take action against the officials responsible for the deaths of students in the March incident, to release all those arrested, and to allow student unions to form in universities across the country. Although the government did not satisfy all these demands, it did release some students and take nominal action against a few officials supposedly responsible for the students' deaths.

Political development in the first half of 1988, however, gave activists the confidence they needed to persist in their antigovernment activities. At the special party congress held in July, Ne Win, chairman of the Burma Socialist Program Party, stepped down after proposing a referendum on whether Burma should adopt a multiparty system.[5] To many people's surprise, the congress voted down Ne Win's proposal. For the first time in the history of the BSPP, an irreconcilable split had occurred between the party's chairman, Ne Win, and his comrades. Until then, the congress had been a mere rubber stamp, and party members had meekly followed Ne Win's instructions. Those who defied him were fired immediately. This is why Burma watchers jokingly remarked that the BSPP did not have a chairman; rather, the chairman had a party. The congress feared losing the privileges it had acquired. Although party delegates officially asked Ne Win to remain in power, he prudently chose not to stay on.

Political activists sensed the opening up of a window of opportunity. They found Ne Win's disappearance from active politics especially significant, because none of his potential successors seemed as capable as he was. "The government at the time," says a leading member of an opposition group, "was very unstable. Most high-ranking officials did not know Ne Win would resign. The government was caught in an almost untenable position. We thought the time was right to organize a nationwide demonstration."[6] Another activist said, "Ne Win resigned because of our protests. We concluded that if we could bring him down, we could bring down the entire government as well."[7] In fact, Ne Win also helped political activists set the goals of the movement. Until Ne Win mentioned holding a referendum for the country's party system, political activists were not asking for democracy. After listening to Ne Win's speech, however, political activists began calling for the people to fight for democratic transition in Burma. Furthermore, SMOs began receiving moral and material support from major foreign embassies, including those of the United States, Japan, Germany, and Australia.

Despite the new political opportunity and the support accorded by major foreign embassies, SMOs still had trouble disseminating informa-

tion about a nationwide movement. Ne Win's successor, Sein Lwin, was
not very conciliatory. Because of his alleged involvement in dynamiting
the student union building at Rangoon University in 1962 and in the
forceful suppression of subsequent antigovernment protests, he was
nicknamed "the butcher" by the people. He mentioned in a speech given
to state and divisional council members that he would try to restore discipline in the country.[8] A retired BSPP official recalled that Sein Lwin
was prepared to do anything to get things right.[9] Even late in July 1988,
many people, especially in rural areas, did not know that the opposition
groups were trying to organize a nationwide democratic rally on August
8. A survey of one hundred rural people and one hundred urbanites
conducted in 1999 indicated that only fifteen of the rural people and
twenty-five urbanites knew about the Four-Eights movement two weeks
before the rally began. The rest did not learn about it until the following week. The problem was resolved when members of an independent
student SMO happened to run into the BBC correspondent Christopher
Guiness. On August 6, 1988, the BBC aired an interview with a group of
Rangoon University students. In the interview, the student leaders first
described how students were tortured in prison. They then called for
the whole nation to rise up for democracy. It was this BBC broadcast
that helped the movement turn bystanders into participants. At about
the same time, the Voice of America (VOA) came to serve as a source
of information about the movement. SMOs used both the BBC and
VOA as a coordination mechanism between the summit and the base.
In fact, student activists framed the BBC interview exactly in the way
they wanted. Taking advantage of rumors circulating in Yangon regarding students being tortured and raped in prison, they convincingly portrayed how they had suffered. In reality, none of the students involved
in the interview had been tortured or raped (at least at the time of the
interview). They simply made it up "to provoke the whole country to
rise up against the government."[10]

On August 8, 1988, the SMOs in Yangon and Mandalay had mobilized enough people to begin the movement. For the first few days, however, the government fired on demonstrators. If the security forces had
kept shooting, the movement might have collapsed at once. The restraint
was shown in part because of differences between some senior BSPP government officials and in part because of Ne Win's order that they should
not use excessive force against demonstrators.[11] Although Ne Win had

stepped down, he was still running the government from behind the scenes.[12] Therefore, BSPP government officials could not do much without getting his approval. No one really knows for sure why Ne Win did not allow them to crack down on the demonstration forcefully at that time. In any case, their change of policy enabled SMOs to mobilize even more people into the movement.

SMOs, however, suffered from an "organizational deficit"—that is, the network of the BCP's affiliated study groups was not large enough to organize a nationwide movement. To make up for this deficit, SMOs tried to find a way to appropriate existing social organizations. BCP-affiliated SMOs first tried to appropriate the associations in which members of their "brother reading groups" were involved. In places where there were no affiliated reading groups, BCP-affiliated SMOs sent out their agents to establish contact with well-respected figures with the intent of using them as brokers who could help them turn local organizations into SMOs. By the second week of the movement's inception, a number of conventional religious and social organizations had emerged as SMOs. At the same time, popular figures like Daw Aung San Suu Kyi, the daughter of the national hero Aung San, and U Nu came to join the movement.[13] BCP agents then tried to unite the movement by forming general strike committees in various parts of the country. At about the same time, Sein Lwin was replaced by Attorney General Dr. Maung Maung. Many protestors interpreted the fall of the butcher as the harbinger of the victory of the movement and started shouting "victory" in the streets.[14] At that time, Dr. Maung Maung, the last president of the socialist regime, declared to the nation that the government would hold a multiparty election. Dr. Maung Maung also asked the people to call off their demonstration so that the government could make the necessary arrangements for holding an election. Dr. Maung Maung's apologetic and seemingly compliant manner on national television made many assume that the government was no longer the confident leviathan it used to be.[15] Meanwhile, former prime minister U Nu formed an interim government. Then veteran politicians and Suu Kyi tried to form a national consultative committee.

In the last week of August 1988, the socialist government stopped functioning, and the country found itself in a state of anarchy. Many government officials joined the protests by forming strike committees. While government newspapers started publishing news articles in support of the protests, many strike committees took control of electric power stations and petroleum depots. Because they received conflicting orders and instructions from their superiors, police, military and other security officers could not take any action. Some protestors surrounded government offices and military headquarters and verbally attacked senior government officials. While some called for the execution of Ne Win and other political and military leaders, others called for the transfer of power to an interim government. On September 9, U Nu formed an interim government with his former colleagues. Aung San Suu Kyi and some veteran politicians also tried to form a committee that could serve as an intermediary between the government and the people.

Meanwhile, in some major cities, thugs and unruly people started destroying government office buildings, storage places, factories, and public stores and stealing things from them. The military, after it took control of the country, announced that the value of the public properties destroyed by the protestors amounted to 620.46 million kyat (based on a six-kyat-to-a-dollar exchange rate).[16] In many parts of the country, some unruly protestors attacked police stations and military units. Thirty security officers were reportedly killed by rioters.[17] In Yangon, some protestors arrested retired military officers after accusing them of spying for the government. Some protestors conducted public executions of some of these alleged government spies. According to a government report, unruly thugs either beheaded or burned to death twenty-three people who, they thought, were government spies. Student and community leaders tried to control these unruly protestors. However, students proved to be quite powerless to deal with unruly people. One former student leader said, "Those people were totally violent. We tried to tell them not to kill anybody. They would not listen to us. They looked really scary. We could not even stop the people who were destroying our university. We asked soldiers who were guarding the television and radio station to do something about it. Soldiers just said, they were ordered not to take any actions against protestors."[18] Veteran politicians and leading activists pressured the socialist government to transfer power to an interim government so as to restore law and order in the country and to undertake a real democratic transition by holding credible, free, and fair elections.

Then-President Maung Maung refused to hand over power to an interim government but promised to hold multiparty elections. The protestors were determined to continue with street demonstrations until the government complied with their demands. After witnessing the anarchic situation in the nation's capital, then–Commander-in-Chief Saw Maung and Intelligence Chief Khin Nyunt reportedly became frustrated with their powerless position. A source close to these two officials noted, "Both Generals Saw Maung and Khin Nyunt personally saw government buildings being destroyed." They were very upset with the fact that their soldiers were being chased by rioters. Saw Maung was verbally abused by the protestors demonstrating in front the War Office. Many veteran military officers who had joined the protests were also calling for military officers to join them. There were rumors about the air force planning to bomb regional military headquarters in upper Myanmar. General Saw Maung strongly felt that he must do something before the *tatmadaw* (armed forces) split up. Khin Nyunt agreed with him. As far as they were concerned, the people who orchestrated the protests were themselves being controlled by the BCP or Western countries. When a government ship detected the presence of American navy ships near Myanmar territorial waters, officials felt strongly about doing something before the government fell apart.[19] They then reportedly explained the situation to Ne Win at the latter's residence and asked him what they should do. At that time, Vice President Aye Ko and the secretary general of the State Council, Kyaw Htin, reportedly wanted to crack down on the protests by imposing military rule throughout the country. Ne Win told the older generation that it was time for them to let go of power and let the younger generation deal with the situation. President Maung Maung wholeheartedly supported the plan. On September 17, 1988, the tatmadaw took control of the government.

Many military leaders at that time believed that although many citizens had joined the protests simply because they truly wanted democracy, it was the presence of the BCP cells and of the lackeys of manipulative Western governments (whom army officers referred to as ax handles) and Western media that contributed to the country's state of anarchy. They also believed that their continued presence could contribute to a repeat of the Four-Eights movement. The then-chairman and the first secretary of the SLORC, Saw Maung and Khin Nyunt, repeatedly mentioned in their speeches and press conferences that the provocation of external forces like the BCP and Western governments had led many gullible and naive people to turn against their own government.

THE MILITARY GOVERNMENT'S MISSION TO RESTORE
LAW AND ORDER IN THE EARLY 1990S

When Commander-in-Chief Saw Maung announced on national radio that the tatmadaw had taken over the government and would take all necessary actions to restore law and order in the country, many protestors thought that the new military council would not be able to revive the dying leviathan. Many defied the order to disband. Some even prepared to fight against the soldiers with *gin-ga-lee* (nails or sharp bicycle spokes fired from catapults) if the latter forced them out of their makeshift headquarters. On the day the formation of a new military government was announced, the tatmadaw did not take any actions against protestors. Around noon the next day, however, military battalions moved into all cities and towns where protests were taking place. While marching into their assigned areas, soldiers also fired guns into the air continuously for about fifteen minutes to half an hour. They removed all roadblocks and ordered residents to bring them all antigovernment pamphlets in their possession. In some places, strike committees refused to move out of their headquarters. In a few cases, they shot gin-ga-lee at soldiers who approached them. A handful of soldiers reportedly died of gin-ga-lee wounds. However, when soldiers fired back and killed a number of protestors, the strike committees called off all their activities. Soldiers also shot at the people who broke curfew, which lasted from 6:00 P.M. to 6:00 A.M. Although the government announced that 691 people were killed during this time, protestors and some eyewitnesses speculated that more than 3,000 people were killed by government security forces. Within a week, the military government managed to clear all roadblocks, and the tatmadaw was in control of the country. Many activists then decided to continue activities within the country, while many others went to border areas to start exile movements against the military government.

As soon as it managed to get the state apparatus functioning again, the government went after the people who had been involved in destroying public properties and killing others, prominent informants of foreign journalists, and government officials who had joined the protests. Those found guilty of destroying public properties or committing murder and informants of foreign journalists were summarily tried and given severe punishments, ranging from ten-year prison terms to death. Although police and military officials who had joined the protests were dismissed soon after the protests were subdued, the government did not dismiss civilian employees immediately. Some retired government officials surmised that about two hundred people lost their jobs for giving answers military leaders did not want to hear. At the same time, all midlevel government servants whose children were actively involved in the protests were either forced to retire or dismissed.

Meanwhile, the government asked the public, especially political activists, either to join a political party if they wished to remain involved in political activities or to stop all political activities and live as law-abiding citizens. This new parameter enabled the government to start taking action against those who had tried to organize political activities outside its legally sanctioned space. Many political activists and veteran politicians formed more than two hundred political parties within the next six months. However, student leaders continued to criticize the government and call for the people to continue to fight for democracy. They also worked covertly with exile groups based in Thailand. Not surprisingly, the government arrested and sentenced many student leaders to lengthy prison terms. The first chairman of the SLORC, General Saw Maung, once famously or infamously said, "In seeking out enemy what is the basic act? We must first locate the enemy. If we cannot locate the enemy, we must open searching fire."[20] Government agents readily arrested the student leaders who responded to their searching fire. Those who showed repentance either received short prison terms or were released. Those who cooperated with the agents only after they were tortured usually received five- to ten-year prison terms.

At about the same time, the government also turned its attention to leading political activists who, it thought, were either linked to the BCP or received assistance and advice from Western embassies and informants of foreign media, especially BBC and VOA. Among these people were journalists, writers, retired government officials, Buddhist monks, schoolteachers, lawyers, factory workers, and small businessmen. A former activist noted, "It was impossible to hide anything. They beat us with belt and cane. They would also knock us down to the ground after blindfolding us. They would then kick all over our body until we started saying what they wanted to hear. Sometimes they put our head into a bucket and poured water into it until we were completely choked. We ended up saying things that we were not even asked to say. The suffering was so immense that we lost self-control."[21]

After illegal student and political organizations were subdued, the government turned to political parties. The generals repeatedly warned members of political parties that if they did not abide by the laws adopted by the government, then they would be punished severely. The government also warned citizens not to help politicians with their illegal activities. As the NLD, which was made up of the intelligentsia (writers, lawyers, journalists, doctors) and veteran military officers and led by prominent figures like Aung San Suu Kyi and well-respected ex-military officers such as Tin Oo and Aung Gyi, emerged as the main opposition party, the government came to treat it as an enemy organization that had to be monitored. As an organization formed of former participants in the Four-Eights movement, the NLD, especially its intelligentsia, continued to act like a social movement organization. Many NLD members felt that the democracy movement that had begun on August 8, 1988, was not yet over. When the NLD managed to convince forty-three other political parties to elect Aung San Suu Kyi as their representative to deal with the government, the government came to see the NLD as an organization that could jeopardize its attempt to restore law and order and began to arrest its members. A good example was the detention of the leading NLD member Win Tin, who was known to have been the mastermind behind many NLD activities in early 1989. Win Tin was subsequently sentenced to an eleven-year prison term. The government also placed the two NLD leaders Aung San Suu Kyi and Tin Oo under house arrest.

After the NLD won a landslide victory in the elections in 1990, the military had to decide if it would transfer power to the NLD as it had earlier promised or find a way to delay the power transfer. Military leaders initially thought about transferring power to the NLD. However, after the attempt of a group of impatient NLD members to call their own parliament and form an interim government, the junta decided to delay the power-transfer process by holding a constitution-drafting convention without setting a deadline. On December 7, 1990, the first secretary and intelligence chief, Khin Nyunt, explained in one of his marathon press conferences that left-wing (BCP) and right-wing (pro-Western political activists based both inside and outside the country) political forces that had tried to take over the government in 1988 had come together to plot against the government again.[22] Khin Nyunt also noted that this was the continuation of what they had started in 1988. In concluding his speech, Khin Nyunt said in a somewhat angry tone that the government would take punitive action against anybody who tried to challenge its rule and jeopardize its plan for political transition in Myanmar.[23] The government did not even tolerate prominent and highly respected Buddhist monks. When Buddhist monks in Mandalay organized a boycott against military officers by not performing religious rituals for them and their family members, the government sent highly respected monks to labor camps. They were also forced to wear prison uniforms even though they continued to live like monks.[24] Between 1990 and 1995, more than a thousand political activists and politicians were reportedly sentenced to five- to fifteen-year prison terms.

In sum, the military government's harsh repression of the Four-Eights Movement aimed at teaching its citizens a lesson: if they associated with external forces of which the regime did not approve or if they challenged its rule, the state would punish them severely. The government's punitive actions against challengers produced the desired results. By the early 1990s, a large majority of the population had come to accept that the opposition was no match for the government. Although many of them supported Aung San Suu Kyi, they were not willing to take to the streets for her. All 250 participants in a survey I conducted in the early 1990s noted that they were afraid of the government; 87 of them said they were so afraid of the government that they dare not listen openly to BBC and VOA broadcasts. Interviewees also said that since the early 1990s, it had become utterly impossible to organize large-scale demonstrations that could be sustained for several weeks. They also said that by 1993, they had come to realize that the government was stronger than the movement.

THE MILITARY GOVERNMENT AND THE YEAR OF SELECTIVE REPRESSION

In the middle of the 1990s, the government became quite confident about its position in the country. It had successfully cleansed the NLD of intelligentsia-group members. Most members of the NLD intelligentsia had been detained because of their connection to BCP cells. The party was left with aging retired military officers who mainly wished to keep the party alive. The party had even expelled Aung San Suu Kyi in order to please the government. The government also deregistered the political parties that had not won any seats in elections. In addition, the generals successfully controlled discussion in the national convention that they started in 1993. While the country enjoyed some economic growth, the government also managed to make ceasefire arrangements with seventeen ethnic insurgent groups. The powerful Burma Communist Party split into four ethnic groups in 1989 and stopped functioning as an effective antigovernment force in the early 1990s. Although the Karen National Union (KNU) did not have a ceasefire agreement with the government, government forces had occupied most of its major strongholds in the 1990s. As a result, exiled pro-democracy groups could not operate along the border as freely as they used to. In the international arena, India had stopped supporting pro-democracy groups after deciding to improve relations with the military government. ASEAN countries had invited the Myanmar government to join the regional association in 1997. China has unconditionally supported the regime from the beginning. The government appears to have then thought that it could rule the country without keeping many political activists in jail.[25] It subsequently released many political activists, including Aung San Su Kyi and Tin Oo. Government agents also tried to reach out to political activists by offering them the help they might need to make a living. In addition, the government stopped arresting family members of the activists they could not arrest. The government also came to tolerate those people who provided refuge or financial support to political activists. These conciliatory gestures were meant to defuse the tense political situation that had evolved after 1988.

Because the democracy movement was still going on and political activists from inside and outside the country continued to challenge the government in any ways they could, the government had to continue at least to undertake regime-construction activities. A former government official noted, "In the second half of the 1990s, the government was already in firm control of the country. However, we were still surrounded by enemies. We had to monitor the activities of our enemies and made sure that they did not do anything that would undermine the government."[26] In 1996, the NLD walked out of the national convention, saying that it did not have any freedom to make the proposals it favored. It then pressed for dialogue between Aung San Suu Kyi and military leaders. The government responded by suspending the national convention. In 1996, students from the Rangoon Institute of Technology organized protests after some students had a fight with a local restaurant owner. Because the 1988 movement occurred in the wake of a fight between RIT students and some people in the neighborhood, some had expected that the protests might spread to every corner of the country again. Although the protests spread to some universities in upper Myanmar, the government quickly cracked down on them. All leading participants of the protests were arrested and sentenced to seven- to twelve-year prison terms. In 1998, the NLD organized the Committee Representing People's Parliament (CRPP), with nine other political parties, which won some seats in the 1990 elections. When the CRPP called a meeting in Yangon, the government arrested all 110 parliamentarians-elect. Most of them were released a few months later, after they agreed not to participate in any meeting organized by CRPP. In 1998, the government also arrested a student leader who wrote about the history of the student union in Myanmar and all former student leaders who read the manuscripts. They were all given ten- to twenty-year prison terms. As a result of these repressive measures, the attempt of several exile groups to mobilize the Four-Nines movement on September 9, 1999, came to naught.

The Military Government and Ongoing Repression

In the early 2000s, the military government ruled the country without clearly explaining to the public how it would introduce political reforms in the country. Although the generals allowed some civil society organizations to undertake development activities, it did not do anything with the political opposition other than placing restrictions on the movements of Aung San Suu Kyi and arresting anybody who tried to organize anti-government meetings and activities openly. Things started to change after Aung San Suu Kyi, out of frustration, tried to make trips to up-country areas in defiance of travel restrictions. The government responded by placing her under house arrest again.

The NLD's aging leadership gave an ultimatum to the government to release Aung San Suu Kyi. However, they could not do anything when the government did not comply. Their attempt to organize protests in the country ended in vain. In 2002, the government released Aung San Suu Kyi after some top generals had secret meetings with her. There were rumors that the government and Aung San Suu Kyi had found a way to work together and that political prisoners would soon be released.

However, the generals merely wanted Aung San Suu Kyi to help them with their development programs and to convince Western countries to lift sanctions. A source close to the government revealed that General Khin Nyunt allowed her to travel around the country mainly because he believed that they could control the situation.[27] Apparently Khin Nyunt believed that her travels would also have some positive effect on the country's international reputation. However, some powerful ministers in the government were uncomfortable with the situation and tried to disrupt Aung San Suu Kyi's trips. Eventually there was a showdown between Aung San Suu Kyi's supporters and government supporters at Deepayin in central Myanmar. According to opposition sources, as many as seventy pro-democracy people were killed by government supporters. However, the government insisted that only four people had died. Regardless of which figure is correct, this proved to be one of the most violent encounters between the NLD and the government. The government subsequently placed Aung San Suu Kyi under house arrest again.

In the wake of the Deepayin incident, the government appointed intelligence chief Khin Nyunt as prime minister and resumed the national convention. The government also announced a seven-step roadmap to democracy.[28] This was part of an attempt to allay international criticism against its violent repression of Aung San Suu Kyi and her supporters. However, it also served as the government's plan for democratic transition in Myanmar. The government invited the NLD and other legal political parties and all ceasefire groups to participate in the convention. Both the NLD and a major ethnic political party, the Shan National League for Democracy (SNLD), boycotted the convention. Although the US government had imposed economic sanctions on Myanmar in response to the government's detention of Aung San Suu Kyi, the NLD and exile groups could not do much to influence political developments within the country. During this time, the government had to take severe punitive actions against only two groups of people. One worked with an exiled labor union in giving information about forced labor to the International Labor Organization; the other worked as a journalist for the Democratic Voice of Burma, an exiled radio station based in Norway.

In 2004, a power struggle between the military intelligence corps and army officers led to the disbandment of the entire intelligence agency and the dismissal of Khin Nyunt and all other powerful intelligence officers. At the end of 2004 and in early 2005, the government released many prisoners, including prominent student leaders who had been jailed since 1989. Meanwhile, the government sentenced five leaders of the SNLD to lengthy prison terms ranging from 79 to 103 years, for they had tried to encourage the ceasefire groups that were attending the national convention to take a tough stand against the government guidelines for the new constitution.

In the middle of 2005, there emerged a new influential organization known as the 88 generation group, consisting of former student leaders who had been released from prison. Government agents reportedly encouraged the members of the 88 generation group to engage in community development activities and to stay away from political parties. The government also allowed some leaders of the group to travel to foreign countries. Although they interacted with the NLD and exiled political groups, the 88 generation group initially confined its activities to helping citizens get their legal rights in the country. Some government agents reportedly kept in touch with some members of the group. The government briefly detained them in late 2006, after they celebrated the anniversary of the Four-Eights Movement. When they were released about four months later, the government apparently warned them not to engage in any activities that would destabilize the country. In August 2007, the government suddenly suspended the fuel subsidy without any prior notice. The 88 generation group then organized protests, demanding that the government do more for the welfare of the citizens. All leading members of the group were immediately arrested and sentenced to fifty- to sixty-five-year prison terms. A government official noted that "the government was willing to allow members of the 88 generation group to organize meetings and engage in community development activities. However, since they were almost as popular as Aung San Suu Kyi, the government could not tolerate them when they started organizing demonstrations. The long prison terms given to these former student leaders were designed to dissuade younger people from trying to mobilize demonstrations."[29]

In mid-September 2007, Buddhist monks in some major cities organized peaceful demonstrations. A series of events that took place in early September led to one demonstration. On September 5, a group of monks from Pakokku staged a peaceful demonstration against higher fuel prices.[30] Local officials tried to disperse the protest, reportedly using members of two government-organized nongovernmental associations—the Union Solidarity and Development Association (USDA) and Swan

Arshin—to do so. Many were reported to have been beaten by supporters of the government, and three monks were arrested. Soldiers also tried
to disperse the protests by firing guns into the air. On the following day,
when local officials went to one of the main Pakokku monasteries to apologize for what had happened the day before, the monks, angered by the
mistreatment of the peaceful demonstrators, burned the officials' cars and
held the officials hostage until the local government had agreed to release
the detained monks.[31]

Meanwhile, an underground organization known as the Alliance
of All Burma Buddhist Monks emerged. The alliance made its presence
known by distributing leaflets asking the government to apologize for the
mistreatment of monks in Pakokku.[32] The alliance warned the government
that if it did not issue a formal apology by September 17, the monks would
hold *patam nikkujjana kamma;* that is, they would boycott the receipt of
alms from family members of the armed forces.[33] The junta ignored the
alliance's ultimatum. On September 17, 2007, several hundred monks
staged peaceful protests. To the surprise of many inside Myanmar, the
government did not immediately crack down on the protesting monks.
As a result, the number of participants grew from a few hundred to a few
hundred thousand and generated public sympathy for their cause.

Originally, the monks had not planned to prolong their demonstrations. According to an activist monk from Yangon, many senior monks
feared that the government would brutally repress the protests if they
dragged on. Some monks therefore wanted to stop the demonstrations
after a few days.[34] But growing public support swayed many younger
monks toward continuing to protest until the government complied
with their demands.[35] Some monks also wanted to enlarge the protests
by allowing lay political activists to join in. The alliance finally agreed on
both counts: the protests would continue, while remaining peaceful, and
other citizens would be allowed to join them.[36]

The demonstrators' ultimate goal was to pressure the government
into working for national reconciliation and genuine political reform.
But the alliance and other protest groups did not voice their political
demands in a united manner. Protesters in Pakokku made more political
demands than their counterparts in Yangon and other places. As the size
and momentum of the demonstrations swelled, the prospect of political
change began to seem more plausible to many in Myanmar. On September 25, 2007, the junta finally decided to stop the protests. First, a curfew

was imposed in the cities where major demonstrations had taken place. Immediately thereafter, large contingents of soldiers burst into these cities. The soldiers initially ordered the protesting monks and lay people to disperse. When the protesters did not obey these orders, the soldiers began to lob tear gas and fire guns. In some places the soldiers fired warning shots in the air before opening fire at demonstrators. At other locations, however, soldiers allegedly shot at protesters without prior warning. Soldiers also beat monks and lay protesters with bamboo sticks.

It is clear that several hundred protesters were beaten in Yangon. The number killed outright became a matter of dispute between the generals and their opponents. The junta told the UN human rights envoy that fifteen people had been shot dead, but opposition groups claimed that soldiers had killed more than one hundred.[37] As far as we know, no protesters were killed in the other cities. This was due in part to instances of cooperation between military officers and some senior monks. The demonstrations did not stop right away, but around the country their size and number had diminished significantly by September 27. On the following day, monk protesters who had not yet been arrested were interned in their monasteries. Security forces then raided the main monasteries in cities where major protests had taken place and detained the protest leaders. By the end of September the monks' peaceful protests had been subdued. A few months later, the monks who led the protests were sentenced to twenty- to sixty-five-year prison terms.

In May 2008, the delta area in lower Myanmar was badly hit by Cyclone Nargis. Since it could not cope with the relief and recovery activities, the government allowed several citizen groups to help the victims. While doing disaster-relief work, many of these citizen groups emerged as civil society organizations. The government did not allow political activists to engage in disaster-relief work, because the activists did not simply engage in disaster-relief activities. While helping victims, they also tried to expose the failure of the government's relief programs by giving interviews to the BBC and VOA. One government officer noted, "It seemed that their intention was not simply to help the victims but to embarrass the government."[38] When the government sentenced some prominent activists who had tried to embarrass them to forty- to forty-five-year prison terms, most political activists stopped openly criticizing the government's relief programs. An activist noted, "Those who are strong and ruthless win."[39]

By the middle of 2010, the junta's plan was moving forward without any major disruption. The junta had concluded the national convention after adopting 104 principles for the new constitution in late 2007. A committee formed by the government then drafted the constitution on the basis of these principles. The government then held a referendum for the new constitutions in May and September 2008. Amid the accusation that there were irregularities in the referendum, the government announced that more than 92 percent of the voters had approved the new constitution. The junta then announced that it would hold elections in 2010. When the election commission started accepting applications for party registration, the NLD decided not to re-register with the government and stopped being a legal political party on May 6. A group of leading NLD members then formed a new political party known as the National Democratic Front (NDF). Unlike in 1990, the government also formed its own political party, known as the Union Solidarity and Development Party (USDP), which was the simple conversion of its former mass organization.

Needless to say, Myanmar's ruling military government has been quite ruthless in dealing with societal groups and individuals that it considers to pose a serious threat to its rule. Naturally, the degree of the government's repressiveness depends upon the magnitude of the threat posed by challengers. During the Four-Eights movement, protestors not only broke the rules set by the government but also allied themselves with groups that challenged the then-government from areas that were out of government control. Because a large number of people actively participated in the Four-Eights movement, it was not easy for the government to isolate only the people who really belonged to external organizations. Therefore, whenever they could identify a BCP cell, they arrested not only the cell members but also all the people associated with it.

The government eventually came to consider the opposition groups less threatening than before. Although the military government did not want to be viewed as weak and indecisive, it apparently did not want to resort to violent repression all the time. A source close to the government noted, "If possible, our generals wish to be loved by the people." As far as pro-democracy activists are concerned, the movement they started in August 1988 is still going on, and they will not end it until the country becomes democratic. The tatmadaw, on the other hand, does not plan to give up its political power. The generals are now trying to extend the role of the military in the government through the new constitution that guarantees the tatmadaw institutionalized representation.

The elections that were held in November 2010 have given the government a veneer of internal and international legitimacy. Opposition groups and politicians accused the government of cheating in the elections, primarily by way of counting pre-election ballots to tilt the numbers in its favor. The government also utilized the nationwide Union Solidarity and Development Party (USDP) for political mobilization and vote aggregation. Additionally, a large number of serving and retired military officers were mobilized to take part in the elections. The NLD and four other parties that chose not to contest the election were dissolved by the Union Election Commission, and those contesting the election had to pay a hefty fee of five hundred dollars per candidate. Voter turnout for the election was in excess of 75 percent at all levels, and as expected, the USDP won handsomely, with 79.7 percent of the seats in the People's Assembly, 76.8 percent in the National Assembly, and 74.9 percent in the Regional Assembly. Opposition seats were won by an NLD splinter party, the National Democratic Front, the National Union Party (NUP, a relic of the pre-1988 BSPP government), and ethnic political parties. Consequently, opposition political parties do have a measure of representation in the new parliament. It remains to be seen how the political opposition functions in the parliament and how the military, through the USDP, manages with the new norms of parliamentary government. The election itself marks a major turning point in the country's political evolution and has effectively sidestepped the 1990 election results, which are unlikely to be honored in the future. The major agenda item on the tatmadaw's timetable is how to effectively deal with the ceasefire groups that have thus far resisted induction into a border-guard force under its control and command. In fact no election was held in many of these rebel-controlled areas.

As the country undergoes structural political changes, there may well be some opportunities for the political opposition and in particular ethnic parties to register their views. It is entirely possible that a more confident government will allow for greater civil and political liberties insofar as the military's stranglehold on power is not challenged. In fact, Aung San Suu Kyi was released from house arrest shortly after the election, and although the NLD has been declared illegal, it continues to operate in defiance of the government. If the military feels threatened by the activities of the NLD, in particular its collaboration with foreign embassies and ethnic insurgent groups, the military is likely to forcibly shut the NLD down. In this regard, threats to the regime and in particular to the state are taken very seriously, and the state is likely to unleash violence as it has previously done. Violence that is related to consolidation of territory would constitute instrumental violence, although it may have an exemplary angle to it as well, since there are a large number of insurgent groups to deal with. In fact the government's defeat of the Myanmar National Democracy Alliance (MNDA, Kokang) in August 2009 was interpreted by many other insurgent groups as performing an exemplary rather than an instrumental function. On the other hand, the skirmish with the Kachin Independence Army (KIA) over the site of a dam in June 2011 certainly had the potential to deteriorate into instrumental violence. And violence that is aimed at regime detractors, such as the 1988 Uprising and the 2007 monk-led demonstrations, is more likely to be exemplary and to send a strong deterrent message to observers and potential participants. Nonetheless, the military government is acutely aware of Suu Kyi's international stature and is likely to avoid an open confrontation with her and her supporters, as occurred in 2003. The greater likelihood, and the military's preferred outcome, is that both the cause of the NLD and Suu Kyi will eventually fade over time. Although the regime remains essentially military authoritarian, it is trying to metamorphose into a democratic regime, if only procedurally.

The Myanmar government's aim is to press ahead with its own goals for political development. In so doing it hopes to paint over the electoral defeat of 1990. As for the 1988 movement the government is unlikely to concede to excessive use of force. The events of that year will simply go down in government annals as a law-and-order issue that had to be sternly dealt with, not unlike the Chinese government's interpretation of the Tiananmen incident. Consequently there is nothing to resolve. It has since released most political prisoners who were detained in the 1990s and after, just as Suu Kyi was released after the USDP won the elections. The April 2012 by-elections that were handsomely won by Suu Nyi's NLD, which captured forty-three out of the forty-five seats up for election, has strengthened opposition representation in parliament. The Thein Sein government has won widespread praise for its efforts at political and economic liberalization since then, and many Western countries have dismantled sanctions against the government. The only wild cards remaining in the present situation are how the ceasefires with the insurgent armies hold up and how the fighters are eventually demobilized. Given that the ceasefire arrangements essentially challenge government control of the country's territoriality, the situation will be resolved one way or the other over time. Since much of the contested territory borders China, it is likely that China will become involved in the settlement process. And as time has gone on, the government has gotten stronger at the expense of the political opposition and its detractors. Some members of the democracy movement from 1988 are either in prison or exiled abroad, while others have returned after an offer of government amnesty. A few of them have repented and are no longer involved in political activities. Over and above its increased legitimacy, the Myanmar government has also benefited immensely economically from the major finds of oil and gas off its coast. And through Chinese developmental assistance, it continues to try and enhance its domestic legitimacy on the basis of modern infrastructural development and traditional renovation of Buddhist pagodas.

NOTES

1. Ne Win made this comment in the final speech he gave at the emergency party congress on July 23, 1988; see *Working People's Daily,* July 24, 1988.

2. See Vince Boudreau, "Interpreting State Violence in Asian Settings," in this collection.

3. Moksha Yitri, "The Crisis in Burma: Back from the Heart of Darkness," *Asian Survey* 29, no. 6 (1989): 543.

4. *Guardian Daily,* Nov. 8, 1986.

5. *Guardian Daily,* July 24, 1988.

6. Interview with the author, June 8, 1994.

7. Interview with the author, Oct. 7, 2006.

8. *Working People's Daily,* July 27, 1988.

9. Interview with the author, Sept. 12, 1999.

10. Interview with the author, Aug. 19, 1995.

11. Interviews with the author, 1998, 2004, 2005.

12. Interviews with the author, 1999, 2004, 2005, 2006.

13. Hereafter, Daw Aung San Suu Kyi will be referred to as Daw Suu.

14. Interviews with the author, 2004, 2006. I also personally witnessed some protestors in Mandalay shouting "victory" on that day.

15. Interviews with the author, 2004, 2005, 2006.

16. Army Officer, *Nga-ye-khan-atwin-ka-phyan-than-ke-taw-myan-mar-gyi* [The experience of Myanmar when it went through hell] (Yangon: News and Periodical Enterprise, 1990), 9.

17. Ibid., 7.

18. Interview with the author, Oct. 25, 2006.

19. Interview with the author, Aug. 12, 2009.

20. *Working People's Daily,* July 6, 1989.

21. Interview with the author, Nov. 9, 2008.

22. Khin Nyunt, *Ba-ka-ba-ug-dab-n-l-d-gaung-saung-acho—naing-gan-daw-anar-ya-yu-ye-tha-put-u-ka-lain-chun-zat-lan-son* [The story about the evil attempt of the leaders of BCP, DAB, and NLD to attain political power] (Yangon: News and Periodical Enterprise, 1991), 1–69.

23. Ibid.

24. Interview with the author, Oct. 19, 2004.

25. Interview with the author, Sept. 8, 2008.

26. Interview with the author, Dec. 25, 2008.

27. Personal communication with the author, Nov. 3, 2009.

28. The Seven Step roadmap announced by the government includes: "(1) Reconvening of the National Convention that has been adjourned since 1996. (2) After the successful holding of the National Convention, step-by-step implementation of the process necessary for the emergence of a genuine and disciplined democratic system. (3) Drafting of a new constitution in accordance with basic principles and detailed basic principles laid down by the National Convention. (4) Adoption of the constitution through national referendum. (5) Holding of free and fair elections for Pyithu Hluttaws [legislative bodies] according to the new constitution. (6) Convening of Hluttaws attended by Hluttaw members in accordance with the new constitution. (7) Building a modern, developed, and democratic nation by the state leaders elected by the Hluttaw; and the government and other central organs formed by the Hluttaw."

29. Personal communication with the author, June 28, 2009.

30. See *BBC News,* "Q&A: Protests in Burma," Oct. 2, 2007, http://news.bbc.co.uk/2/hi/asia-pacific/7010202.stm.

31. Shah Paung, "Monks Take Officials Hostage for Hours in Upper Burma Standoff," *Irrawaddy,* Sept. 6, 2007, http://www.irrawaddy.org/article.php?art_id=8524.

32. "Burmese Monks Demand Government Apology," *Irrawaddy,* BurmaNet News, Sept. 10, 2007, http://www.burmanet.org/news/2007/09/10/irrawaddy-burmese-monks-demand-government-apology-yeni.

33. Ibid.

34. Interviews with the author, Oct. 27, 2007.

35. Radio Free Asia (Burmese Language Program), "Thousands Protest in Burma," Sept. 19, 2007, http://www.rfa.org/english/news/social/burma_fuelprotest-20070919.html?searchterm=None.

36. Political activist, interview with the author, Oct. 28, 2007.

37. Thomas Fuller, "At Least 15 Died in Crackdown, Myanmar Tells Envoy," *New York Times,* Nov. 17, 2007, http://www.nytimes.com/2007/11/17/world/asia/17myanmar.html.

38. Ibid.

39. Interview with the author, Jan. 18, 2009.

Conclusion

Comparing State Violence and Reconciliation across East Asia

N. Ganesan and Sung Chull Kim

A careful reading of the recent history of East Asia indicates that there are indeed many examples of state violence in the region. As noted at the outset, many instances of the worst examples of such violence occurred during the Cold War, and violence was often directed against those who were regarded as enemies of the regime in power and by extension of the state. This conflation between regime and state security that was common during the Cold War continues to obtain in many countries. Countries with authoritarian regime types often use such broad conceptions of security to legitimize violence against critics. In fact economic development in East Asia has often not been accompanied by political development that distinguishes between state and regime interests and political norms that allow for a plurality of interests and their subsequent contestation within clearly established structural and procedural norms. Rather, political elites often seek to entrench their power base and broaden it if possible. Additionally, positive economic performance is often used to strengthen political legitimacy through performance-based criteria than enhance political pluralism.

An important issue is how to systematically think about state violence in East Asia. Similarly, how does one account for the different conditions under which such violence occurred and for how regimes and countries have dealt with the past? Do such episodes have symbolic value in identifying transgressions and unacceptable behavior, and how were they reconciled in the national psyche of the countries involved? Do they fall into certain categories, and can we create a schema of sorts to better analyze these important episodes in the region's history? In other words, are such events comparable at some analytical level, or are they simply too discrete and diverse to offer any form of useful comparative information that can guide research? Whatever the case may be, the best starting point is perhaps to identify aspects of the violence that make them similar as well as different in order to at least arrive at some attempt to catalog them.

In some senses the Okinawan case is unique because it occurred during conditions of actual war. Interestingly, however, the violence that was directed by the Japanese military against civilians was aimed not at foreigners but rather at local citizens. The evidence also indicates that the military treated the Okinawans with suspicion regarding their loyalty to the state and the government in power. So atrocious was the motivation behind such thinking and so horrendous the crime inflicted on an innocent civilian population subjected to the perceptions of its own military that the topic was left unattended and conveniently forgotten. The fact that the Okinawans were an insignificant minority within the national scheme of things and had little impact on domestic politics made such behavior and denial easier. The Okinawans continue to retain memories of the atrocities inflicted on them by the military, owing to their standing as a minority community, and they see the incident as part of a larger pattern of the exercise of state power by a dominant majority. In fact, the location of US bases and troops on their territory has also become a major point in both local and national politics. Okinawans regard hosting US bases as a disproportionate burden borne by them and have regularly voted in local elections against the continued presence of foreign troops and bases on their soil. Unfortunately for them, however, even well-intentioned local politicians like Hatoyama Yukio, who led the Democratic Party of Japan to victory in 2009 on the promise of renegotiating the base agreement, have been unable to change the situation. And his successors Kan Naoto and Noda Yoshihiko appear less interested in pursuing the matter after US support in coordinating Operation Tomodachi in March 2011, in the aftermath of the massive earthquake and tsunami in the Tohoku region of Japan. If anything, the Japanese government has been far more concerned with reconstructing the damaged areas, resettling the affected population, controlling and monitoring the nuclear fall-out, and restarting the devastated regional economy.

The Thai and Korean cases occurred under rather similar conditions. Both countries were ruled by military authoritarian regimes, which perceived a domestic challenge to their monopoly on power. In both cases, it is clear that the nature of the violence was indiscriminate and that what was perceived as challenges did not constitute a significant threat to the regime in power. The monopoly on violence was clearly utilized as a demonstration of power and the ability to stifle dissent through the use of force. In this regard, the violence that ensued was exemplary in nature and aimed at both primary and secondary constituencies, while retaining the regime in power. The trajectory of domestic political developments in Korea was strongly determined by the fate of the two generals-turned-president who were responsible for the 1980 Kwangju massacre, and the movement and generation that harnessed inspiration from the suppression has paved the way for rising anti-American sentiment since the early 1980s. In fact, it may be argued that this generation has had a profound effect in undermining the security compact that used to previously exist between the United States and South Korea. The Kwangju incident served as a source of intense embarrassment to the military and helped facilitate and entrench an activist political culture as well.[1]

Conversely, in the case of Thailand, the state never dealt with past episodes of violence, and the military continued to use lethal force against its own citizens with impunity. The Red Drum massacre in the 1970s was only part of a pattern of widespread abuse of power by the army and enforcement agencies. However, the events did lead to sufficiently widespread social unrest that the military junta in power was forced to abdicate and allow for a brief democratic interlude from 1973 to 1976. The fact that the military has never been called to task for its behavior until today, while having undergone a measure of democratic transition, is perhaps indicative of the sway that the institution still holds in domestic politics. And the inability of the country's social activists, citizens, and state agencies to hold the military accountable for its excesses also reveals the weakness of these constituencies. The coup against the Thaksin government in 2006 and the unfolding evidence of the deep linkages between the military and the monarchy, especially through the military-dominated Privy Council, provides ample testimony to the position of the military.[2] The utilization of the constitutional and administrative courts to weaken the political opposition and disqualify it from political contestation has also greatly weakened the more neutral bureaucratic apparatuses of the state. In this regard, Thailand has not undergone the social transformation that accompanies economic and political development at the national level compared to other countries in the region, although a measure of such consciousness does obtain in urban areas.

Another way to interpret the evidence is that the realization of such consciousness in rural areas is steadily being thwarted by elites in order to retain them in a subordinate and pliant position. Consequently, violence used against the civilian population has both instrumental and exemplary value—at the former level it entrenches a certain conception of the state that is held to be sacrosanct and not subjected to challenge. During the 2011 election that led to the victory of the Pheu Thai Party and its leader, Yingluck Shinawatra, the military commander General Prayuth Chan-Ocha continuously reminded the electorate to vote in favor of the monarchy—a curious call in a democratic election in a constitutional monarchy. And the military continues to treat the 2011 violence against the Red Shirt movement that led to the death of approximately ninety persons as a law-and-order issue and prevents attempts to hold it accountable for the use of excessive force against mostly unarmed civilian demonstrators. It has also thwarted attempts by the political elite to negotiate terms with the Cambodian government in resolving differences over the Preah Vihear temple complex that have led to sporadic outbursts of violence between the two countries.

The Indonesian case involves violence against civilians within the context of Cold War ideology, since it was primarily directed, at least at the outset, against members and sympathizers of the Indonesian Communist Party. However, a military authoritarian regime was certainly not in place when Sukarno was in power. Sukarno's notion of Guided Democracy, which characterized the Indonesian political system from 1960 to 1965, was rule by presidential decree. Sukarno's linkages to the military lay in the nebulous relationship between the nationalist faction in domestic politics and the early paramilitary units that engaged the Dutch from 1945 to 1949 during the so-called revolutionary period in the country's political history. But the military linkages were significantly different from those that obtained from military elites in the Thai and Korean cases, who were professional soldiers. In what was interpreted to be a coup attempt against the government after the assassination of a number of top generals, the blame was squarely placed on the PKI. The military involvement in the violence was initially to secure the capital city, Jakarta, before the violence spiraled out of control. The situation was aided and abetted by paramilitary and Muslim youth groups opposed to the PKI. Douglas Kammen's chapter in this volume indicates that leading military commanders often took the initiative regarding whether they should be involved in the violence and how severely the purge would be carried out. As a result of this initiative, Kammen thinks that it would be unfair to identify the state as the source of the violence. The outbreak of violence was left unchecked for a long period of time and clearly had a certain pattern that lasted until 1968 in Kalimantan.

The massive violence that resulted in almost five hundred thousand deaths eventually paved the way for regime transition, leading to the installation of Soeharto's New Order government in 1967. This case quite clearly concerns regime transition, and the violence was exemplary, with the PKI as the primary audience and other potential future challengers as the secondary audience. Soeharto's personal involvement in the restoration of order as the head of the Army Strategic Command in Jakarta and his staunch anti-communist credentials meant that the massacres were not investigated. In fact, if anything, the state continued to purge those accused of communist leanings, and communism became an easy way to brand political opponents as enemies of the state. Soeharto's lengthy tenure in office and the relative success of his corporatist developmentalist regime also meant that he decided how history was to be interpreted. The ban on research and alternative interpretations of what had transpired between 1965 and 1968 has for the most part sealed the New Order regime's interpretation of events as sacrosanct. Since many of the country's senior military commanders were implicated in the violence and Soeharto's own support base derived from the military, there was no question of any kind of fact finding regarding what actually transpired during the transitionary period. And although Indonesia has been a stable democracy since the election of the Yudhoyono government in 2004, there has been little effort at uncovering the past. The military is keen to retain its corporate identity and remains an important player in domestic politics. Leading figures in the present government as well as the opposition were also previously from the military, which makes investigation of past misdeeds problematic.

The Cambodian mass killing, by far the worst of the cases documented here, in terms of both the number of casualties and the extended period of violence, occurred under a military regime of sorts. The Khmer Rouge was clearly a military force with hierarchical command and control structures and a clearly defined strategy of warfare tailored along the Maoist model of rural insurgency. Whereas there was some attempted ideological justification of the sustained and large-scale violence directed against civilians, the general understanding of the situation is that the regime was motivated by extreme xenophobia against those of non-Khmer ethnicity but also sought a grotesque purity within the general population that quite simply defies logical explanation. This regime appears to have utilized violence to terrorize the entire population into general submission in order to reorder society and its structural norms with a seeming emphasis on proletarian values and a clear disdain for education and the arts. Sorpong Peou also mentions an ideology of radical egalitarianism, marked by extreme suspicion of urban dwellers and those engaged in capitalist enterprises. The violence also served as a cover for the inability of the Khmer Rouge to govern the country after the guerrilla victory.

The sustained nature of the violence in the Cambodian case far surpasses that of Indonesia in terms of total death toll and has often been classified as genocide. Evidence suggests that more people in the country perished as a result of malnutrition, starvation, and disease than outright killing. Whereas the Cambodian case falls under violence associated with regime transition, it is different to the extent that the Khmer Rouge was keen to erase all practices and memories associated with the past. Hence the violence and hardship had a far more pervasive and sinister character. And since the entire population was involved in the violence, it was clearly more than exemplary, in the way the term has been used thus far. Sorpong Peou tells us that the Khmer Rouge was motivated by extreme anxiety about its vulnerability in the urban areas and regularly purged its own cadres, so that the violence occurred within the state guiding the "revolution," as well as against its perceived enemies. And since the violence went all the way to the top and the movement was broad-based, there was a very real sense in which the situation spun out of control and the violence was nihilistic in character.

The Burma/Myanmar case presents a rather unique situation: a country where a military junta being challenged by the collapse of its socialist-style government was also challenged by a segment of the local urban population. A nervous government, unable to cope with the challenge, used indiscriminate violence against its own citizens, with seeming disunity within the ranks of the military on the proper course of action. The closed nature of the state allowed for the incident to draw much less publicity than it would have otherwise, and there has been little serious effort to deal with this episode in the country's recent history. In 2007 the military brutally crushed an uprising that was led by the monkhood and subsequently detained a large number of monks. The military elite have demonstrated from their response to Cyclone Nargis in 2008 that human security is not high on the agenda. In fact, the manner in which the referendum on the new constitution was rushed through in the aftermath of the cyclone indicates the regime's obsession with its own longevity and security. And the election of November 2010 was intentionally designed to sideline Aung San Suu Kyi and the NLD and privilege the military's Union Solidarity Development Party (USDP), which was in turn represented by military elite who simply changed into mufti. It is therefore clear that the military has no interest in relinquishing its power anytime soon and is in fact trying very hard to ensconce its position while attempting to gain a measure of international credibility through applying minimalist democratic procedures.

The Tiananmen incident in China is not unlike the Burma/Myanmar case in that the regime in power felt threatened by public demonstrations in urban areas calling for greater democratization. Unable to cope with the rising tide of dissent, the regime in power deployed the military and resorted to violence. Unlike the Burma/Myanmar case, however, the Chinese incident attracted widespread publicity internationally, because the timing of the violence coincided with the period when communism was being challenged in Eastern Europe and even the Soviet Union, under the Gorbachev government, had proclaimed its policy of perestroika and glasnost. Consequently, protestors may well have been taken in by the euphoria of broader global developments that appeared to suggest the weakening of left-leaning ideologies. There is some evidence to suggest that the protestors in Burma/Myanmar were similarly inspired.

Finally the Mendiola Bridge massacre in the Philippines shares a number of traits with the other cases as well, although the contestation of what actually transpired is probably much more troubling. Like the Thai case, the state in the Philippines appears to commit acts of political violence with impunity and is never brought to account for its actions.

The massacre also occurred within the framework of a democratic polity that had just entered the political fray against the background of a military authoritarian regime that was deeply embedded in the Cold War and supported by the United States. Whereas the number of victims was the least in comparison to the other cases examined here, the new democratic regime's reliance on the military for its stability and legitimacy appears to have compromised President Aquino. Importantly, the structuration of the Philippine political economy, which draws on its Spanish colonial past, appears to make the country impervious to any form of structural economic and social changes. If so, it is likely that instances of political violence in the Philippines will never be resolved and that the state and its organs have effectively been captured by the ruling elite, who then determine their interests and enemies. Rommel A. Curaming, however, does not apportion willful behavior that regularly legitimizes violence to the elite. Rather, he takes note of the impossibility of any form of resolution of past violence under existing structural conditions.

INSTRUMENTAL VERSUS EXEMPLARY VIOLENCE

Vincent Boudreau argues in his chapter that East Asian states were much more prone to violence at the time of state formation as a result of a larger number of contenders for power, compared to the European experience. Yet as essentially postcolonial states, East Asian states were under pressures that were ameliorated by colonial structures and practices and the demonstration effect of old states and international norms within the broader global context. He also argues that since states in Northeast Asia evolved from an absolutist authoritarian tradition, subsequent regimes were less prone to instrumental violence. In other words, certain norms associated with political hegemony and attendant practices had already been established, and subsequent actions emphasized regulations for mass participation.

The absence of the distinction between state and regime security in many parts of East Asia meant that it was not uncommon for violence to be directed against detractors or challengers to state power. The interesting question that arises from such considerations is: when can a state's use of violence be regarded as legitimate? Presumably conditions that warrant the exercise of such violence are those that truly jeopardize the state and perhaps the regime in power. Yet it would be difficult to arrive at an acceptable definition of what constitutes a threat. The reason for this assertion is simply the fact that such calls are invariably an exercise in judgment, and authoritarian systems typically tend to err on the side of their own safety. And if the incumbent regime monopolizes power and discourse during the outbreak of violence, to redress it afterward becomes problematic. Some cultures also appear more prone to violence than others, and violence inflicted on marginal or marginalized communities is more easily explained and accepted, as Boudreau contends. Such violence is also more likely to be instrumental and more intense since the mainstream political community remains unaffected by it. Additionally, even democratic regimes have been prone to excesses in the past, and ideological considerations and broadly defined notions of "national interest" have been loosely used against those deemed a threat.

If it is indeed true that violence perpetuated during state-building is functional and therefore perhaps justified in the evolution of the state, then almost all of the cases examined in this volume would not strictly qualify as state-building enterprises. There are two possible exceptions to this generalization. The first is the Japanese case, where center-periphery tensions appear to have exaggerated the Japanese military's feeling of vulnerability when fighting US troops in Okinawa. Quite apart from Okinawa being a marginal community, a state of war with foreign forces on its soil would surely have constituted an existential threat to the state as previously constituted. The second case of a functional claim to violence can be made in the Myanmar case. After all, the military does not control the entire country and has negotiated peace agreements with seventeen different ceasefire groups that retain control over contiguous territory and the weapons in their possession. In fact, if anything, the cards have fallen in their favor, since the terms require the military to serve them notice when there is encroachment into these areas. The government's attempts to try and convert these private armies into a Border Guard Force (BGF) have not succeeded, and in 2011, when the government attempted to construct a dam in Kachin state with Chinese assistance, there was an outbreak of conflict between the Kachin Independence Army (KIA) and the military; the situation has been stalemated since, and the fighting has spread to other parts of the state. The larger of these groups are clearly unprepared to give up the territories that they have controlled for over half a decade. Consequently, the process of state construction remains incomplete even with regard to territoriality in Myanmar. The military is therefore understandably harsh toward those who would challenge the regime in power and threaten its legitimacy, which is being given a democratic varnish.

The Philippine case provides clues to a number of other difficult considerations. Can we apportion blame onto the state if the political executive did not condone the outbreak of violence and would likely have acted to prevent it? In other words, the assumption that the state is a unitary one may well be problematic in some cases. Curaming also alludes to another important consideration. He argues that at the time when the violence broke out at the Mendiola Bridge in 1987, both the perpetrator and the victims had much to gain in terms of political leverage if violence actually broke out. In such a situation, it will clearly be much more difficult to apportion blame. And it is for this reason that the state's version of the events that transpired is subjected to careful scrutiny. And if differing interpretations of what actually transpired cannot be effectively brought to a close, then resolution becomes all the more difficult, worsened in the Philippine case by embedded elite interests within the state's executive and judicial institutions. Douglas Kammen also points out how the scale and intensity of the violence in Indonesia were a function of whether regional military commanders were allied with Sukarno and how the navy and the air force were much less complicit in the violence than the army and the RPKAD. Hence, the evidence from these two cases does appear to suggest that the state may not be unitary when violence is utilized. Or to put it differently, elements within enforcement agencies have some leeway in determining the nature of the response when confronted with challenges.

The linkage between state and regime is nebulous in many parts of East Asia, and some elite in difficult situations may well truly believe that challenges to those in power constitute an existential threat. For example, when the Burmese military resorted to violence in 1988 to quell student protests, it was a regime with a deep sense of insecurity and one that had not been openly challenged in urban areas for a long time. Added to this was the fact that the collapse of the Burma Communist Party (BCP) and the defection of its sword arms, the Wa and the Kokang, clearly threatened the territoriality of the state. The Burmese military, since the coup that placed it in power in 1962, had not been able to control many of the highland areas that were inhabited by ethnic minorities. It was in light of this threat that the military government quickly negotiated ceasefire arrangements with the major ethnic armies from 1988 onward. Additionally, the military regards itself as the champion of the state and its citizens against local detractors and foreigners, as Mary Callahan informs us.[3] Consequently, in the Burmese case, the conflation between state and regime security clearly obtains.

If the distinction is between segments of a target audience rather than actions, as Boudreau suggests, then two more cases examined here will also qualify as examples of instrumental violence, albeit state formation was not the motive for the violence. The case of Kwangju in Korea targeted the inhabitants of a specific locale, while the violence directed against the PKI in Indonesia was equally instrumental in identifying the members of an organization and its sympathizers. In the Indonesian case, however, the violence acquired its own momentum after some time, and as Douglas Kammen tells us, there was much settling of private scores as well. Both examples qualify in terms of categorical violence, rather than violence directed at the general population at large. Nonetheless, Namhee Lee regards the Korean case as an example of exemplary rather than instrumental violence.

There were a number of other factors that aided widespread and systematic abuse of state power. The monopoly of power exercised by the state and those who led it implied that such power could be abused with little consideration of norms of proper or ethical governance. There were few structural or institutional restraints; even where such obstacles were present, they could have been totally ignored. More important, individuals and agencies that were involved in and directed state violence invariably exercised traditional power in the Weberian sense. In other words, elements of power and its availability were associated with specific individuals and often agencies that they led. In many instances such agencies were those tasked to preserve order and that therefore could claim a legitimate use of state power as well. Since there were often no clear distinctions made between internal and external security functions, the task of maintaining state security more often than not actually fell on the military. Internal and external security was viewed as indivisible, especially during the Cold War; as a result, enemies of the state were present inside the country as well. Consequently, military authoritarian regimes that were guided by ideological considerations of threat definition would have regarded the use of force against "subversive" elements as necessary and justifiable. As a result of such tendencies, it is arguable that state violence that occurred under military authoritarian regimes was regarded as justifiable under the circumstances in which the state and international community then existed.

Even in the most widespread case of violence documented in the region—that associated with the Khmer Rouge in Cambodia—Sorpong Peou argues in this volume that the regime suffered from a general perception of vulnerability and weakness at the individual and corporate levels. The Chinese "counterrevolutionary riots" in Tiananmen Square are said to have stemmed from insecurity resulting from reform-era initiatives. In the Thai case, although there was the threat of communist insurgency, personal antagonisms at the local level clearly appeared to have played a part. To recognize such justification does not necessarily mean to condone it, however. Rather, it merely introduces the importance of time- and situation-specific considerations into the equation.

While dealing with military-authoritarian-regime types, it may be useful to note that such regimes often employ armed groups with which they maintain loose linkages. In fact, history has shown that authoritarian, totalitarian, and communist regimes often employ idealistic and energetic youth groups to further their ideological goals. Nazi Germany and Communist China under Mao Zedong were notorious for the use of such youth groups. These groups enabled the state to mobilize resources to engage in activities that might be regarded as unlawful or extra-legal. There is sufficient evidence to indicate that paramilitary and youth organizations were often involved in such indiscriminate violence in East Asia. The Indonesian and Thai cases bear this out clearly. And both countries continue to mobilize such resources when their security forces are stretched or when their governments desire to retain some distance from indiscriminate violence. The Indonesian military mobilized many such groups before and after the Timor referendum, like Aitarak, Besi Merah Putih (Red and White Iron), and Pemuda Pancasila (Pancasila Youth), and Thailand did the same to counter the violence in its southern provinces. The use of such vigilante paramilitary and youth groups is clearly detrimental to the proper pursuit of law and order.

The exercise of traditional power in the states examined came with other connotative values as well. These included the fact that the appropriation of power and its exercise, no matter how illegitimate, could not be challenged. There were quite simply no mechanisms for changes and challenges. It is noteworthy that in a number of instances, a single individual was often associated with the lengthy tenure of an abusive government. This was certainly the case with the Soeharto government that rose from the violence against the PKI and its sympathizers and went on to cement a thirty-one-year leadership of the country. Additionally, the military, from which Soeharto first obtained power before consolidating his independence, remains well entrenched in Indonesian politics. Alternatively, the continuation of an existing structural situation that perpetuated power in a particular institution, as in the case of the Communist Party in China and embedded elite interests of the political executive in the Philippines, would also have thwarted addressing state violence.

If the state and its exercise of power were unrestrained, conversely, society was emasculated. Since the state often targeted specific groups or individuals as its enemies, it could generally continue its activities without broad-based challenges. And even in instances where resistance to such violence obtained, it was often muted or easily repressed. What societal structures existed were often co-opted by the state or placed under intense scrutiny for "subversive" activities that threatened the state. At best, some of these traditional structures could offer solace at the individual or very low levels of organization. In this regard it would make little sense to speak of state-society relations as we understand them today. The state quite simply existed independent of society and was often able to exert its will on society and attendant structures on its own terms. The only contingent conditions were probably the collapse of the regime from internal fissures; an uprising against it; or, in some cases, the withdrawal of external legitimacy. Alternatively, if the violence was exemplary and related to certain types of proscribed behavior, as Boudreau argues, then the general population learns to live by such proscriptions over time and internalize them.

Perpetrators and Victims of Violence

The apportionment of blame for violence and the identification of victims are also central to this book. The military appears to have played a key role in an overwhelming number of cases of violence; military involvement was clearly the case for the Northeast Asian countries discussed here, although subtle differences obtain. For example, in the case of China, the military acted under the orders of the leadership of the Communist Party. In Southeast Asia, some distinctions surface: in the Philippines, the marines and the police were responsible for the violence, whereas in the Cambodian case, the Khmer Rouge, responsible for the ongoing massacre, constituted both the regime and the military. Sorpong Peou also mentions the faceless organization "Angka," a creation of the Khmer Rouge to which blame was attributed for both the violence and the identification of victims.

As for the victims, in China, they were predominantly "cross-class" demonstrators; in Japan, the violence was aimed at Okinawans; in South Korea, the victims were from Kwangju. The Japanese and Korean cases share similarities in that the violence was directed against a region-specific target. The Cambodian case, despite having a large number of victims, targeted urban dwellers, intellectuals and artisans, minorities, and religious groups in more systematic ways. In Indonesia, although the victims were initially members of the PKI and their sympathizers, there is also evidence of violence that targeted political enemies at a time of general turbulence and regime transition. The Myanmar case points to students and their sympathizers as the general targets of violence, and in the Philippine case peasants bore the brunt of the violence. The Thai study suggests that average citizens who were labeled as communists were subjected to violence.

An interesting correlation is that between state violence and the status of the regime in question. Four broad categories emerge from the case studies: regime crisis, regime transition, regime defense, and law-and-order considerations. The Chinese Tiananmen incident was clearly justified as a law-and-order issue, while the Japanese case appears to have been regarded as wartime defense of the state. The Korean case is a little complicated: it involved power transition within an existing regime, although it could be construed as regime defense as well, if the detractors are thought of as contenders for a different regime type. The Indonesian and Philippine cases also point toward violence associated with regime transition/consolidation, while the Cambodian and Thai cases tend toward regime defense. The Myanmar case differs from the others in that the regime was in crisis. The collapse of the BSPP government and Ne Win's "official" retirement created the crisis, which in turn spawned the protests and subsequent violence.

Whatever the specific circumstances of the situation may have been, it is clear that regimes engaged in violence against their own citizens sensed a threat to their authority and the exercise of power. Unwilling to give up power and framing the national discourse against protestors or challengers by defining them as enemies of the state, these regimes resorted to the use of force. Given the conflation between state and regime interests that typically obtained and in the absence of competing structures at the political and social levels, they were well placed to exercise the monopoly on the "legitimate use of force." In other words, as far as the regimes in power were concerned, their response was justified in returning the state to normalcy. And since police and military functions were not kept discrete, as in democracies, the military, with its far greater capacity for violence, was often utilized. The claim that those against whom violence was used threatened the regime in some way appears to have provided both sufficient provocation and subsequent rationalization for the use of force. Whereas the Cold War provided an ideological cloak in a number of instances, especially in the case of military authoritarian regimes, socialist and communist states also appropriated violence. In this regard, state violence has been a phenomenon of both the extreme right and the extreme left.

RESOLUTION OF STATE VIOLENCE

As for political transition and reconciliation in the aftermath of the violence, it has not always been forthcoming. In fact, as mentioned earlier, only the Korean and Cambodian cases have been attended to with some amount of rigor. Of these two, only the Cambodian case has emphasized retribution, and this approach was largely inspired by pressures emanating from the international community. The Korean attempt at resolution, which involved an admixture of retribution and reconciliation, obtained within the framework of a democratizing polity. And Japan, which counts itself as a well-developed democracy today, has yet to address some of its past episodes of state violence. A deep culture of taboo continues to obtain, although past misdeeds have transformed the nature of the state and led in turn to far greater recognition of fundamental liberties at the state level. Important gains have also been made by community-based lobby and interest groups. And in the case of Japan, the courts have also been engaged in interpreting state powers in the face of legal challenges. This separation of powers between the judiciary and the political executive may well be the harbinger of greater changes to come, if civic and interest groups force the state to respond to citizen-initiated lawsuits.

As for questions regarding the postviolence situation and how states have attempted to deal with it, there is a wide range of outcomes in the manner of resolution. China has been able to deflect some of the pressures associated with Tiananmen as a result of rising affluence and a youth culture that cements regime legitimacy. Although there have been no formal attempts at resolving the situation, the regime may well address it at some point in the future when it feels more confident. In the meantime, the regime has permitted far greater levels of associational life through civic organizations. A major reason why states have not addressed previous episodes of violence also has to do with state priorities and challenges. For example, it is arguable that in the Chinese case, the threats, or the regime-perceived threats, deriving from peripheral areas and minority communities, particularly in Xinjiang and Tibet, constitute a much more urgent matter than trying to reconcile the Tiananmen incident. After all, within the Chinese government's perception of priorities the maintenance of the state and its sovereignty is an overriding consideration. The same argument could be made with regard to the Taiwan issue. In the perception of the government, these are all issues that may well be regarded as state-building rather than aimed toward regime consolidation or transition, to borrow Boudreau's terms. Then there are tactics that regimes continually utilize to try and make amends with victims of state violence, albeit in an often piecemeal and opaque manner. Expressions of Chinese national pride at the country's new place in the international order and the breathtaking pace of socioeconomic changes blunt calls to address state violence, as demonstrated in Jeffrey N. Wasserstrom and Kate Merkel-Hess's chapter. In fact, public sentiment almost justifies the path taken, since it constitutes a demonstration effect of the successful path taken, as opposed to that which was not.

In Japan, the government has attempted a backhanded apology by honoring the war dead as heroes, and revisionist history textbooks have been allowed to coexist alongside official scripts. In the meantime, however, the Okinawan community has introduced a unanimous demand for recognition of wartime forced suicides. South Korea has been the most progressive in resolving past violence through compensating and honoring its victims. The initiators of this policy were the regime under Roh Tae Woo, which came to power in 1988, and the more recent regime under Kim Young Sam. The political opposition took up the cause, and acts to commence resolution of the situation were legalized.

As for Southeast Asia, the new regime under the Hun Sen government

in Cambodia committed itself to a resolution of the situation in cooperation with the United Nations, and tribunals to address the situation are
ongoing at the time of writing. The resolution has adopted the European
Commission's type of retributive justice, which seeks to prosecute the
perpetrators of violence. However, the government has placed some limits on whom the courts may try and has warned international prosecutors
and the community that extending the mandate and the target group to
be prosecuted risks unraveling the peace that has obtained thus far. This
intervention and threat naturally serve regime interests, since Khmer
Rouge collaborators are in power at the present time. The Indonesian situation remains unresolved up until now, although it appears to be a matter
of time before civic groups and NGOs place resolution firmly on the country's political agenda. The residual fears of the families of victims are also
an important reason why there have been few calls from that quarter to
address the violence and mete out some form of justice. The military also
continues to remain an important national institution, with territorial-
deployment and administrative functions, despite serious attempts at
administrative and fiscal decentralization in the post-Soeharto period.

In the case of Myanmar, the regime is preoccupied with reestablish-
ing a modicum of domestic and international legitimacy that was lost
after the collapse of the Burma Socialist Program Party–led government.
Additionally, there is the important issue of integrating territories and
peoples that are currently being controlled by ethnic armies that challenge the sovereignty and legitimacy of the state. As in the Chinese
case, these are issues that may well fall within the ambit of state building. The patronage of the Buddhist Sangha by the regime in Myanmar
and its expenditures and upkeep of pagodas in the country are meant to
grant the regime traditional legitimacy in accordance with Buddhist virtues. In the Myanmar case, the state continued with a repressive policy
while slowly increasing tolerance toward local and foreign NGOs. Initial
attempts at multiparty democracy were frustrated, and tension continues to exist between the regime and the political opposition. Elements
of the political opposition, however, have tried to break the impasse by
participating in the 2010 election to structurally attempt the introduction
of opposition in parliament, and Aung San Suu Kyi was released from
house detention. The government started negotiations with Suu Kyi, and
it released some two hundred political prisoners in late 2011. And in
April 2012, the NLD was allowed to register as a political party and suc-

cessfully won forty-three out of the forty-five seats that were available for contestation. Consequently, Suu Kyi is now a member of parliament and has been issued a passport for overseas travel as well. At the time of writing she is in the middle of a European tour that includes a stop in Norway to collect her Nobel Prize for Peace. Within the country many reforms are ongoing, and the international community has significantly relaxed its sanctions. In fact, many Western countries are now spearheading investment in Myanmar.

In the case of the Philippines, much has been done by way of symbolic resolution of the situation. President Corazon Aquino conveyed her condolences as head of state to the families of the victims of the violence, although there has been no conclusive outcome from the fact-finding mission that was commissioned. This mission continues to remain unsatisfactory to interested parties, and violence is ongoing over the issue of agrarian land reform, even though a monument to honor those who died at Mendiola has also been built. The incident remains a major political issue that regularly crops up on the national agenda. In Thailand, induced testimony brought the Red Drum incident to the fore, although there are still disagreements over the actual number of victims. Student organizations, the Interior Ministry, and elements within the military initiated the process of resolution, but no concrete actions have followed. As a result, whereas the military has admitted to the violence, there has been neither accountability nor reconciliation. Rather, victims have been reconciled to the "inevitability" of the situation and the culture of impunity, as described by Tyrell Haberkorn in this volume.

The initiation of retributive justice generally appears less likely in the East Asian cases examined thus far. There are multiple reasons for this assertion, including, importantly, retaining the memory of violence and summoning the political will to have it addressed at some point. The advocacy of such justice may suffer from disinterest and lethargy over time, especially when confronted with an authoritarian state. Notably, those who seek to keep such issues alive may themselves be branded as subversives and harshly dealt with. After all, repression is the easiest means of erasing negative memories associated with the state. As for the question of political will, successor regimes may naturally not see it as in their best interest to address past misdeeds. Regimes may regard such acts as unnecessary or beyond their purview. They may also paper over such events in order to demonstrate their willingness to forge a new social compact that is devoid of the emotional baggage associated with the past. The political will to address past crimes may be forthcoming if a new regime is committed to specific changes in policy output and acquires its political mandate on the basis of campaigning for such changes prior to coming into power. Such drastic changes in regimes and their orientations are unlikely to obtain in states with more authoritarian structures and values. In any event, the regular conflation of interests between state and regime security makes the possibility of such changes in developing countries even more remote.

For all the reasons mentioned above and others that may be unique to specific countries, we conclude that East Asian countries are far more likely to engage in restorative rather than retributive justice. This is not to suggest that such states and societies are not keen to punish those associated with state violence and clear the names and memories of those persecuted. Rather, it appears to be the likely path toward some form of reconciliation that is intended to have a longer-lasting and less contentious transformative effect on state-society relations. This situation is likely to eventuate, especially if the previously hypothesized dichotomy between retributive and restorative justice corresponds broadly to the liberal and nonliberal traditions regarding law and human rights. Nonetheless, as mentioned at the outset, the restorative approach has its detractors too, who are interested in bringing those responsible for the abuse of state coercive power to account. Enforcing such accountability early on also has the demonstration effect of establishing norms of conduct for state and regime utilization of coercive power. Whatever approach is deemed necessary and workable, some form of neutral truth- or fact-finding commission is necessary at the outset in order to establish the terms of reference for both the perpetrators and the victims of violence.

POLITICAL TRANSITION AND RECONCILIATION IN THE EAST ASIAN CONTEXT

The case studies that have been examined in this study yield no conclusive evidence about the nature of the relationship between political transition and reconciliation. The South Korean and Cambodian cases present starkly different findings. In the former, democratization was the major spur of attempts to deal with past violence, whereas in the case of communist Cambodia, the pressure of international opinion and the United

Nations led to the efforts at meting out retributive justice. And in the case of all the other countries examined, no settlement has been attempted or realized thus far. In any event, it is likely that states will find it easier to deal with events that did not involve large numbers of deaths in the first instance. For this reason, the Philippines may well find past violence easier to deal with: the Mendiola Bridge massacre resulted in relatively few casualties, although structural factors appear to have inhibited such an outcome. Conversely and notwithstanding the Cambodian example, it is likely that countries like China, Indonesia, and Myanmar will take much longer to deal with their past. Whereas it appears illogical that events involving mass casualties will not be accorded priority, the reality of the situation is that the number of affected and interested parties makes such an undertaking a large national one. And for this reason alone, only strong states with significant political will and the proper mindset are able to attempt to deal with past injustices. "Proper mindset" may seem an odd phrase in this context, but it refers to the regime's legitimacy and general principles of governance. For example, the Chinese and Myanmar governments continue to regard those who were subjected to state violence as essentially subversive elements that sought the overthrow of state power. Whatever the lexicon may be, it is important to realize that unless the discourse of the state shifts from emphasizing regime security to stressing some conception of human security, reconciliation is unlikely to be forthcoming. And as noted earlier, if the violence was indeed large-scale, elements of the state's coercive agencies that were responsible for the violence are likely to be still embedded within the social structure or to continue to have their interests structurally represented and protected.

And what is the nature of the relationship between reconciliation and regime transition? We posit that it is unlikely for states, especially authoritarian ones, to undertake reconciliation unless it serves regime interests in some way. A hybrid regime that is not entirely authoritarian and that seeks to entrench a corporatist or developmentalist ideology may well find some interest in undertaking such a task. This would especially be the case if sufficient time had elapsed to distance or disassociate the regime from past abuses of state power. Apart from changes to regime-specific characteristics and legitimacy, reconciliation may take place within the framework of revolutionary change inspired by a mass protest movement or alternatively by a regime that opts to drastically change its policies, even at the risk of its own potential displacement, as happened in the

South African case. However, in epochal terms, the period of revolutions appears to be over, and authoritarian regimes with benevolent and progressive leaders rarely exist. In light of such international norms, political transition is far more likely to lead to attempts to address past state excesses.

In any event, to draw this discussion to a close, regimes must abide by certain international norms of conduct, and there must be structural restraints on the exercise of coercive power. There must also be much stronger state-society relations and interaction, and the state must better reflect the constitution and will of its people. It is hoped that as countries examine their past and history is recorded, matters involving state violence will be seriously addressed. Failure to do so will invite legitimizing an essentially illegitimate use of power and violence. Ethical conduct at the individual, societal, and state levels requires nothing short of such redress.

NOTES

1. Jung-kwan Cho, "The Kwangju Uprising as a Vehicle of Democratization: A Comparative Perspective," in *Contentious Kwangju: The May 18 Uprising in Korea's Past and Present,* ed. Gi-wook Shin and Kyung Moon Hwang (Lanham, MD: Rowman and Littlefield, 2003), 67–85.

2. See Duncan McCargo, "Network Monarchy and Legitimacy Crises in Thailand," *Pacific Review* 18, no. 4 (2005): 499–519.

3. See Mary P. Callahan, *Making Enemies: War and State Building in Burma* (Ithaca: Cornell University Press, 2004).

Acknowledgments

We, the editors, have benefited from the generosity and efforts of many individuals and organizations to bring this project to a close. Above all, we would like to thank all the contributors to this volume not only for their cooperation on writing the chapters, but also for revising them at least three times. The project benefited immensely from the input of the invited discussants at the workshops. Robert Taylor, Meredith Weiss, and Khoo Boo Teik made the workshops rich and engaging; they guided the efforts of the writers and challenged them on many occasions about central issues regarding state violence. We are equally thankful to the four anonymous reviewers, whose comments and criticisms helped in the revisions and tightening of the entire volume.

The chapters that appear in this volume are drawn from two workshops, one held in Hong Kong in December 2009 and the other in Seoul in August 2010. The bulk of the funding for the project was borne by the City of Hiroshima and the Hiroshima City University. We are deeply grateful for their financial support and commitment in the convening of the workshops.

Additional funding for the first workshop was borne by the Center for Southeast Asian Studies at the City University of Hong Kong. For this generosity and support, we owe thanks to William Case. Supplementary funding for the second workshop in Seoul was borne by the Konrad Adenauer Stiftung in Seoul, and for this arrangement we are grateful to Colin Duerkop and Lee Ju Hong. In addition, the Asian Political and International Studies Association provided generous support for both workshops as well, and we are especially indebted to Hari Singh. Also, we are grateful to Huh Moon Young and Park Hyeong Jung at the Korea Institute for National Unification for logistical and voluntary support for the Seoul workshop. Michiko Yoshimoto at the Hiroshima Peace Institute performed an excellent job in coordinating the entire project from afar. Finally, thanks also go to Shiping Hua for his scholarly leadership of the Asia in the New Millennium series at the University Press of Kentucky, and to Stephen Wrinn and Allison Webster for their excellent editorial guidance.

Contributors

Vince Boudreau is a professor of political science at the City College and at the City University (CCNY) Graduate Center. He is also the director of CCNY's Colin Powell Center for Policy Studies and was until recently chair of the CCNY Political Science Department. He is a specialist in comparative politics, with a regional emphasis on Southeast Asia. He writes about protest movements, state repression, and democratization, both with specific reference to Southeast Asia and more generally. His latest book is *Resisting Dictatorship: Repression and Protest in Southeast Asia* (2004). His most recent research seeks to explain divergent patterns of post-transition politics in Indonesia and the Philippines and patterns of collective violence across Southeast Asia. He also serves on the editorial boards of *Comparative Politics* and *Kasarinlan.*

Rommel A. Curaming is a lecturer in history and Southeast Asian Studies at University of Brunei Darussalam (UBD). Before joining UBD, he was with the National University of Singapore as a postdoctoral fellow and La Trobe University as Research Fellow under Endeavour Award Australia (2008). He completed his PhD at Australian National University with a thesis that compares the dynamics of state-scholar relations in Indonesia and the Philippines. His research interests include the politics of memory, comparative historiography, state-scholar relations, the politics of scholarship, and state violence in the islands of Southeast Asia. His most recent publications have appeared in *Critical Asian Studies* and *Time Society.*

N. Ganesan is a professor specializing in Southeast Asian politics at the Hiroshima Peace Institute, where he has been since 2004. Concurrently he serves as a visiting professor at the National Graduate Institute for Policy Studies (GRIPS) in Tokyo. His teaching and research interests are in Southeast Asian politics and foreign policy, especially sources of tension and conflict within and between states. His most recent major publications are *Realism and Interdependence in Singapore's Foreign Policy*

(2005); *Myanmar: State, Society, Ethnicity,* coedited with Kyaw Yin Hlaing (2007); *East Asia Facing a Rising China,* coedited with Lam Peng Er (2010); *Southeast Asia in International Relations,* coedited with Ramses Amer (2010); and the edited collection *Conjunctures and Continuities in Southeast Asian Politics* (2012).

Tyrell Haberkorn is a research fellow in the Department of Political and Social Change, School of International, Political, and Strategic Studies, Australian National University. Her work is located at the intersection of critical archival and ethnographic practice and activism around state and parastate violence in Southeast Asia. She is the author of *Revolution Interrupted: Farmers, Students, Law, and Violence in Northern Thailand* (2011). Her work has also appeared in *Critical Asian Studies, Stance,* and *Article 2,* and on *openDemocracy.*

Hayashi Hirofumi is a professor of history at Kanto Gakuin University in Japan. He is an expert on modern history and has published a number of books on war crimes and war histories. Representative writings include *Sabakareta Senso Hanzai* (Tried war crimes: British war crimes trials of Japanese) (1998), *Okinawasen to Minshu* (The Battle of Okinawa and the people) (2001), *Okinawasen: Kyosei sareta "Shudan Jiketsu"* (The Battle of Okinawa: Forced "mass suicide") (2009), *Okinawasen ga Toumono* (Questions from the Battle of Okinawa) (2010), and "Japanese Deserters and Prisoners of War in the Battle of Okinawa," in *Prisoners of War, Prisoners of Peace: Captivity, Homecoming and Memory in World War II,* edited by Bob Moore and Barbara Hately-Broad (2005).

Douglas Kammen earned his PhD in the Department of Government at Cornell University and taught at the University of Canterbury (Christchurch), Universitas Hasanuddin (Makassar), and Universidade Nacional Timor Lorosae (Dili) before joining the Southeast Asian Studies Programme at the National University of Singapore. His research interests include social movements, the military and politics, and human rights in Indonesia and Timor-Leste. He is coauthor (with Katharine McGregor) of *The Contours of Mass Violence in Indonesia, 1965–1968* (2012).

Sung Chull Kim is Humanities Korea Professor of Peace Studies in the Institute for Peace and Unification Studies at Seoul National University.

Before holding this position, he served as a senior fellow at Korea Institute for National Unification and a professor at the Hiroshima Peace Institute. Kim has written widely on transitions in Asian socialist systems, domestic-regional linkages, and democratic transition. He is the author of *North Korea under Kim Jong Il: From Consolidation to Systemic Dissonance* (2006), the editor (with Edward Friedman) of *Regional Cooperation and Its Enemies in Northeast Asia: The Impact of Domestic Forces* (2006), and the editor (with David Kang) of *Engagement with North Korea: A Viable Alternative* (2009). He has contributed a number of articles to academic journals, including *Systems Research and Behavioral Science* (formerly *Behavioral Science*).

Kyaw Yin Hlaing is an assistant professor in the Department of Asian and International Studies at the City University of Hong Kong. His teaching and research interests are in Southeast Asian politics, state-society relations, comparative democratization, and foreign aid and poverty. Kyaw is the coeditor (with N. Ganesan) of *Myanmar: State, Society, Ethnicity* (2007). His articles on Myanmar and Laos have appeared in such academic journals as *Asian Survey,* the *Journal of Southeast Asian Studies,* and *Contemporary Southeast Asia.*

Namhee Lee is an associate professor of modern Korean history at the University of California, Los Angeles. She is the author of *The Making of Minjung: Democracy and the Politics of Representation in South Korea* (2007), as well as of a number of articles on Korean historiography, on the Park Chung Hee period, and on social memory and historical novels and films. She is currently working on a book project tentatively titled "Social Memory and Public History in South Korea," which explores the production of historical knowledge in the public arena over the last three decades, examining the debates, tensions, and exchanges generated from historical novels, films, museum exhibitions, festivals, historical restorations (or destructions), and civic historical movements.

Kate Merkel-Hess is an assistant professor of history and Asian studies at Pennsylvania State University. She received her PhD from the Department of History at the University of California, Irvine, in June 2009. Merkel-Hess studies modern China, and her dissertation, which she is currently turning into a book, examines global efforts to reform and modernize rural people in the 1920s and 1930s. Her writing has been published in the *Times Literary Supplement, Current History, History Compass,* and *World History Connected,* and she is the coeditor (with Jeffrey Wasserstrom and Kenneth Pomeranz) of *China in 2008: A Year of Great Significance* (2009). Merkel-Hess has received numerous awards to support her research, including a Mellon/ACLS Recent Doctoral Recipients Fellowship, a Mellon/ACLS Dissertation Completion Fellowship, and a Fulbright-Hays Doctoral Dissertation Research Abroad Grant.

Sorpong Peou is a professor of politics (international security) and the chair of the Department of Politics at the University of Winnipeg, Canada. Many of his family members, including his grandparents, perished during the Khmer Rouge reign of terror. His father (a government official under the Sihanouk and Lon Nol regimes) was taken away for execution in 1975 but was found alive after thirty-five years. Sorpong himself is a survivor of the Khmer Rouge killing fields and left the country after the Vietnamese invasion of Cambodia late in 1978. His most recent major publications include *International Democracy Assistance for Peacebuilding* (2007), the edited collection *Human Security in East Asia* (2009), *Peace and Security in the Asia-Pacific* (2010), and *Human Security Studies: Theories, Methods and Themes* (forthcoming).

Jeffrey N. Wasserstrom is a professor of history and the chair of the Department of History at the University of California, Irvine, and the editor of the *Journal of Asian Studies.* He is the author of four books, including *Student Protests in Twentieth-Century China: The View from Shanghai* (1991) and *China in the Twenty-first Century: What Everyone Needs to Know* (2010), and has edited or coedited several others. His work has appeared in many academic journals and newspapers, as well as in magazines such as *Time* and *Newsweek.* He blogs for the *Huffington Post*; is a cofounder of the electronic magazine *China Beat*; and served as a consultant for *The Gate of Heavenly Peace,* a prize-winning film about 1989.

Index

ASIA IN THE NEW MILLENNIUM

SERIES EDITOR: Shiping Hua, University of Louisville

Asia in the New Millennium is a series of books offering new interpretations of an important geopolitical region. The series examines the challenges and opportunities of Asia from the perspectives of politics, economics, and cultural-historical traditions, highlighting the impact of Asian developments on the world. Of particular interest are books on the history and prospect of the democratization process in Asia. The series also includes policy-oriented works that can be used as teaching materials at the undergraduate and graduate levels. Innovative manuscript proposals at any stage are welcome.

ADVISORY BOARD

William Callahan, University of Manchester, Southeast Asia, Thailand
Lowell Dittmer, University of California at Berkeley, East Asia and South Asia
Robert Hathaway, Woodrow Wilson International Center for Scholars, South Asia, India, Pakistan
Mike Mochizuki, George Washington University, East Asia, Japan and Korea
Peter Moody, University of Notre Dame, China and Japan
Brantly Womack, University of Virginia, China and Vietnam
Charles Ziegler, University of Louisville, Central Asia and Russia Far East

BOOKS IN THE SERIES

The Future of China-Russia Relations
Edited by James Bellacqua

Contemporary Chinese Political Thought: Debates and Perspectives
Fred Dallmayr and Zhao Tingyang

The Mind of Empire: China's History and Modern Foreign Relations
Christopher A. Ford

State Violence in East Asia
Edited by N. Ganesan and Sung Chull Kim

Korean Democracy in Transition: A Rational Blueprint for Developing Societies
HeeMin Kim

Modern Chinese Legal Reform: New Perspectives
Edited by Xiaobing Li and Qiang Fang

Inside China's Grand Strategy: The Perspective from the People's Republic
Ye Zicheng, Edited and Translated by Steven I. Levine and Guoli Liu

Challenges to Chinese Foreign Policy: Diplomacy, Globalization, and the Next World Power
Edited by Yufan Hao, C. X. George Wei, and Lowell Dittmer

www.ingramcontent.com/pod-product-compliance
Lightning Source LLC
Chambersburg PA
CBHW020752300326
41914CB00050B/142